# Re(Dis)covering Our Foremothers

# Re(Dis)covering Our Foremothers

Nineteenth-
Century Canadian
Women Writers

Edited and with an
Introduction by
Lorraine McMullen

University of Ottawa Press
Ottawa • London • Paris

**REAPPRAISALS**
Canadian Writers

LORRAINE McMULLEN
General Editor

**Canadian Cataloguing in Publication Data**

Main entry under title:
Re(dis)covering our foremothers

(Reappraisals, Canadian writers; 15)
Includes bibliographical references.
Papers presented at a conference held at University
of Ottawa, April 29–May 1, 1988.
ISBN 0-7766-0197-0

1. Canadian literature (English) — Women authors —
History and criticism — Congresses. 2. Canadian
literature (English) — 19th century — History and
criticism — Congresses. I. McMullen, Lorraine,
1926-   . II. Series.

PS8089.5.W6R43 1989    C810.9'003'082    C90-090037-7
PR9188.R43 1989

UNIVERSITÉ D'OTTAWA
UNIVERSITY OF OTTAWA

©University of Ottawa Press, 1990
Printed and bound in Canada
ISBN 0-7766-0197-0

Typeset by Nancy Poirier Typesetting Ltd., Ottawa
Cover design by Judith Gregory

# Contents

# Introduction

LORRAINE McMULLEN

The essays in this volume explore an area in which scholarly work has only begun. They look at Canadian women writers in the nineteenth century and point to the need to recover those once known but now
forgotten and to discover those never publicly known whose diaries, letters,
and autobiographical writings are—or should be—a valued part of Canadian
tradition. Several essays broadly assess aspects of this topic; others are concerned
with research methodology; and still others with theoretical critical modes for
looking at individual writers.

There are many references to pioneer women, so it is appropriate that
Clara Thomas opens the volume by recalling her own pioneer journey into
this area in 1960, her study of Anna Jameson, and her first graduate course
on Canadian women writers in 1976, a course which included, and therefore
linked, contemporary writers with their neglected forebears. Thomas now makes
a similar connection, introducing two of today's distinguished writers, Carol
Shields and Donna Smyth, who by "thinking back through our mothers"
become part of that linking of present with past.

Shields and Smyth are scholars as well as creators. Both have done
archival and critical work on early nineteenth-century women writers, and,
in their creative work, both have rewritten women writers of that era, Shields
in a novel and Smyth in plays. Bridging the creative and the critical, they manifest the link between today's writers and their foremothers. And they introduce motifs which recur throughout this volume. Shields reminds us that, while
we were obliged in school to read "that dark dense sort of book," the "classic,"
our real tradition goes beyond the canonized writers to include women who
produced juvenile stories and sentimental novels. Smyth calls our attention
to women who probably never thought of themselves as writers, women whose

moving records of their lives in letters and diaries form a part of our lost heritage. Such motifs contribute to a pattern which links these essays.

An inescapable conclusion emerges: Canadian literary history will be read very differently when women are re-inscribed in its rolls, for the women express a different vision of Canada and Canadian experience than is conventionally held. Helen Buss's central thesis, that women's autobiographical writings are at variance with the popular Canadian myth of the garrison mentality, is a demonstration of the disparity between what women's voices say and what has been accepted as a central Canadian statement.

Genres and themes frequently used by women writers have been devalorized by a patriarchal culture which values most the concerns and the literary genres popular with male writers. Such gender-specific valuations account in part for the disappearance of women writers from reference works and anthologies. In various ways, the essays of Carole Gerson, Marjory Lang, Helen Buss, and Donna Smyth confront the issues of canon and genre. The omission of women writers from key texts is carefully documented by Carole Gerson who points out, citing Lynne Spender, that when women writers are lost, "someone has lost them." Someone has made a decision to exclude them, and it is easier to lose than to recover writers.

Not least among lost women writers is the first generation of women journalists, as Marjory Lang tells us. These women grasped the opportunities provided when, late in the nineteenth century, newspaper publishers created the "women's page" to increase circulation by luring female readers. Given their entrée, women journalists often did not restrict their columns to so-called "women's issues" but explored a variety of topics. Have Canadians forgotten Kathleen Blake Coleman, a.k.a. Kit of the Mail? Her lively "Women's Kingdom" boosted the Toronto paper's circulation by a third. She included among her fans Prime Minister Wilfrid Laurier, who bought the staunchly Conservative *Mail* only in order to read Kit's column. Have we forgotten the Kit Coleman who covered the Spanish-American war as the first accredited woman war correspondent?

The essays of Buss, Lang, Gerson, and Smyth indicate the generally unnoticed but very large number of women producing poetry, fiction, journalism, letters, and diaries. Finding these lost women is a major focus of several other essays. The research required to locate even the barest essentials of a woman's life and to find her poems, essays, short fiction (which often appeared in ephemeral publications), and her books (which are long out of print) is a major challenge for today's scholars. Marion Beyea, Francess Halpenny, and James Doyle provide some helpful strategies.

Halpenny's discussion of the extensive research needed to produce accurate biographical and bibliographical entries for the *Dictionary of Canadian Biography* and of the difficulties encountered and the persistence necessary is a forewarning of the challenges the would-be researcher on nineteenth-century women can expect to encounter. Beyea's paper complements Halpenny's by providing step-by-step directions for the search through archives to assemble the bits and pieces of information that will create a picture of the writer and her times. Carrie MacMillan's account of her own search for material on one writer indicates the combination of analytic skills, determination, and ingenuity required. And with women writers, the researcher all too often finds that, despite every effort, many pieces are still missing from the mosaic of the writer's life.

While rescuing nineteenth-century women writers from anonymity is one of the tasks of today's scholars, another challenge is the reassessment, in light of new knowledge and new critical modes, of those few women who survive in the canon. By looking at Catharine Parr Traill's nature writing, Michael Peterman takes a step in the valorization of genres outside the traditionally popular forms of fiction and poetry. David Bentley considers how the psyches and writings of nineteenth-century women were affected by their emigration from Europe to Canada, from the centre to the periphery. And Misao Dean gives a narratological analysis of Sara Jeannette Duncan's lesser-known novels.

The one nineteenth-century Canadian woman who has most captured the imagination of both creative writers and literary critics is Susanna Moodie. Margaret Atwood's *The Journals of Susanna Moodie*, for example, has done much to make Moodie's name known internationally. Three contributors to this volume suggest new approaches to Moodie. Carl Ballstadt comments on the extent to which newly discovered Moodie letters will further illuminate her text. Alec Lucas questions earlier modes of looking at Moodie and argues for an essential unity in *Roughing It in the Bush*; the arrangement of the sketches, Lucas maintains, was carefully planned by the author for subsequent publication in book form. And Bina Freiwald gives a sophisticated feminist reading of Moodie's text.

While taking a broad approach—exploring the problems of research, questions of genre and canon, incorporation of the newer critical modes in reassessing the few women in the canon along with those women we seek to return to or introduce into the canon—this volume is more than the sum of its parts. Despite their varied range, a number of important ideas resonate from one essay to another. Despite first appearances, this is not only a linear collection. Although it begins with creative writers who assert the existence of a ''foremother'' tradition of writing in Canada, then moves into an exploration of the research required to re(dis)cover these women, and finally looks at critical approaches to them, there is an insistent, recurring subtext throughout.

No matter what topic is being explored, key motifs appear: that genres preferred by women writers, such as journals and letters, have been devalorized, have become ''underprivileged'' genres, as Elizabeth Waterston calls them; that women once included in anthologies and reference books have been dropped, lost, and must now be recovered; that sentiment, a significant element

*4*

of much women's writing in the nineteenth century, has been denigrated; and that male dominance of the community of publishers, editors, and academics is accountable for the makeup of the canon, and thus for the exclusion of many women's voices.

Nathaniel Hawthorne was not referring to Canadians when he complained of "that damn'd mob of scribbling women," but he could have been. There was certainly a mob of women writing in Canada in the nineteenth century, a much larger mob than is generally appreciated. To return them to their rightful place in our consciousness requires both scholarship and activism. The kinds of scholarship needed—from difficult research, to rehabilitation of non-canonical genres, to feminist and theoretically sophisticated readings of individual writers—are discussed and demonstrated in these pages. And, implicitly or explicitly, activism is demanded by these essays. They make it clear that, however much is achieved by research and scholarship, Canada's lost heritage of women writers will not be restored until the re(dis)covered writers become part of the canon included in the reference works, in anthologies, in reprint series.

Only when this is achieved, when the voices of now-silent women are heard, can the final step be taken—a rewriting and reinterpretation of Canadian literary history, a reshaping of the literary institution to include the voices of all Canadians, women and men. This volume is a manifesto, a call for the action that is needed.

I wish to express my appreciation to the Social Sciences and Humanities Research Council of Canada for its support of this project. Thanks as well to the Faculty of Arts at the University of Ottawa for its continuing support of this series and to my colleagues at the Department of English, University of Ottawa, for their co-operation and assistance. Special thanks to my colleague Frank Tierney, for his ongoing encouragement and support.

# "Thinking Back Through Our Mothers": Tradition in Canadian Women's Writing

CLARA THOMAS
CAROL SHIELDS
DONNA E. SMYTH

*Clara Thomas*

**W**hen, in 1838, Anna Jameson published *Winter Studies and Summer Rambles in Canada*, she chose as its epigraph these lines from Book III of *The Faerie Queene*:

> How over that same door was likewise writ,
> *Be bold, Be bold,* and everywhere *Be bold*;
> That much she mus'd, yet could not construe it
> By any riddling skill or common wit.
> At last she spied at that room's upper end
> Another iron door, on which was writ,
> *Be not too bold.*

I might well have chosen the same epigraph for my thesis, "Anna Jameson: The Making of a Reputation," written for the University of Toronto between 1960 and 1962. In fact, I wish I had. Both Northrop Frye, my supervisor, and A.S.P. Woodhouse, the legendary head of the English Department and reigning czar of English studies in Canada, would, I think, have seen the joke and laughed. Both those men had given me great encouragement, from the day in 1958 when I arrived in Frye's office scared to death, all too aware of the anti-female reputation of English graduate studies at the University of Toronto. A week or so later, Woodhouse met me in the corridor outside his office in the cloisters, the place all those of my vintage remember so well, and congratulated me heartily on my thesis proposal and outline, adding that Professor Frye had agreed to be my supervisor. On the day of my thesis oral, Woodhouse even made a point of coming early, to see me before any other examiner arrived and to reassure me that "it will be all right."

So, what Susan Jackel wrote in *Gynocritics* about the determining of our literary canon and the Toronto department's anti-woman bias is part of the truth and is certainly true to the legend that has grown with the years. But it is not my truth.

There are myriads of wonderful stories embedded in that legend, and who would be without them? I think of the anecdote Henry Kreisel, one of Canada's best sources and raconteurs of Woodhouse stories, tells in his memoirs: "Kreisel, I shall send you to Alberta. And I shall send them only one name." Woodhouse "sent" me to York and for that continuing adventure I am always in his debt. He "sent" everyone in those days.

Nevertheless, as I wrote the thesis and later as I extended it into the biography, I was—and was conscious of being—inhibited, certainly not because of anything Northrop Frye said or did, but because of my own time and place. I thought that Anna Jameson was much more of a feminist than I thought it prudent to proclaim—in the independence of her life and her travels, overtly in some of her works, and covertly in all of them. She filled to perfection two of Ellen Moers' major categories—the educating and the travelling heroines. Mme de Staël was the role model of her entire adult life, as I speedily found out, but in 1960 no one was doing much about that prototypical feminist and her enormously influential and suggestive *Corinne*. In fact, it was not until Ellen Moers reviewed *Love and Work Enough* in *Victorian Studies* and then corresponded with me until she died that I realized that anyone at all involved in English studies was busy tracking the influence of the formidable de Staël.

In Canada at least, these were very early days for the women's movement, so much a part of our lives for the past fifteen years. There was no busy sisterhood in women's studies and no networking as we know it today, though I did have a staunch friend and fellow student, Jane Campbell of Wilfrid Laurier University, who was working on Coleridge and in much the same time period. We spent hours and days talking about the nineteenth century, trading anecdotes and information, until we felt ourselves moving in the literary circles of the time as among old friends.

Even in 1976, when I taught my first graduate course in Canadian women writers, such an undertaking was something new in this country. York University has always been notably experimental, however, and because it was still a young institution, we were as yet relatively unencumbered with heavy faculty and departmental bureaucratic structures. I got used to colleagues from other parts of the country telling me that they could never "have got such a course through"—but I had no trouble.

There were thirteen of us in that graduate class. We had a wonderful time. As well as studying our contemporary women writers, each student adopted one neglected novelist. There were many to choose from—Lily Dougall (about whom Lorraine McMullen has now done so much), Mary Anne Sadleir (a continuing interest of Michèle Lacombe), May Agnes Fleming, Joanna Wood, Sui Sin Far (Evelyn Eaton), Onoto Watanna (Winnifred Reeve), Emily Murphy, Margaret Marshall Saunders, Nellie McClung, and at that time even Sara Jeannette Duncan could still be called "neglected," for *The Imperialist* was the only one of her works ever looked at seriously. We learned an enormous amount, including respect for the work of these women, and we laughed a great deal at our own adventures in tracking down their works and bringing back to life such a diverse band of sisters.

This volume is, then, a wish-fulfillment for me, as was *A Mazing Space*, which we used this past year as a text for yet another graduate course in Canadian women writers. All its essays give me great joy, and especially close, of course, is Bina Freiwald's on Anna Jameson. I also have an art historian friend, Adele Holcombe of Bishop's University, who is nearing the completion of a book on Anna Jameson, the first professional female art historian.

Nearly thirty years ago, I did not say, thought I could not say, and in fact did not have the words and the techniques to say: Sisters and colleagues, we *have* advanced. I rejoice to have been and to still be a part of it all.

This essay is followed by those of Carol Shields and Donna Smyth. A key word in any description of these two writers is certainly versatility. For many years I have known Carol Shields for her novels: *Small Ceremonies*, *The Box Garden*, *Happenstance*, *A Fairly Conventional Woman*, and now, *Swann: A Mystery*. I have enjoyed and admired them all. In addition, there is that extraordinary collection of short stories, *Various Miracles*, of which "Mrs. Turner Mowing her Grass" is a wonderful example. Then there is the poetry—*Others* and *Intersect*—and, to top it off, the first critical work, *Susanna Moodie: Voice and Vision*.

I have just finished writing an article on *Swann* for a special issue of *A Room of One's Own*, and in the final paragraph, an apologia really, I wrote: "To try to analyse *Swann: A Mystery* is rather like dissecting a butterfly with a hoe . . . it is a novel whose hallmarks are wit, wisdom, play, skill and great good nature, one to be enjoyed and remembered." Those words apply to all of Shields' work.

I first knew Donna Smyth as an academic, a free-thinking young feminist, and the founding editor of *Atlantis*, a journal we are all proud of. Then I knew of her as a brave and committed environmentalist, one who was harassed for years, her very future threatened, because of her willingness to speak out for, and fight for, our fragile world.

Then, with the publication of *Quilt*, I knew her as a novelist, writing of old Sam Stanford, her dignity, her humour, and her secret. *Quilt* makes the village of Dayspring with all its characters come alive, not as the Arcadian idyll of Avonlea, for instance, but, to paraphrase what Janice Kulyk Keefer says in *Under Eastern Eyes*, as an intriguingly problematic manifestation of desire for that which we can never have, and knowledge of that which we cannot help but desire.

Then there is *Subversive Elements*, a novel that its dust-jacket says deals with a romantic love story and the uranium mining controversy in Nova Scotia. So it does—but it also deals with goats, and the cover does not mention that. I love the goats. There are the dramas, *Susanna Moodie* and *Giant Anna*. I have not seen either of them—my loss, because I am quite sure that they are written and staged with the freshness and wit that are characteristic of Donna Smyth.

And that brings me back to these two women writers together—they are both so witty. They say, they do, and they write wise things and often sad ones, but they both have humour and hope. They know how to rejoice and they know how to laugh.

## WORKS CITED

Freiwald, Bina. 1986. " 'Femininely Speaking': Anna Jameson's *Winter Studies and Summer Rambles in Canada.*" In *A Mazing Space: Writing Canadian Women Writing*. Ed. Shirley Neuman and Smaro Kamboureli. Edmonton: Longspoon-NeWest. 61–73.

Jackel, Susan. 1986. "Canadian Women's Autobiography: A Problem of Criticism." In *Gynocritics/Gynocritiques: Feminist Approaches to Canadian and Quebec Women's Writing*. Ed. Barbara Godard. Toronto: ECW Press. 95–110.

Keefer, Janice Kulyk. 1987. *Under Eastern Eyes: A Critical Reading of Maritime Fiction*. Toronto: Univ. of Toronto Press.

Moers, Ellen. 1976. *Literary Women*. New York: Doubleday.

Shields, Carol. 1972. *Others*. Ottawa: Borealis.
——— . 1974. *Intersect*. Ottawa: Borealis.
——— . 1976. *Small Ceremonies*. Toronto: McGraw-Hill Ryerson.
——— . 1977. *The Box Garden*. Toronto: McGraw-Hill Ryerson.
——— . 1977. *Susanna Moodie: Voice and Vision*. Ottawa: Borealis.
——— . 1980. *Happenstance*. Toronto: McGraw-Hill Ryerson.
——— . 1982. *A Fairly Conventional Woman*. Toronto: Macmillan.
——— . 1985. *Various Miracles*. Don Mills, Ont.: Stoddart.
——— . 1987. *Swann: A Mystery*. Toronto: Stoddart.

Smyth, Donna. 1979. *Giant Anna*. Toronto: Playwrights Canada.
——— . 1982. *Quilt*. Toronto: Women's Press.
——— . 1986. *Subversive Elements*. Toronto: Women's Press.

*Carol Shields*

There is a time in our reading lives when we read anything, when we are unsupervised, when we are bonded to the books we read, when we are innocent of any kind of critical standard, so innocent and avid and open that we do not even bother to seek out special books, but read instead those books that happen to lie within easy reach, the family books, the in-house books. These books have a way of entering our bodies more simply and completely than library books, for example, which are *chosen*, or school texts, which are *imposed*.

It is a literary cliché, largely aristocratic, largely male, that writers in their young years are "given the run of their father's library." You imagine oak panelling, a fire, sets of leather-bound volumes, Shakespeare of course, but also the Greek dramatists, the Latin poets, the Fathers of the Church, the Waverley novels, Dickens—an almost exclusively masculine offering and with little visible connection between book and reader.

My parents' library was a corner of the sunroom, a four-shelf bookcase stained to look like red maple which had been "thrown in" with the purchase of the 1947 edition of the *World Book Encyclopedia*. This bookcase also had room for a set of *Journeys Through Bookland*, black binding stamped with gold, published in the early 1920s, and ten books, oddly uninviting, with cheap red covers and an absence of illustration, entitled *The World's One-Hundred Best Short Stories*, put out by Funk and Wagnalls in 1927. There were two volumes of poetry, the works of James Whitcomb Riley and next to them *A Heap o' Living* by Edgar A. Guest. The rest of the shelf space, only a few inches, was filled with my parents' childhood books.

My father was represented by half a dozen Horatio Alger titles, *Luck and Pluck*, *Ragged Dick*, *Try and Trust*, and so on, which I read, loved, and never thought to condemn for didacticism, for did I not attend a didactic Methodist Sunday School, sit in a didactically charged classroom at Nathaniel Hawthorne Grammar School, absorb the didacticism of my well-meaning parents? This was the natural way of the world, half of humanity bent on improving the other half. Nor did it seem strange that I, in the 1940s and 1950s, should be reading books directed at a late nineteenth- and early twentieth-century audience. I scarcely noticed this time fissure, entering instead a seamless, timeless universe, scrubbed of such worldly events as wars, elections, and social upheavals with which we mark off periods of history. Occasional archaisms were easily overleapt, since the child's world is largely a matter of missing pieces anyway, or concepts only dimly grasped.

Horatio Alger aside, it was mainly the books of my mother that I read, four of them in particular, two of which were Canadian (not that I noticed at the time). In the last month or so, I have looked again at these four books:

*Anne of Green Gables*, *A Girl of the Limberlost*, *Helen's Babies*, and *Beautiful Joe*. No Shakespeare, Hawthorne, Poe, no Virginia Woolf, Gertrude Stein, Willa Cather—just these four.

My mother, the youngest child of Swedish immigrants, grew up on an Illinois farm, attended Normal School and, as a young woman, went to Chicago to teach school. She and three other girls roomed for a year on the third floor of the Hemingway house in Oak Park. Ernest was away in Paris writing *The Sun Also Rises*, though my mother did not know this, of course; she only knew that his parents spoke of him coldly. The Hemingways were difficult; they were stingy with hot water, and they would not allow the four young women to entertain their boyfriends. So, in a year they moved on, ending our mother's accidental brush with the world of real literature, which always excited her children more than it did her. In fact, she never read Hemingway; he was not, despite her thrilling connection, a part of *her* tradition.

It is easy enough to see what she found in *Anne of Green Gables*. She found what millions of others have found, a consciousness attuned to nature, a female model of courage, goodness, and candour, possessed of an emotional capacity that triumphs and converts. Unlike Tom Sawyer who capitulates to society, Anne transforms her community with her exuberant vision. She enters the story disentitled and emerges as a cherished daughter, with loving friends and a future ahead of her, and she has done it all without help: captured Gilbert Blythe, sealed her happiness, and reshuffled the values of society by a primary act of re-imagination.

Gene Stratton-Porter's *A Girl of the Limberlost*, published in 1909 and in many subsequent editions, presents another heroine of pluck (that wonderful word) and creativity. Elnora Comstock, like Anne, is poor and powerless, attending high school in shabby old-fashioned clothes. (Her first suffering day, standing at the blackboard, is engraved on the hearts of millions of readers and may be one of the reasons why my own mother always made me a new dress for the opening of school.) Elnora is a sort of half-orphan, the daughter of an abusive mother who is herself a victim. Occasional subtlety in the mother-daughter relationship is what gives substance to this terrible book, as does Elnora's indomitable spirit. She wins hearts by instinctive kindness, giving away her lunch each day to those more needy even than she, touching the same emotional chord we find in *The Secret Garden*, the dispossessed coming to the aid of the even more flagrantly dispossessed. In addition, Elnora conquers the wilderness around her, the very swamp that took the life of her father and twisted the mind of her mother, by patiently and knowledgeably classifying its flora and fauna, breaking down the threatening universe into elements that are meaningful and, in Elnora's case, profitable, for it is her collection of moths that provides her with money, wins her her prince, and captures at last the inhospitable heart of her mother.

There is a moment of high drama, almost lost in a welter of high drama, in *A Girl of the Limberlost* when Elnora at last confronts her mother and rages against the injustice of her situation. It is a scene not unlike Anne Shirley's confrontation with Mrs. Rachel Lynde, who insists that Anne is ugly and ungraceful. Anne, unlike Elnora, later apologizes, but slyly revels in the drama of her abasement; her sense of herself as heroine gives *Anne of Green Gables* the shading and grace that *A Girl of the Limberlost* never achieves. Anne's and Elnora's confrontations bring to mind, straining only a little, Elizabeth Bennett's showdown with Lady Catherine in *Pride and Prejudice*. It is as though virtue and imagination, those prized weapons, must at times be thrown to the ground so that these protagonists can escape their helpless dependence and achieve control of their lives.

But what can my mother, and generations of other readers, have seen in *Helen's Babies*, John Habberton's 1876 novel? Helen, a young married woman, writes to her brother Harry, imploring him to come and look after her two little boys while she and her husband enjoy a holiday. Harry is seen as an endearing boy-man, selfishly devoted to cigars and claret and short on the patience and sensitivity needed to nurture infants. His baby-sitting experience is mildly cathartic, and he is rewarded by the love of Alice Mayton, a strong-willed local beauty who takes him in hand in somewhat the same manner as Helen, a mother indulging and rebuking an infantile sensibility. This novel, excruciating to read today because of the baby talk of the two little boys, plays with certain ideas of obedience and submission, how they are traded off between the sexes, and I can only guess that this submerged text accounted for the book's huge popularity.

Then there is *Beautiful Joe*, Margaret Marshall Saunders' 1884 autobiography of a mongrel dog. Can I risk a comparison here? It is unlikely and ludicrous, but I will press on. Like Anne, the ironically named Beautiful Joe is not conventionally beautiful. His name is both his shame and his glory. Like Elnora, he is cruelly treated but, through virtue, temperance, and courage, he finds love, and he tells all this through a voice that is characterized by the most delicate, undog-like tints of feeling—though as a child I never questioned his right to a voice, nor to his insights.

Nor did I worry about sentimentality in my mother's books. Sentimentality, like coincidence, seemed to be one of the strands of existence; it could be detected every week, after all, in the last two minutes of "Amos and Andy"; it was a part of the human personality.

Nellie McClung, in her autobiography, recounts how she burst into tears when reading a piece entitled "The Faithful Dog" in the Second Reader, and how her response was reinforced by a teacher who pronounced: "Here is a pupil who has both feeling and imagination; she will get a lot out of life." (And we all know that she did.) She was also much taken by a novel called *Meadow Brook* by Mary Jane Holmes, a book about a misunderstood daughter who talked too much (chatty girls posed a threat) and who attempted to punish her family by exposing herself to the elements and making herself ill. Nellie McClung claimed that she herself did not understand the appeal of the novel, but from our distance we can perhaps guess at the awakening of a rebellious spirit.

Sara Jeannette Duncan was also devoted to the romantic novels of Mary Jane Holmes, as well as to those of Mary Cecil Hay, and undoubtedly the determination of these romantic heroines contributed to her passion, forged early in life, to become a writer.

Laura Goodman Salverson was urged to acquaint herself with Elsie Dinsmore, but preferred the earlier oral tradition of her household—her uncle's salty tales or her mother's accounts of Brynhild the Warrior Maid, Isolde the Unlucky, Gudrid the Fair.

Anne Shirley adored "The Lady of the Lake," *The Seasons* by James Thomson, and "The Dog at His Master's Grave" from the Third Reader, an eclectic sampling, typical of the randomness of early reading lists. All Anne demanded of poetry, she said, was that it should give her a "crinkly feeling" up and down her back.

The young Strickland sisters of Reydon Hall, Catharine and Susanna, attempted the rigorous classics of philosophy and history, but were also enchanted with old astrological magazines dating from the middle of the previous century.

For most of us, our early reading is random and ill-assorted, an almost laughable mélange of the popular and the established. All the senses are open to it. Judgement is suspended because we do not yet suspect that judgement is demanded. Are children damaged or nourished by eclectic reading? We can only say that they are influenced, not least because the inherited readings, and the books themselves, connect them to their mothers and to their mothers' mothers.

As a child, I was intimidated by that dark dense sort of book described as a classic, though a kindly high-school teacher, speaking of *Silas Marner*, demystified the term by telling us it referred to books that people had liked rather a lot for a long time. Later, though, I found that some of these so-called classics refused to open up to me because they projected a world in which I did not hold citizenship.

Childhood itself seemed a powerless interval when one bided one's time, preparing for the confrontation that might or might not occur, though its possibility, shining in the future and winking off the pages of books, gave promise. I never dreamt then that my own confrontation with a withholding world would take the form it did—the writing of novels.

What does a female literary tradition mean and who gets to name it? I see it as still growing towards its definition, investigating the question of reclaimed language and redeemed experience. Because I did not have the run of a father's prescribed library, but rather the run of my mother's bookshelf,

I am persuaded that the popular tradition must be taken into consideration, since it echoes and even interrogates the established tradition, taking liberties, offering models of behaviours, and gesturing—crudely, covertly, often unconsciously—towards that alternate sphere.

## WORKS CITED

Austen, Jane. 1813. *Pride and Prejudice*. London: T. Egerton.

Habberton, John. 1876. *Helen's Babies*. Boston: Loring.

McClung, Nellie. 1936. *Clearing in the West*. Toronto: Thomas Allen.

Montgomery, Lucy Maud. 1908. *Anne of Green Gables*. Toronto: Ryerson.

Saunders, M. Marshall. 1884. *Beautiful Joe*. 1894; rpt. Toronto: McClelland and Stewart, 1918.

Stratton-Porter, Gene. 1909. *A Girl of the Limberlost*. New York: Grosset and Dunlap.

*Donna E. Smyth*

> *—You don't have to die to prove your existence.*
> *—All your clothes go to the Salvation Army.*
> *—And the next wife gives your furniture to her poor relatives.*
> *—That's the tradition.*
> *—Thank god for tradition. Otherwise we wouldn't ever know what to do with our worldly goods.*
> *—Tradition is all right as far as it goes, but it can go too far. Suppose you want to be cremated with all your possessions, down to your blender and your cat, then tradition is a nuisance.*
> *—Perhaps I didn't make myself clear: so long as there's tradition, we're free to break it. Do away with the conventions, then everything becomes conventional, even going up in smoke with your pets and your appliances. This way, with marriages and funerals and forks to the left and thank-you notes and daily baths, we have sign-posts to guide us.*
> *—Or we can ignore them.*
> *—At your own risk.*
> *—Everything is.*
> *—What?*
> *—At your own risk.*
>
> HELEN WEINZWEIG, *Passing Ceremony*

> *The problem is no longer one of tradition, of tracing a line, but one of division, of limits; it is no longer one of lasting foundations, but one of transformations that serve as new foundations, the rebuilding of foundations.*
> MICHEL FOUCAULT, *The Archaeology of Knowledge*

> *Good old Pythagoras.*
> LOUKY BERSIANIK, "Aristotle's Lantern: An Essay on Criticism" *in A Mazing Space: Writing Canadian Women Writing*

**W**hich traditions? Whose? Who is writing/reading, speaking/listening? Text and context, being and time. Being in Time. In the complexity, richness, muchness, whatness, thingness of Time. Facticity.[1] And the multiplicity of identities into which we are thrust by women's work, our mother/s giving birth to Time. Born again writer-woman from mother tongue/s creating, exploring, generating selves. Do the dead speak to the living? If we crawl into basements, up to attics, burrow in trunks and archives, to find these treasures, to bring them to light, do we find ourselves cursed like those imperialistic invaders of imperial Egyptian tombs? Weighted down with our booty, our loot: here's a piece of embroidery, a quilt, a snapshot of Anna aged ten.

Here's the butter churn pounding out the rhythm of our days. And the factory where she was a lady stitcher. Historicity.

Or do we find an opening, openings, possibilities, probabilities of being? Where is Being hiding from us? An old lined scribbler reveals a world. Personal, familial, familiar everyday world. Anonymous scribbler. Not like those we already know and cherish: Susanna Moodie, Catharine Parr Traill, Anna Jameson, Frances Brooke, Sara Jeannette Duncan, Isabella Valancy Crawford. Word shapers in the public eye. Rescued from time: excavation, reclamation. This is work well done but the project is not to canonize a difference, "différance."[2] This fix fixes us to what we already know and that's not much.

Presence/absence.[3] What she sees depends on who she is. Where she is. Time and space. We can be so specific we refuse to speak: I'm from the Maritimes, you (who live in Upper Canada) can't possibly understand. I'm from the working class. I'm black. I speak French but not like they do in Quebec or France. I am a woman. Differences define and separate us. We are sensitive to them now in a way we were not in the early, heady days of the 1970s when Helen Reddy could sing "I am Woman!" Or white, middle-class American feminists could speak of "women's experience," meaning their own, and so elide the absence of those already on the margins of the dominant discourses/cultures.

Words/silence.[4] Women's writing always escapes categories. Jailbreaks and re-creations: Margaret Avison knew a thing or two.[5] What is Literature is not a question that ought to plague us. Our multiple identities have given rise to multiple forms, protean creations, and public and private meditations. And, at times, the weight of that which is not written has been unbearable. What has not been said? What is hidden between the lines? Text and subtext. To say nothing of those who have left scant traces in Time but must have: talked, gossiped, chattered, mumbled, sang, told stories, jokes, exchanged recipes. Must have had Being in the fullness of a lifetime. Are now missing, concealed, withdrawn, obscured, dead.

Public words are visible, are published. Written with an audience in mind, in view. Cultural baggage on display. Gentlewomen claimed a century and a half later by other gentle women writing (Laurence: Parr Traill; Atwood: Moodie) as ancestral voices. Self-conscious voices filtered through literary conventions even when the conventions are evoked to be disrupted and displaced. A kind of tradition which claims and names literary mother/s. The work of art transforming difference to map a territory: woman-space; to chart new constellations: woman-time.

Yet women writing private words/worlds are writing too. Diaries, letters, journals construct self/selves hidden from public view but voices nevertheless that whisper to us messages of kinship and community. Speak to us, it may be, of other kinds of traditions. Textures of lives, the roll of the seasons. How goes the weather? Who was born/died last night? This morning when I got up . . . . Was I some tired when I went to bed!

This project, for example, in which I have been involved for about eight years: a collection of Nova Scotia women's diaries and letters.[6] From 1776 to 1938. The dates arbitrary, the texts randomly salvaged from rubbish and archives and families and walls. We begin with Loyalist women and end with Ella Liscombe, a secretary in the Bank of Montreal in Sydney, Cape Breton, in the 1930s. Time travel throws up difference: Rebecca Byles, upper middle class, Boston family, moves with her Loyalist clergyman father to Halifax, relocates herself and her culture. There and then transform here and now. Mrs. Cottam opens her school for young ladies in the new place. Cultural transmission is not broken by a Revolution. Rebecca reads Alexander Pope, translates Terence from the French, takes to heart Dr. Gregory's advice to young women about to be married. In 1824, Eliza Chipman experiences conversion and baptism in the Annapolis Valley. She who once thought of herself as ''a vile worm in the dust'' is born again and marries a man old enough to be her father, a widower with eight living children, some of whom are older than Eliza who later has twelve children, eight living. When Eliza's first two children die, she struggles to accept the loss and to see them as ''lent favours'' from God. She regrets that she is so ''much of a Martha'' and not more of a Mary who would spend time making her soul rather than maintaining a busy and large household. When she does have time to read, of course, it is the Word.

In the late 1800s, Margaret Marshall Saunders takes up the cause of social reform in Halifax in a genteel and patronizing manner characteristic of her time and class. She also fills her house with birds and animals (like Emily Carr) and writes the classic *Beautiful Joe*. She never marries.

In 1901, Rebecca Chase Kinsman Ells runs an Annapolis Valley farm with the help of her eighteen-year-old son while her husband is absent—up in the Klondike searching for elusive gold. Which he never finds.

Within difference, between these differences, patterns emerge: delicate weavings, strong bindings. A regional ontology[7]—*No place like home.* Waves of Maritime outmigration have not uprooted. Away from home, our writers record the rush of nostalgia, the homesickness of the traveller. Not only for a region but also for a special locale, a place of birth, where the ''dear loved ones'' still gather without the absent one. Home as the house which a woman makes her own or loses to another woman. How easy it is in 1904 for Rebecca Ells to welcome her son's young bride as part of an extended family. How hard it is for Lauretta Kaulback Slauenwhite to lose her husband and her home in the 1930s and have to work in other people's homes as a domestic.

Archaeology of names: generations have lived in one place, generations have lived together, have built new homes close by, have come back to live.[8]

Continuity of generations. Kinship networks. The ties are stretched but never broken. In the 1870s, Margaret Connell of Pictou County lives with her husband and daughter in Fall River, Massachusetts. Both husband and daughter work in the textile factories. Her sister Mary is also living there, other family members come and go, and Margaret writes always to her sister back in Pictou, struggles to save enough money to get home for a visit, sends money home instead to help out the folks.

In these personal documents, mother-daughter love transcends Time as daughters mourn their mothers' death or lament their absence. Sisters, too, are interwoven with each other's lives. When Annie Rogers Butler voyages with her sea-captain husband in the 1870s, she has vivid dreams of her sister Rie:

> I laid and slept again but the ship rolled so I could not keep steady and I was tossed from side to side of the berth, and again I sprang up and called Rie. John, I thought I was with my dear sister and in our girlhood days once more but alas too soon came the knowledge I was far far away from her out at sea.

Ella Liscombe lived with her mother and her sister all her life. Rebecca Ells misses her dead mother and two sisters. Matilda Churchill, a missionary in India in the 1890s, has a tearful, all-night farewell with her sister in Truro before she embarks for the mission field.

Female friendship is part of community. Community is part of life. So is religion. As these women experience it, women's spirituality develops within traditional Christianity: Protestant, for the most part, and, for many during the eighteenth and early nineteenth centuries, radical—Dissenting and what George Fox calls "experiential." The New Light movement and then the Baptists shake up the old-line churches and establishment. The upper middle class and professional élite, especially those in Halifax where power is located, remain aloof. When Rebecca Byles is older, a mother and grandmother, she is disturbed by one of her children's conversion to the Baptists. She herself remains Anglican. At the same time, Eliza Chipman in a rural community discovers she has a soul.[9] Sense of sin, guilt, suffering. Christian rhetoric. Self suppressed, self-sacrifice an ideal. Comfort of belief a reality when faced with hardship, hard work, loss. Matilda Churchill arises up out of Truro to go forth to bring the light to the nations lost in darkness. By the late 1800s, the Baptists are established and extending spiritual domination in the wake of Empire. Spiritual imperialism. Yet Matilda and another lady missionary go out into the public world to work in the name of Christ and it is that work they crave. They march into medical wards, attend anatomy lectures, learn childbirthing. Insert themselves into the male world where they have no right to be and where they would not go unless impelled by what they understand to be a spiritual imperative. A Calling.[10]

The deep structures of these women's lives are conservative and patriarchal. Developed within an economic and political economy over which they have little or no control. Neither do many of the men with whom they share their lives. After 1867, the Maritime region becomes one of the marginalized parts of the nation. After World War I, of course, political, economic, and social change becomes more rapid and more intrusive into personal lives. Industrialization and capitalism transformed our self definitions. For some of our women, this is liberation. Betsy Hall, a university student during the Great War, went on to get a Ph.D. and a job as a social worker in the United States. On the other hand, traditional working-class women, like Lauretta Slauenwhite, suffer losses, are hired by middle-class women to do traditional women's work in the home. Working women, like Ella Liscombe in the Bank, are lucky to have a job, even one they hate, during the 1930s. By this time, women working outside the home are a fact of life.

These women are our mothers too. The conflicts and contradictions of their lives live on in us, their daughters. By attempting to decode their lives, we learn how to read our own traditions. So much that is hidden within us, that is silent in us, still awaits discovery, uncovering. If the personal is truly political, then personal documents, fragmentary, incomplete, elusive as they are, must be read as Texts as carefully as more crafted, conventional utterances.

Sometimes these private texts are boring, monotonous. The language of commonsense and experience does not often provide a numinous window on Being/beings. The "work-shop" is not often "lit up."[11] There are clichés, evasions, suppressions, ellipses. Personal names with hidden identities. Hannah Richardson, working in a shoe factory in Lynn, Massachusetts, in 1872, records on Saturday, March 18: "Fine and cool. Hard at work all day. Kiss Patterson and I went down to Mrs. Crowells in the evening to see Joe. Had a nice time eating oranges and mending Joe's pants and coat. Also a pleasant walk home."

The reader familiar with this discourse will note the length of time taken to describe paid work as contrasted with the pleasures of after-work social life. The feminine assumption of mending men's trousers as part of social routine when a group of young Nova Scotians are in exile together. But who, really, is Kiss Patterson? We will never know. Those who might know are dead or have disappeared or don't remember or confuse identities: was that X who married Y, or was it her cousin? Frustrations with the opaque surfaces of being-in-the-world.

But, if we think of the tiny trickles of snow which signal an avalanche, what accumulation can do is overwhelm us with a sense of beingness. Mundane, repetitive realities, domestic rituals, patterns that mark the self's interactions on a daily basis.[12] Mood shifts and sighs: Annie Rogers Butler, on board ship, writes on April 22: "Last night I was dreary enough. I don't know when I have felt so homesick before. I had a real good cry to myself after tea, then I felt better. Every woman knows the blessedness of tears. After that I killed three mammoth roaches; and settled down to my work. How I did wish for someone to speak to but no, there I sat sad and alone on the River Plate.''

Disruptions of crises, large and small: the birth and death of children, the farm horses bloated because they get into the oats, Ella Liscombe sick with the flu and feeling guilty/glad she cannot finish the accounts at the Bank.

Small narrative episodes that mark any life. Larger, more dramatic stories that mark the biological frame of each life story as we ''crawl,'' in Rebecca Ells' words, through Time to The End.

And even here, where life-as-Text is recorded, more or less unfaithfully, even here are epiphanic moments where a phrase, a word, reveals a world of self: On March 20, 1877, Margaret Connell, in Fall River, Massachusetts, writes to her sister in Pictou, Nova Scotia: ''The 17 and 18 we had a regular snowstorm and very cold the seasons come and go and the years roll round and when we look back it seems but a little while since we was all children together and now we are growing old and are scattered over the world.''

## NOTES

1.   I am ''playing'' with some of Heidegger's ontological-exploratory terms as a way of framing the essay. The following is a preliminary definition of facticity as it relates to *dasein* or human existence—Being-There: ''*Dasein* understands its ownmost Being in the sense of a certain 'factual Being-present-at-hand.' And yet the 'factuality' of the fact . . . of one's own *dasein* is at bottom quite different ontologically from the factual occurrence of some kind of mineral, for example. Whenever *dasein* is, it is as a Fact; and the factuality of such a Fact is what we shall call *dasein*'s 'facticity.' ''

2.   Identity and Difference, as analyzed by Heidegger and Jacques Derrida, become more problematic in the coming-to-Being of feminist ethics/aesthetics. See, for example, Godard, and Ricci.

3.   Cf. Krell: ''*Sein* and *aletheia* remain the key words, *sein* meaning coming to presence, and *aletheia* the disclosedness or unconcealment implied in such presence. Of course this double theme has its reverse side. Coming to presence suggests an absence before and after itself, so that withdrawal and departure must always be thought together with *sein* as presencing; disclosedness or unconcealment suggests a surrounding obscurity, Lethean concealment, so that darkness and oblivion must be thought together with *aletheia*.''

4.   This is not to condone the arbitrary binary opposition, that Manichean system which Louky Bersianik deconstructs in ''Aristotle's Lantern,'' in *A Mazing Space*, but to listen to the silences surrounding texts, within texts, texts not uttered, not-There. Tillie Olsen's silences, the silences of dominant texts regarding that which is Other.

5.   Nobody stuffs the world in at your eyes.
     The optic heart must venture: a jail-break
     And re-creation. (''Snow,'' by Margaret Avison)

Interesting that Margaret Atwood also uses this quotation as part of her conclusions to *Survival*.

6. The project originally covered the Maritime region. Many women helped along the way but the core group now consists of myself, Toni Laidlaw, a psychologist at Dalhousie University, and Marg Conrad, a historian at Acadia University. The Nova Scotia collection will be published under the title *No Place Like Home* in the fall of 1988 by Formac in Halifax. All quotations from the collection are from original documents which will be available in the Nova Scotia volume.

7. I have lifted this phrase from Michel Foucault and am here "playfully" re-materializing it in the Canadian context. The original usage refers to Foucault's thesis that: "The domain of the modern *episteme* should be represented rather as a volume of space open in three dimensions." The third dimension is "philosophical reflection, which develops as a thought of the Same" but also reveals, "if we question these empiricities from a radically philosophical point of view, those regional ontologies which attempt to define what life, labour, and language are in their own being . . . ." (346–47)

8. In place names, individual, family, and local histories can be uncovered layer by layer. Space contains Time. Genealogy is an essential part of archaeology.

9. Cf. Cott for a discussion of the meaning of women recording their religious meditations in terms of self-awareness.

10. See Merrick, and Hill.

11. For Heidegger, "equipment" is those things ready-to-hand in the world. When we become frustrated with equipment, this frustration can become a new way of seeing: "we catch sight of 'towards this' itself, and along with it everything connected with the work—the whole 'work-shop'—as that wherein concern always dwells. The context of equipment is lit up, not as something never seen before, but as a totality constantly sighted beforehand in circumspection." (105)

12. Cf. Heidegger: "The theme of our analytic is to be Being-in-the-world, and accordingly, the very world itself; and these are to be considered within the horizon of average everydayness—of the kind of Being which is closest to *dasein*. We must make a study of everyday Being-in-the-world; with the phenomenal support which this gives us, something like the world must come into view." (94)

## WORKS CITED

Cott, Nancy. 1977. *The Bonds of Womanhood*. New Haven: Yale Univ. Press.

Foucault, Michel. 1970. *The Order of Things: An Archaeology of the Human Sciences*. London: Tavistock.

Godard, Barbara. 1986. "Voicing Difference: The Literary Production of Native Women." In *A Mazing Space: Writing Canadian Women Writing*. Ed. Shirley Neuman and Smaro Kamboureli. Edmonton: Longspoon-NeWest. 87–107.

Heidegger, Martin. 1967. *Being and Time*. Trans. John Macquarrie and Edward Robinson. Oxford: Basil Blackwell.

Hill, Patricia R. 1985. *The World Their Household: The American Woman's Foreign Mission Movement and Cultural Transformation, 1870–1920*. Ann Arbor: Univ. of Michigan Press.

Krell, David Farrell. 1977. Introduction. *Martin Heidegger Basic Writings* by Martin Heidegger. New York: Harper and Row.

Merrick, E. C. 1970. *These Impossible Women—100 Years—The Story of the Union Baptist Women's Missionary Union of the Maritime Provinces*. Fredericton: Brunswick Press.

Ricci, N. P. 1987. "The End/s of Woman." *Canadian Journal of Political and Social Theory/Revue canadienne de théorie politique et sociale* 11, no. 3: 11–27.

# Research—
# Problems and Solutions

## Archival Sources for Research on Nineteenth-Century Women Writers

MARION BEYEA

$\mathbf{A}$rchives are no longer primarily the domain of academic historians. To their number have been added the family historian, the lawyer, the author, the television producer, the town planner, and many others. As archivists introduce descriptive standards and computer terminals in their effort to develop better ways of bringing the appropriate records to the attention of a myriad of researchers, it is valuable to have an opportunity to explore with users and potential users the archival sources relevant to their subject, in this case nineteenth-century women writers. For the purposes of this essay, the sources fall into two categories: the papers created by these writers and their families—their literary manuscripts, diaries, housekeeping accounts, and the letters they wrote and received; and secondly, the documents that record their activities—marrying, working, voicing concerns, dying. The examples have all been taken from the province of New Brunswick.

Women have been anonymous in history. They were not involved (or their involvement was not recorded) in wars, commerce, politics, or the other epic events that are traditionally chronicled and, indeed, that generated the records. Fortunately, this situation is less true of women writers. They were articulate, they wrote, they published, and in some cases they left papers that have been preserved. However, locating these papers can present many challenges. They may be preserved in more than one repository, and these locations are frequently obscure.

The starting point for research on individuals who have gained some prominence is the *Union List of Manuscripts in Canadian Repositories (ULM)*. This guide, which is available in most major archives and research libraries, describes the manuscript holdings of archival repositories across Canada. The information is provided by the institutions themselves, and the coverage is as comprehensive as time will permit. The entries, which are arranged alphabetically by the title of the collection, summarize each manuscript or record group in the contributing repositories. Where a writer's name does not appear as the title of a group of papers (as, for example, in the case of Julia Catherine Beckwith Hart), access to relevant material is provided through the index. The *ULM* was first published in two volumes in 1975, and four supplements have appeared since, in 1977, 1978, 1980, and 1981.

In addition to providing data for the *ULM*, individual archives have prepared and published guides to groups of records or papers in their repositories. These publications have a format and contents similar to those of the national guide, but the treatment is often more detailed. This is also the case with thematic guides that focus on sources relating to a study area, such as labour, immigration, or women. These guides may describe papers focusing on a particular topic in one repository, or they may span a number of institutions, usually within a specific geographic area. A good example of the thematic approach is the computerized guide to papers of writers and publishing houses held at Queen's University Archives, which was prepared as part of the ''Can Lit'' project. Unfortunately, the existence of such finding aids has been the exception rather than the rule. However, financial support from the Research Tools Program of the Social Sciences and Humanities Research Council and the Arrangement and Description Program of the Canadian Council of Archives has made more descriptive work possible in Canadian archives.

Nevertheless, even where such descriptive tools exist, they may not be readily available, and considerable effort may be necessary to locate a writer's papers. If records are not listed in the *ULM*, the search can require detective work. Fortunately, there is some logic to the location of archival records: they are usually found in a repository that is close to where the individual lived or worked, since archives generally acquire material within specific geographic or institutional perimeters. This is the case unless the writer was sufficiently prominent to have had her papers sought out by the special collections division of such libraries as those at Toronto, Calgary, or Queen's universities, which have manuscript holdings that cross regional boundaries. These centres, and the focus of their collections, are, of course, well known to literary scholars.

Provincial archives may provide the starting point for a search. However, in New Brunswick and in some other provinces, the archives had a late start, and it was historical and literary societies, museums, and special collections departments of university libraries that acquired the papers that might otherwise have gone to provincial institutions. But even if provincial archives do not hold the papers of a particular woman writer, their staff frequently know which repository does, or might, hold them. Some provincial archives are taking the lead in gathering together the guides and other finding aids to all archives in their area of jurisdiction. Archivists are discussing ''distance access'' and an automated *ULM*, and there are hopes that repositories will eventually be linked by computer, so that access for the researcher will be greatly simplified. Other helpful tools are the *Directory of Canadian Archives*, which provides addresses, hours of operation, and information on holdings for over 400 repositories, and provincial and city directories of archives.

Problems in locating manuscript material may arise because the papers of a woman writer are not always preserved together or easily identified. If they form part of the papers of her family or of a family with a name different from hers, they may not be easily located under her own name. If they were left with her estate papers or those of her family in a lawyer's office, they may have to be identified by the lawyer's name. If the papers ended up in the local newspaper office or form part of the correspondence of a friend or relative, their existence may remain hidden. Good indexes are the answer, but these are not as plentiful as they should be.

In such circumstances, it is to the archivist that the researcher must turn. "I am seeking information on Hannah Maynard Pickard, a nineteenth-century New Brunswick writer, whose novel *Procrastination* was published in Boston in 1840. I have been unable to discover the existence of her papers or of complete biographical information . . ." is the kind of letter that could be sent to an archivist. Or a visit to the archives could be arranged. Most archivists are willing to help, although the many demands on their time conspire to curtail the public service they can give. These pressures include volume of work; the acquisition of other important records; the arranging and description of extensive existing collections; the bureaucratic responsibilities of planning, reporting, and justifying decisions; the need to keep abreast of and introduce new technologies; and the sheer number and variety of researchers— lawyers, architects, local historians, and genealogists—who now crowd the reading rooms.

It may be that the researcher of the nineteenth-century woman writer will be required to join the ranks of the genealogist. Once stigmatized by archivists and historians—such as Philip Jordan, who wrote of "a dabbler, a rag-picker who works the alleys, a fuss-budget of an antiquarian, even a genealogist" (30)—this group is gaining new respect. Academics, archivists, and other researchers are impressed by the tenacity, ingenuity, and diligence of the genealogist, who often finds dates and facts that they themselves have despaired of discovering. This fact has particularly been remarked on by writers seeking biographical data for entries in the *Dictionary of Canadian Biography*. The researcher of nineteenth-century women writers may need exactly the same qualities. For basic facts concerning a writer, for the information she did not provide about herself, sometimes for any information at all, the researcher must turn to the records most commonly used by the genealogist: records of vital events (births, marriages, and deaths) and of government administration (land transactions and court and census records); records relating to occupation (teachers' licences and nursing-school attendance) and health and social care;

records of organizations in which women were involved; and "secondary" sources such as genealogies, transcriptions of epitaphs, collections of news clippings, scrapbooks, and other ephemera. Again, regrettably, these sources are not complete, nor are they usable without deduction, interpretation, and occasional frustration. But by relating the writer to other people (her family members, for instance), to the places where she lived, and to what she did in addition to writing, a researcher will be led to the information that does exist and, in the process, will be able to place her in context and understand what and why she wrote.

A more detailed examination of some of the resources I have described will illustrate their usefulness. The records that I have termed records of vital events (fondly called the "hatch, match, and dispatch" records by genealogists) include: church registers of baptism, confirmation, membership, marriage, and burial; civil registers of birth and marriage; municipal burial permits; death certificates; cemetery records; marriage bonds; and other documents. These records vary according to the bureaucratic practices of the particular jurisdiction. For instance, in most provinces during a certain period only the Church of England, as the established church, was authorized to perform marriages, although the Roman Catholic Church was sometimes granted a dispensation that permitted recognition of marriages performed by its priests. This means that, in most cases, Church of England marriages are not recorded in civil registers for the period and the church registers must be sought. There are other problems inherent in these sources. The records may not begin early enough or be comprehensive enough to meet a researcher's need for that crucial date of birth or that elusive maiden name. In New Brunswick, government registration of births began only in 1888, and compliance was very irregular until the 1920s. Even if the record is extant, it usually contains only basic data. Occasionally, though, it may provide a gratuitous gem of information, such as the name of a sponsor at a baptism which would link a woman to the family of her in-laws at a date earlier than she was thought to have known them. Or the record may contain a clue that will lead to other records. The route can be tortuous: the researcher goes from oft-repeated "fact" to inaccurate secondary source, to newspaper obituary, to original source.

Other records deriving from government administration include those of the court and land grants, ownership, and transfer. Some records, such as the census and assessment rolls, serve only to fix a person in a certain place at a certain time. It was, of course, usually men who were involved in legal transactions. However, some of these documents may contain valuable information about women. A dramatic example (although not involving a woman writer) is Ebenezer Slocum's petition for compensation for losses suffered as a result of his and his father's loyalist stand in the American Revolution. His testimony and his mother Sarah's provide details about their experiences during the revolution:

His father Charles Slocum was killed by a rebel mob in 1778. He left no will, but his wife is alive in this Province and ten children alive . . . . Likewise proceedings against Sarah Slocum for having issued forged paper money and certificates from the sheriff, that she stood half an hour in the Pillory and had her ears cropt (Ontario Archives, 303).

Court records may also provide information on women. They include the records of the various divisions of civil and criminal courts (perhaps reflecting the individual's propensity to litigation), and particularly those of the probate court. Women made wills, were named in wills, and received bequests. An excellent example of the first is the will of New Brunswick writer May Agnes Fleming, which Lorraine McMullen uncovered in her extensive research. Fleming makes specific recommendations for the education of her children:

> I hereby direct them, absolutely and without condition to have all of my children educated at Roman Catholic Schools, under the charge of the Religious Orders of the Catholic Church, and it is my wish and desire that the girls be educated at Mt. St. Vincent, on the Hudson River, under the charge of the Sisters of Charity, and the boys at St. John's College, Fordham, under the charge of the Jesuit Fathers, and I wish them all to be kept at school until they are twenty years of age respectively . . . . Should my husband refuse to allow our said children to remain under the control of the said guardians or either of them, or himself assume the control and management of our said children or render inoperative the foregoing provisions for the care and education of our said children, then and in such case, and whenever and as long as he shall do so, I will and direct the said trustees that they shall not pay, use or apply any part of my said estate to the support or education of any of the said children who may be thus taken from their control, and held under the control of their said father.

This excerpt gives an indication of Fleming's religious values and the importance of education to her, and it speaks volumes about her attitude towards her estranged husband. Her point of view perhaps extended to include men in general, as her instructions for payment suggest:

> [if] any one or more of my said daughters should marry before attaining the age of twenty-one years . . . the share [must] be immediately invested for her benefit . . . for her sole and separate use, and as her separate estate, not to be under the control or subject to the debt of her husband.

Not all wills contain such dramatic or detailed information as May Agnes Fleming's, but the names of parents, spouses, and children, estimates of worldly wealth, and a hint of familial relations are usually found.

In the nineteenth century, it was the exception for women to work outside the home, but women writers were among the most likely to be employed. One of the most common occupations was teaching, and the training of teachers, their certification, licensing, and pensioning required government records.

Usually teachers had to submit applications at each of these stages. Although these documents are often no more than a completed form, the information can be helpful and sometimes detailed. In New Brunswick in the early part of the nineteenth century, teachers had to petition the legislature for payment of their annual salaries. For several years in the 1820s, the request of one woman teacher was made in verse. Teachers sometimes corresponded with their local school boards, the provincial board, or the Department of Education, and these bodies also exchanged letters concerning individuals. Hannah Rogers of Charlotte County, New Brunswick, who was "degraded from the rank of a licensed Teacher of Youth" and then reinstated, was the subject of such correspondence. Some 113 trustees and other inhabitants of the parish of St. James, *all men*, petitioned the lieutenant governor to rule against her reinstatement, citing an investigation that had resulted in "clearly convicting her of atheism, and of blasphemy couched in the most gross and indelicate terms." Careers in nursing and in the religious orders were also open to women and records of their training, registration, and work have survived.

Health care and social assistance records for the nineteenth century exist in some jurisdictions, though there are few for this period in New Brunswick. A case file from the 1940s provides information on a certain writer's illness from tuberculosis, as well as evidence that his mother died from the same disease, and other facts that were not available elsewhere. Such government records are restricted because of the confidentiality of the information they contain, but the restrictions do not usually extend beyond ninety years and would therefore not be applicable to most documents relevant to nineteenth-century women writers.

Records of societies and associations in which women were involved may also be helpful to the researcher. Women writers were likely to be participants in, if not organizers of, such bodies as the Women's Christian Temperance Union; mission societies and other church-related organizations; historical, library, and literary societies; maternal associations; and disaster, immigrant aid, and patriotic societies. However, these organizations became more prevalent in the twentieth century as women emerged from the home and moved into volunteer and philanthropic roles. Consequently, more twentieth- than nineteenth-century records have survived even for those groups established at an earlier date. Often the preserved records are not very illuminating even about the objectives and activities of the organization itself; they may merely consist of routine motions passed, membership rolls, and financial records. But again, such material may at least locate a woman writer in a particular place and time and indicate her interests or provide valuable clues to other likely sources for research.

Other potential sources which are found in libraries as well as in archives may be both a last resort and a vital key. They include genealogies (published, unpublished, or in note form); obituaries from newspapers; local, church, and association histories, which are sometimes inaccurate but often direct a researcher to factual information; maps locating a lot or dwelling; city directories and gazetteers, which list families by street and make it possible to trace their movements; scrapbooks of clippings and memorabilia; and transcriptions of epitaphs, which occasionally provide amusing, if not helpful, information— such as "O Lord, she is thin."

Fortunate is the researcher who finds the odd touch of humour, for searching can be a discouraging and frustrating task. Archivists will admit that researching in archives is not easy. They can recite a litany of reasons for this: a lack of resources; the unique nature of archival materials; the difficulties of acquiring records; even inadequacies in the researcher and perhaps in the research topic itself. Although archivists continue to produce more comprehensive finding aids and fight for more resources, research in archives remains a challenge. Records, unlike books, were written not to inform but to document. With an understanding of the nature of archival records, hard work, and perhaps some luck, information may be uncovered which will elucidate the life of a writer: her background, the influences that shaped her, and her reaction to them. This is an important step to understanding her work.

## WORKS CITED

Jordan, Philip D. 1958. *The Nature and Practice of State and Local History*. Service Center for Teachers of History, Publication No. 14. Washington, D.C.: American Historical Association.

Ontario. Bureau of Archives. 1905. *Second Report*. Ed. Alexander Fraser. Toronto: King's Printer.

Provincial Archives of New Brunswick. RG 7, RS 71. Saint John County Probate Court Records; will of May Agnes Fleming, May 7, 1880.

——— . RG 11, RS 655. Teachers' Petitions and Licences.

# Research—
# Problems and Solutions

## Canadian Women Writers and the American Literary Milieu of the 1890s

JAMES DOYLE

"The market for Canadian literary wares," wrote Sara Jeannette Duncan in 1887, "is New York, where the intellectual life of the continent is rapidly centralising" (41). American magazines, agreed Archibald Lampman in 1892, "are attracting to them most of our literary and artistic effort" (Davies, 96). Margaret Marshall Saunders, reminiscing in 1921 about the beginning of her literary career in the 1890s, explains: "When I started writing I met with so little encouragement in Canada that I went to [the United States]—but without the slightest resentment. My publishers knew I was a Canadian, they knew I loved my own country best, but it never made any difference to them" (Saunders Papers). Robert Barr, who left Canada for the United States and subsequently for England, exhorted young Canadian literary aspirants in 1899: "Get over the border as soon as you can; come to London or go to New York; shake the dust of Canada from your feet" (10).

It is one of the ironies of Canadian cultural history that, at a time when artistic activity was feeling the impetus of a revitalized nationalism, most of the anglophone writers in the country were looking abroad for publishing outlets and critical recognition. It is rather surprising, furthermore, that historians of Canadian literature have shown little interest in this phenomenon. The circumstances and consequences of this widespread cultural dependency need to be thoroughly researched. Research is particularly needed in the subject of women writers, whose situation, in this generally neglected aspect of Canadian literary history, has been almost completely overlooked.

As Robert Barr indicated in his account of his own youthful employment on the Detroit *Free Press*, one means to literary success in the United States was a staff job with a metropolitan newspaper or magazine. American newspapers, especially in the 1880s and 1890s, provided abundant opportunities for would-be writers, including many enterprising and independent women. Sara Jeannette Duncan, hired by the Washington *Post* in 1885 to write book reviews and cultural articles, is the most prominent Canadian woman writer to achieve success in this direction. Elsewhere in this volume, Marjory Lang cites several other examples of Canadian women journalists who succeeded in the United States in the late nineteenth century. But for writers primarily committed to *belles-lettres*, the hectic demands and stylistic debasement of writing for newspaper deadlines were sometimes regarded as an impediment to creative achievement. "The man [and, presumably, the woman too] who innocently goes into journalism under the hallucination that it has some sort of intermittent relation to literature, sells his soul to the Devil" (170), was the angry complaint of Walter Blackburn Harte, an English-born essayist and critic who began his career writing for Canadian newspapers before moving on to the United States in 1890. Not all Canadian writers would go quite so far in expressing their distaste for journalism, but many would agree that the better opportunities for literary success lay with the magazines. "The literature of the day in America, as far as fiction, poetry, and criticism are concerned," wrote Archibald Lampman, "is concentrated in the magazines" (Davies, 96).

Most Canadian writers of Lampman's generation were not only submitting their work regularly to the American magazines; many of them had gone south to find work in the editorial offices, to be an active part of what were considered the main source and medium of modern literature. In 1891, Walter Blackburn Harte became an assistant editor for *New England Magazine* of Boston, and subsequently worked for *Arena* and several smaller periodicals. Bliss Carman worked for various New York and Boston publications, including *The Chap-Book*, *The Independent*, and *Current Literature*. Charles G. D. Roberts was briefly with *Illustrated American* in 1897, while his brother William Carman Roberts edited *Literary Digest*. E. W. Thomson was on the staff of the Boston family magazine *Youth's Companion*, and Peter McArthur was editor of *Truth* in New York.

In spite of the proliferation of American literary magazines in the 1890s, however, and in spite of the remarkable success of male Canadian expatriates, no female Canadian writers seem to have been able to land similar editorial jobs. This failure is not easy to explain, or even to document conclusively, but a few factors seem relevant. The North American bourgeois attitude of protectiveness towards women may have been a consideration: many periodical offices were unsavoury places where men worked in their shirt sleeves, chomped cigars, used slang and profanity. Even William Dean Howells' rather antiseptic account of this kind of environment in his novel *A Hazard of New Fortunes* (1890) excludes women except as occasional visitors. Jack London's fuller-blooded picture of a typical shoestring literary magazine in *Martin Eden* (1908) includes fist-fights between editors and unpaid contributors.

But even if such dens were more unattractive than the newspaper offices where Canadian women were making inroads, there should have been a more receptive atmosphere in the burgeoning women's magazines, such as *Harper's Bazaar* (established in 1867), *Ladies' Home Journal* (1883), *McCall's* (1885), and *Vogue* (1892), all of which had predominantly female editorial staffs (Mott 1938, 388; 1957, 536, 580, 756). By 1890, furthermore, a few American women had moved into influential editorial positions in other magazines. The most famous was probably Jeannette Gilder, editor of *Critic* for over twenty years. Also worth noting are Susan Ward, literary editor of *The Independent*, and Helen Gardner, co-editor of *Arena* in 1895–96, along with Walter Blackburn Harte.

Perhaps the exclusion of expatriate Canadian women from the editorial offices of American literary periodicals merely reflects the fact that fewer Canadian women than men went job-hunting in the United States. Young Canadian men, with no need of green cards or chaperones, could head for New York to seek their fortune or to live a hand-to-mouth bohemian existence if necessary, as Toronto-born Harvey O'Higgins' 1906 novel *Don-A-Dreams* describes. For a young, middle-class Canadian woman, however, several months of living in a rooming house in an ethnically mixed New York neighbourhood while making the rounds of editorial offices might have raised eyebrows back home. The 1890s was the era of the New Woman in the United States, and the independent cigarette-smoking female writer or artist living on a par with men was a titillating idea, as Arthur Stringer, another Canadian expatriate in New York, indicated in his 1903 novel *The Silver Poppy*. But Stringer's heroine is an American, and American women might be capable of any outrage, even plagiarism, as Stringer's prim provincial hero observes with consternation.

But if few Canadian women followed the men into exile, they did try as eagerly as their male compatriots to break into print with the American magazines and book publishers. Sara Jeannette Duncan's work appeared in *Harper's Bazaar*, *Scribner's*, *Century*, and *Atheneum*, and most of her novels were published by Appleton of New York. Ethelwyn Wetherald was in *Scribner's*, *Harper's*, *New England Magazine*, and *Youth's Companion*, and her book, *House of Trees*, was issued in 1895 by Lamson, Wolffe, a small Boston firm which was also Bliss Carman's publisher. Susan Frances Harrison had poems in *New England Magazine* and *Littel's Living Age*; Agnes Maule Machar appeared in *Century*, although the bulk of her output was placed with Canadian periodicals.

It is impossible, however, to avoid the conclusion that, in their efforts to seek the international prominence and substantial remuneration available in American magazine and book publication, Canadian women writers encountered discrimination—a discrimination compounded perhaps by nationality as well as by sex. American magazines in the 1890s were paying increasing critical attention to Canadian literature through reviews and survey articles, although American critics tended to impose on English-Canadian writers certain stereotyped expectations. Canadian literature was supposed to be a celebration of nature, as established by the Tantramar poems of Charles G. D. Roberts, the lake lyrics of Wilfred Campbell, the wilderness poems of Duncan Campbell Scott. Canadian women writers, it appears, were expected to produce a more delicate version of these stereotypes. The influence of American editors and critics was probably strong enough to make these women conform to their expectations willingly, perhaps even with unquestioning acceptance of the literary assumptions involved. Still, one wonders what individualistic tendencies were suppressed in this authoritarian cultural climate—especially when the authorities were foreign.

This is not to say that American editors and critics paid a lot of attention to Canadian women writers, comparatively speaking. Three survey articles on Canadian literature, which appeared in American magazines of the 1890s, provide a suggestive indication of American responses. An article by a journalist named Joseph Dana Miller, "The Singers of Canada," published in *Munsey's* in May 1895, effused at length over Roberts, Lampman, Carman, and other male writers and then devoted a concluding half-page to Pauline Johnson, Isabella Valancy Crawford, Susan Frances Harrison, and Agnes Maule Machar. A female critic for the New York *Bookman*, Winifred Lee Wendell, mentioned Lily Dougall, Marjory McMurchy, and Margaret Marshall Saunders as well as Johnson and Harrison in her 1900 article "The Modern School of Canadian Writers," but the references were very brief in comparison to her treatment of Carman, Roberts, and other male writers. Walter Blackburn Harte included more detailed appreciations of Duncan, Machar, Wetherald, and Harrison in his "Some Canadian Writers of To-Day" for *New England Magazine* in 1895, but these four are overshadowed by the male writers surveyed in the article.

This kind of discrimination is evident too in the infrequent inclusion of Canadians in American anthologies of the period. A substantial section on Canadian poetry was included in the influential *Victorian Anthology 1837–1895*, edited in 1895 by the New York littérateur E. C. Stedman. But among the generous representations of Roberts, Carman, Lampman, Campbell, and Scott were one poem by Susanna Moodie, two by Isabella Valancy Crawford, two by Susan Frances Harrison, three by Pauline Johnson, four by Ethelwyn Wetherald, and one by Elizabeth G. Roberts. The inclusion of Charles G. D. Roberts' sister was not perhaps an exclusively literary decision: Roberts himself had edited the Canadian section at Stedman's invitation, as correspondence between the two men reveals (Stedman, 1910, II, 199–200). Roberts' editorial policies raise another possibility: that the male Canadians active in the American literary scene tended, albeit without malevolence, to exclude or discourage their female compatriots. Bliss Carman, for instance, as editor of *The Chap-Book*, established in Cambridge, Massachusetts, in 1894, ignored Canadian women writers except for publishing two poems by Ethelwyn Wetherald in 1896. Roberts and Carman were the centre of a rather clubby and bohemian circle of Canadian literary expatriates, where lunches and late-night get-togethers in Greenwich Village restaurants became part of some legendary and predominantly masculine exploits.

But if Canadian women writers had trouble with mainline editors, even among their own countrymen, they could and did seek American publication in the eccentric but innovative little magazines that emerged in the United States by the dozen around the turn of the century. Flimsy in format, limited in circulation and in funds to pay contributors, these pocket-sized ephemeral periodicals, like *Yellow Book* in England, provided outlets for iconoclastic literary and social movements. Bliss Carman's *Chap-Book* is sometimes described as the first of the American little magazines, although it soon lapsed into the conventionalities of the mass-circulation periodicals, leaving the iconoclasm to its imitators. Women writers were not inordinately represented in such publications, although one magazine, *Ebell* of Los Angeles (1898–99), was edited and written entirely by women, and some editors included feminism among the modern causes their publications advocated (Faxon, 72–74, 92, 106–107, 125–126; Heyl, 21–26).

Carman did publish in *The Chap-Book* two poems by Ethelwyn Wetherald, whose work also appeared in *Lotus*, edited in 1895–96 by Walter Blackburn Harte. Harte published the work of another Canadian, Edith Eaton, whose short stories appeared in *Lotus* and in a second short-lived venture of Harte's, *Fly-Leaf* (1896), as well as in a magazine called *Chautauquan* (1905). Harte and Eaton had begun their literary careers together in Montreal, publishing short stories and prose sketches in John-Talon Lesperance's *The Dominion Illustrated News* in 1888. Eaton, the Eurasian daughter of a silk merchant who lived for several years in China, adopted the pen name Sui Sin Far, and went on to publish short stories in a variety of American periodicals until her death in 1914 at the age of forty-seven. Edith Eaton is overshadowed in reputation by her younger sister Winnifred, who in the first quarter of the twentieth century published a series of sentimental novels about Japan under the pen name Onoto Watanna. But Eaton's one book, a collection of stories entitled *Mrs. Spring Fragrance* (1912), reveals a remarkably bold commitment to urban realism and controversial social themes, involving the problems of Chinese and Eurasians in the United States and Canada.

The example of Edith Eaton points up the need for more research in a specialized but vital area of Canadian literary history. The work of other obscure writers, and of better-known ones, needs to be sought out and identified in the back issues of late nineteenth-century American magazines. Many of the more ephemeral publications, in brief and unindexed runs, are housed in the rare periodicals collections of the New York and Boston public libraries and in Princeton University library. Not nearly enough research is done by Canadian literary historians, biographers, and critics in the field of late nineteenth-century American publishing outlets, partly because of an underestimation of the literary importance of periodicals in that era and of the extent and significance of the Canadian involvement with publications in the United States.

The manuscript collections of magazines, editors, and publishing companies also need to be thoroughly searched. The archives of the Century Company in the New York public library contain letters from many Canadian authors, including Agnes Deans Cameron, Sara Jeannette Duncan, Agnes Laut, and Agnes Maule Machar. Much of this correspondence is of considerable biographical and critical interest, since the authors are often writing to introduce themselves to editors and to describe work in progress. One letter from Duncan to the Century editors, for instance, contains an outline of an untitled work-in-progress that is obviously an early version of *The Imperialist*.

Such research should, of course, be part of a comprehensive scrutiny of the whole literary history of late nineteenth-century Canada, including the lives and careers of writers of both sexes, and the editing and publishing milieux on both sides of the Canadian-American border. So little work has been done in this direction that all historical and biographical investigation is to be welcomed. But a concentration on the experience of women writers is especially urgent, for it may lead to important revisions of perceptions of late nineteenth-century Canadian literature. The most widely held notions about this period tend to resolve into two familiar clichés: almost all the work of enduring value was done by three or four male poets, and the prevailing literary medium was a genteel romanticism harking back to Wordsworth, Shelley, and Keats. In fact, the English-Canadian literary milieu from 1867 to the early twentieth century was a turmoil of activity involving the distinctive talents of many now forgotten individuals, as well as various internal and external influences, always and especially including the monolithic and seductive influence of the United States. At the least, research along the lines indicated here should lead to a clearer picture of what it was like to be a Canadian writer in the late nineteenth century. In addition, such research could lead to the rediscovery of important writers and to a better understanding of the social and cultural forces which form part of the explanation as to why Canadian writers wrote as they did at that time.

## WORKS CITED

Barr, Robert. 1973. "Literature in Canada." In *Measure of the Rule*. Toronto: Univ. of Toronto Press.

Davies, Barrie. 1979. Introduction. *At The Mermaid Inn: Wilfred Campbell, Archibald Lampman, Duncan Campbell Scott in "The Globe" 1892–3*. Toronto: Univ. of Toronto Press.

Duncan, Sara Jeannette. 1975. "American Influence on Canadian Thought." In *The Search for English-Canadian Literature*. Ed. Carl Ballstadt. Toronto: Univ. of Toronto Press.

Faxon, F. W. 1903–4. "Ephemeral Bibelots." *Bulletin of Bibliography* 3.

Harte, Walter Blackburn. 1894. *Meditations in Motley*. Boston: Arena.

Heyl, Laurence. 1940. "Little Magazines." *Princeton University Library Chronicle* 2: 21–26.

Howells, William Dean. 1976. *A Hazard of New Fortunes*. 1890. Bloomington, London: Indiana Univ. Press.

London, Jack. 1908. *Martin Eden*. New York: Rinehart.

Mott, Frank Luther. 1938. *A History of American Magazines 1865–1885*. Cambridge, Mass.: Belknap.

———. 1957. *A History of American Magazines 1885–1905*. Cambridge, Mass.: Belknap.

O'Higgins, Harvey. 1906. *Don-A-Dreams*. New York: Century.

Saunders, M. Marshall. 1921. Saunders Papers. Address to Women Teachers' Association of Toronto, 26 Nov. Acadia University, Wolfville, Nova Scotia.

Stedman, E. C., ed. 1969. *Victorian Anthology 1837–1895*. 1895. New York: Greenwood Press.

Stedman, Laura, and George M. Gould, eds. 1910. *Life and Letters of E. C. Stedman*. New York: Moffat, Yard.

Stringer, Arthur. 1903. *The Silver Poppy*. New York: D. Appleton.

# Research— Problems and Solutions

## Problems and Solutions in the *Dictionary of Canadian Biography*, 1800-1900

FRANCESS G. HALPENNY

This paper focuses on problems and solutions in researching the lives of women writers of the nineteenth century for volumes of the *Dictionary of Canadian Biography* (*DCB*). For these volumes, the nineteenth century means individuals who died between 1800 and 1900 and they do not include such writers as Mary Anne (Madden) Sadleir or Sara Jeannette Duncan who lived into the twentieth century. The volumes covering this period have been published, non-sequentially, over a number of years, beginning with volume X in 1972. Work on this volume actually began around 1969, and there has been a burgeoning of research in the twenty-year interval. This research has assisted the work of the *DCB*, and some of it has been encouraged by assignments to write biographies for the volumes. But, inevitably, some research has come after the relevant volumes were completed and will have to be taken into account in re-editions. This paper is, it should be noted, very much an overview based on reading the manuscripts and supporting bibliographies submitted to the project and the correspondence between editors and contributors.

Women, let alone women writers, in the *DCB* for the nineteenth century are not a large group despite earnest striving on the part of the project's staff and its consultants. This is a matter of regret because a greater representation of the undeniably important roles women played in the century's society, roles different from those of men, would have been desirable. But the lack of adequate documentation at the time prevented the writing of even short biographies. References to women in the sources are all too often indirect and fragmentary; the glimpses of a life may be only through the fuller pattern of the career of a woman's father, husband, brother, or son. In a few instances, however, there has been sufficient information to provide expressive portraits. Catherine Honoria (Hume) Blake (volume XI) exemplifies the influence a wife and mother could have in the development of an important family, a woman who found in that role, though not without personal tension, her "main source of self-fulfilment." Another instance is Harriet (Dobbs) Cartwright (volume XI). Of a prominent Kingston family, she made use of obviously considerable talents in organization and intelligence by taking a familiar route for wives in this setting: charitable endeavours on behalf of needy women, temperance, the local hospital, widows and orphans of the epidemics, women in the penitentiary. The biography of Hannah (Peters) Jarvis (volume VII) is another attempt to get at a reality of nineteenth-century life; with her husband, she was caught up in the bickering and jealousies of small-town York (Toronto), but the pattern of her life was finally determined by her long dependence upon her children and her own labour after her spendthrift husband died when she was in her mid-forties.

A group who stand outside this pattern are the female Catholic religious, of whom there are proportionately a considerable number in the *DCB*. They were often women of considerable determination, managerial skill, diplomatic artfulness, and physical courage, as well as piety. Their careers are known because of the annals their congregations recorded and preserved over the years; the documentation thus exists to provide the facts of their service.

Research is not static, and the current activities of researchers with new interests, particularly women, are changing many pictures. Thus the *DCB* has benefitted from the recent work of historians such as Sylvia Van Kirk and Jennifer Brown, who have been adjusting the history of the fur trade to show more fully the lives of Indian, Métis, and white women connected with it and the factors affecting them in social intercourse, marriage, and family. Volume VIII's biographies of Nancy McKenzie, Sarah McLeod, and Frances Ramsay Simpson, wife of Governor Sir George Simpson, offer a reflection of the insights provided by this current approach. Research in the areas of labour, education, social groups, religion, and ethnic communities has already helped and should yield further results (a small foretaste is given in the biography of union leader Katie McVicar in volume XI). The research assistants working on the name lists for the first twentieth-century volumes have found, however, that volume XIII will not differ much from volume XII: there is research on twentieth-century women who broke out of silences, but they usually lived longer than men and often did not die until the 1920s and 1930s.

Something is known of certain other nineteenth-century women because of their writings, not originally intended for publication, which have fortunately been preserved. Studies of these women have been primarily historical or biographical, but they could have more literary implications as well. I am referring here to diarists whose records have been published or have survived in manuscript and to letter writers who confronted the difficulties of communication in their correspondence. The biographies of three religious figures— Elizabeth Dart (volume VIII), Eliza Ann Chipman (volume VIII), and Mary

Coy (volume VIII)—provide examples of the importance of a published journal or memoir in drawing attention to, and providing understanding of, women of unusual force in their communities. Their lives invite new study. The published memoirs and the letters of Susan (Mein) Sibbald (volume IX) offer a sprightly picture of the genteel Family Compact society of Lake Simcoe and Toronto. *Recollections of a Georgia Loyalist*, published only in 1901, is the memoir Elizabeth (Lichtenstein) Johnston (volume VII) wrote in her seventies for her grandchildren. It concentrates on the personal problems she and her family experienced in their wanderings through the American south, Scotland, Jamaica, and Nova Scotia for some thirty years after the outbreak of the American Revolution. A well-read, somewhat puritanical woman devoted to her household, she shows little interest in public affairs. Elizabeth Russell (volume VI) and Anne (Murray) Powell (volume VII) are two of several Upper Canadian women related to leaders in the government about whom Edith Firth has written in the *DCB*. Manuscript letters and diaries in the Ontario Archives (and for Mrs. Powell, a published selection also) have been sources for their stories. Elizabeth (Gwillim) Simcoe (volume VII) is deservedly well known for her writing as a diarist.

One of the more unusual letter writers of the mid-century is Letitia (Mactavish) Hargrave (volume VIII), wife of a Hudson's Bay Company officer, who sent many letters home to Britain, and who became well known when the Champlain Society published her letters in 1947. Published memoranda and a very large archive of lively diaries and correspondence yet to be published for Amelia (Ryerse) Harris (volume XI) of London undoubtedly contain insights into Upper Canadian society through the wife of a public officer. Six of her daughters married Englishmen (four of them officers in British regiments stationed in London) and required letters over the years. It has been customary in Canadian studies to bring within the purview of literary history at least, if not always literature as such, a good deal of material that originally had a private purpose (such as the records of explorers), and the resources I have been describing for nineteenth-century women can be and are being examined from points of view other than the strictly historical.

The number of nineteenth-century women identified as writers in *DCB* volumes is not yet large. This reflects the late growth in literary activity itself and in literature of significance. By way of illustration, for men writers Thomas McCulloch of the Stepsure letters appears in volume VII, John Richardson in VIII, Thomas Chandler Haliburton in IX, James De Mille in X, Archibald Lampman only in XII. William Kirby will appear in XIII; Charles G. D. Roberts and Bliss Carman are projected for XV and XVII. The first significant woman novelist in French, Laure Conan, will appear in XV.[1]

The women writers included in the published volumes provide an interesting study. There are, for example, some who came to North America from an experience of literature and of literary creativity elsewhere and were encouraged and guided by this experience in a variety of ways. Anna (Murphy) Jameson (volume VIII) is a striking example of someone who travelled to Upper Canada from a developed literary environment and returned to it, and who because of that environment could write about her experience in Upper Canada with sophistication and grace. For this undoubted personality and frequent writer, there is much research material available. Juliana Horatia (Gatty) Ewing (volume XI) had a somewhat similar connection with British North America. The daughter of a well-known children's writer, she came to Fredericton with her British officer husband as a published author of children's literature and returned to England to continue this activity. New Brunswick is remembered in the settings of her stories, and attractive collections of her letters and sketches from Fredericton, published in 1983 and 1985 (after volume XI appeared), show something of the colonial society in which she was a brief visitor.[2] It was these colonial connections that made her a candidate for a biography in the *DCB*, and through such sources as the Osborne Collection in the Toronto Public Library and the interest of researchers in the Maritimes and elsewhere, a just account could be compiled. A related yet different sort of comment is appropriate for Susanna (Strickland) Moodie (volume XI) and Catharine Parr (Strickland) Traill (volume XII), figures who command readers by the power and vigour of their accomplished writing. As immigrant and resident authors, they developed Canadian careers. Biographical, historical, and critical information on Moodie and Traill has been rich, and becomes richer by the year, as the story of the publication of *Canadian Crusoes*, unravelled in the CEECT edition,[3] and the recent discovery of a revealing group of Moodie letters attest.

Isabella Valancy Crawford (volume XI) was a resident of Upper Canada from about eight years of age, at one time living in an area which enabled her to know Susanna Moodie and Catharine Parr Traill. She imposes herself upon the attention of today's readers by the quality of her poetry and the special characteristics of her imagination. Fortunately, by the time volume XI was being prepared, there was already available a good deal of biographical and literary information and analysis, particularly from the 1970s, compiled by such researchers as Dorothy Livesay and Penny Petrone. They had uncovered much more of the story of a plain and simple life circumscribed by poverty and seclusion, and also of an imagination that ranged far beyond the popular magazines for which Crawford had to write. There are still gaps in our knowledge of what made her the kind of writer she was, and she will continue to attract our curiosity.

Julia Catherine (Beckwith) Hart (volume IX) has received attention because of the chronological fact that in 1824 she published *St. Ursula's Convent*, the first work of fiction by a native-born Canadian and the first to be published in what is now Canada. There would seem to be more to Mrs. Hart than chronology, however. A family connection with Quebec, for someone who lived in New Brunswick and Upper Canada, made its way into the model of romantic fiction she followed for her first novel. The route to its publication provides an interesting glimpse into the possibilities for writers of the period. Her shift to an American subject and American publisher for her second novel is also significant in practical and literary terms. The bibliography the *DCB* contributor was able to cite in 1976 is not very contemporary. Volume VI has since brought the biography of her Kingston publisher, Hugh Christopher Thomson, proprietor and editor of the influential *Upper Canada Herald*.

The Herbert sisters, Sarah (volume VII) and Mary Eliza (volume X), have received modest attention over the years for their published poetry and romantic tales. Sarah died young and a glow was cast over her sentimental, religious, and temperance pieties, but she was an editor of *Olive Branch* which published Harriet Beecher Stowe. Mary Eliza was involved with *Mayflower*, a genteel periodical with many female contributors. Understanding of these women has been largely through standard compilations, contemporary newspapers, and a few later references. However, Gwendolyn Davies' 1980 thesis, ''A Literary Study of Selected Periodicals from Maritime Canada, 1789–1872,'' made a major contribution to knowledge about this significant genre of literary activity.

A native-born poet and novelist with a prolific and successful record of publication was Rosanna Eleanora (Mullins) Leprohon (volume X). Her career as a contributor of verse and prose to *The Literary Garland* in mid-century, and then as the author of romantic fiction, usually first in serial form and several times over the imprint of John Lovell (volume XII), is noteworthy in a *DCB* context as well as generally because of her introduction through marriage to the French society of Quebec, which gives her writing some continuing interest and which contributed to her rapid appearance in French translation. The bibliography attached to her biography in volume X (published in 1972) could not lead readers beyond the standard reference works of literary history, and there is no reference to documentary resources. The New Canadian Library edition of *Antoinette de Mirecourt*, which appeared in 1973, is now out of print and unlikely to join the revamped series. The *DCB* text hints, however, at intriguing biographical details. One wonders about influences upon her work and about the details of publication history and reception in English and French. One also wonders what personal, social, and literary insights would be revealed in a close analysis of the works themselves by a woman critic, someone who knows the Quebec that appears in the settings of Mrs. Leprohon's novels. Romantic fiction would remain romantic fiction, but is there more to be said about the writer and her work?[4]

Volume X also contains May Agnes (Early) Fleming, who is frequently described as our first outstanding financial success as a professional novelist because of her prolific production of romantic fiction in serial and book form. She and her family left Saint John for the United States in the 1870s, a move that reflects the direction in which her work was aimed: the American and also the British market, where the readership for her style of writing was greatest. In the United States, she could also get the copyright protection that was denied works published by Canadians in Canada. Mrs. Fleming, setting her stories amid high life in England and America, nevertheless introduced Canadian episodes and characters, even some from Quebec, which she certainly did not know first hand. Here again the bibliography in volume X can only refer the reader to standard works, and one remains inquisitive about the publication history from serial to book, about the curious use of her name on title-pages of works written after her death, about what might distinguish her as a woman writer, and about the image of Canada these undeniably stereotyped, but sometimes ingenious, novels present. It is to be noted that the Thomas Fisher Library at the University of Toronto collects everything with a Fleming imprint on it.

Are the hints being thrown up in these paragraphs possible leads? For analysis of content—no doubt at all. In the collecting of detail about biography and publication, advances continue to be made but there may well still be real difficulties.

A group of much less well-known women writers, some of them also editors, who appear in *DCB* volumes are examples of a particular kind of literary endeavour. Their names are often only recognized through local references, contemporary listings, or enumerative bibliographies; their publications are few and restricted; they are not the object of much study today. However, it is only fair to include at least some of these writers of verse, fiction, and other prose in *DCB* volumes in order to fill out the picture of a nineteenth-century society and the lives of women in it. To attempt to write their lives is to take on a difficult assignment. Some examples will illustrate the problems.

Susan Mann Trofimenkoff wrote the biography of Eliza Lanesford (Foster) Cushing (volume XI), whom she learned to call privately "elusive Eliza." Mrs. Cushing wrote frequently for *The Literary Garland*, contributing fiction such as "The Heiress, a Tale of Real Life" or "The Neglected Wife." She became *Garland*'s editor just before its demise in 1851. She was also, with her sister Harriet Vining Cheney, a founder of *The Snow Drop*, a periodical for children which ran from the late 1840s until 1853. Henry J. Morgan mentions her in his *Bibliotheca Canadensis* (1867); she is referred to in a general study for a McGill M.A. in 1929 and in *Literary History of Canada*. Who was she? Her mother had written sentimental novels in the United States; her husband died in 1846. Susan Trofimenkoff was able to find her, through city directories and an 1871 census, living in some eleven houses in Montreal during her forty years of widowhood. Her death at ninety-two got a brief notice in two Montreal papers, and there are oblique references in *The Snow Drop* and one or two letters held by a descendant. Mrs. Cushing remains an elusive, but intriguing figure because of her active period of writing and editing and the long, silent years of genteel living that followed.

Susan Trofimenkoff also researched Ann Cuthbert Rae for volume VIII. Ann, who was born in Scotland, married twice, and the two names she acquired, Knight and Fleming, complicated the search. Her two volumes of poetry, published in Edinburgh in 1815 and 1816, were inspired by a year-long trip to the Canadas in 1811–12, a journey she embarked upon with her six-week-old son. In June 1815 she, her husband, and their son emigrated. The record is sparse. When she became a widow in 1816 at the age of twenty-eight, Ann turned to teaching, the frequent resource of women in her situation. She remarried in 1820. In the 1830s, she taught again, before publishing several educational books for children, which drew the attention of John Strachan and Governor Sir Charles Metcalfe. There are fragmentary glimpses of her life in registry office entries, newspaper advertisements, and occasional references in her books (copies of which are hard to locate). Why did she come to the Canadas in 1811? Why did she and her husband emigrate? How did she get to know her second husband, also from Aberdeenshire, and who was he? How do her books relate to her teaching? Who exactly were her children? What happened in her life between 1845, the last trace available, and her death in Abbotsford, Lower Canada, fifteen years later at the age of seventy-two? Some information about her parentage and family can be gleaned from the career of her brother John Rae (volume X), an Upper Canadian schoolmaster and writer on political economy who emigrated to North America after Ann and who is the subject of a book-length study. A further glimpse of her circle appears in the biography of her brother-in-law John Fleming (volume VI, published in 1987), who died in the cholera epidemic of 1832. He was discovered to be an important Montreal businessman who had a considerable interest in educational texts suitable for Canadian schools, a writer of patriotic verse, and the owner of a large personal library. One may speculate about the social and intellectual relationships between the families of the two Fleming brothers and Ann's own brother and about their particular kind of Scottish-Canadian community.

From public records such as probate papers, newspaper references (including obituaries), some genealogies, and the papers of Phyllis Blakeley, a Nova Scotia archivist of encyclopedic knowledge and interest, Lois Kernaghan was able to put together an account of Mary Jane (Katzmann) Lawson (volume XI). She began to write poetry early and, at twenty-four, she became editor of a superior but short-lived periodical, *The Provincial, or Halifax Monthly Magazine*, which in 1852–53 printed poetry and prose on such topics as foreign travel, local history, rural idylls, and science. We lose track of her until 1866, when she was successfully operating a bookstore in Halifax. After her marriage in 1868, she gave it up to devote herself to charitable causes. In her sixties and nearing the end of her life, she completed an important volume of social history on three Nova Scotian townships. Hers would appear to be a significant contribution for its time.

Much more elusive was Harriett Wilkins of Hamilton (volume XI) whose five slim volumes of verse were printed at the office of *The Hamilton Spectator*. Harriett Annie, as she signed herself, was the well-educated daughter of a Congregational minister; she cared for her widowed mother and conducted a young ladies' school to support the family. She contributed to the *Spectator*'s "Poet's Corner" for thirty years and was also known for her good works. Local historians study her poetry now for its reflections of people and events. There is little to guide a researcher beyond the works themselves, city directories, and incidental references in the *Spectator* during and after her life, as the author of her biography, Katharine Greenfield of the Hamilton Public Library, discovered.

Thomas B. Vincent has dealt with two Maritime writers of nineteenth-century sentimental and religious verse whose lives provide a glimpse of their period. From her works and a descendant's painstaking references to her, we know something of Elizabeth Lockerby (volume XI). She was a Prince Edward Island woman from modest family who sold the first of her two volumes door-to-door in Charlottetown. She tried to make a career as a writer in New York, and then at forty-three, she married a much older, retired lawyer from Indianapolis, where her two volumes were reprinted. Grizelda Tonge's brief romantic story (volume VI), ended early by death of a tropical fever in Demerara, gave her a special place in literary history. She and her few short poems became a symbol "to a generation of Nova Scotian writers" of the promise of a literature and "the tragic fragility of such genius amid the harsh realities of 19th-century colonial life." The symbol was strengthened by tributes from two compatriots. One was Maria Morris and the other Joseph Howe (volume X) who eulogized her in 1828 and again nearly twenty years after her death. Grizelda's story and personality have few details, but her ancestry and an upbringing in the sophisticated society of Windsor, Nova Scotia, allow some speculation about what influenced her and help to account for her literary survival.

Another frustrating figure is Emily Elizabeth (Shaw) Beavan (volume VII). Biographical notes dated 1975, with no indication of sources, are in the University of New Brunswick library; there is a marriage record, an almanac reference to her husband, a mention in an article in *Acadiensis* for 1902. She appears to have come from Belfast, although there is conflicting evidence. She taught in New Brunswick, married a surgeon in 1838, and wrote a few tales and poems for *Amaranth*, the first periodical in the colony to devote itself to literary material. The Beavans left for Ireland in 1843, and in 1845 Routledge of London published her *Sketches and Tales Illustrative of Life in the Backwoods of New Brunswick* (reprinted in New Brunswick in 1980). Fred Cogswell, the author of her biography, compares this work very favourably to Thomas Haliburton's *The Old Judge* and Susanna Moodie's *Roughing It in the Bush* for its information and its rendering of the flavour of life in the settlements, commenting on "the enthusiasm with which she describes nature, and men's and women's attempts to conquer or come to terms with it." But her death date remains unknown, and she may well be in the wrong volume of the *DCB*.

The quest for information on these representative figures does not grow easier later in the century. For volume XII, Lorraine McMullen has struggled with Margaret Murray Robertson, who appears in *Literary History of Canada* only as a name among the prolific writers of fiction. Between 1865 and 1890, she published at least twelve titles, works full of romance, sentiment, and religion. Her Scottish family established itself in Sherbrooke; three of her brothers became distinguished Montreal lawyers and another became treasurer of the province. She taught school and moved in the 1870s to Montreal. Her sister Mary married Daniel Gordon, a Presbyterian minister in Glengarry County, Upper Canada, and their son was the novelist Ralph Connor. Lorraine McMullen could not discover when exactly Miss Robertson made the important move from Sherbrooke to Montreal and out of teaching. Other sources were the standard compendia and local histories. Inquiries at the archives in Ontario and Manitoba, to researchers in Glengarry, and to the Gordon family could provide no records to fill out the connection with Glengarry, although Miss Robertson's novels suggest a strong personal link. The search has been frustrating, yet the biography suggests that the novels should be carefully examined for what they may reveal about their time and place and their author.

This description of some of the minor literary figures in the *DCB* suggests the special problems of research they present. These figures nevertheless deserve a place in the volumes. They should be more than a name in general histories, biographical compendia, public records, and literary surveys. They are part of the social and cultural picture of their age and should figure in its depiction. We may not think of most of their work as a contribution to literature, but it has some part in the story of literary development and of reading taste. And the women writers themselves, however fragmentary our acquaintance with them, can tell us something about what that story was in the nineteenth-century colonies and Canada. We can look at them, without patronage, to try to see what cultural influences affected them, what they were reading, what audience they had, where and how they were published, what the experience of writing was for certain women who had a literary bent but not the commanding gifts of imagination and words or the advantage of tradition and contacts that sustained Susanna Moodie and Sara Jeannette Duncan.

In such a study of minor writers, it is important to recognize certain easy attitudes that lie behind some late twentieth-century comment on Canadian work. For instance, because the views of the world and of society held by nineteenth-century women—from the very purpose of either to their own particular place in them—are not often the views of today, it may be tempting to dismiss these writers as shallow, perhaps even insincere or hypocritical. Certainly their society created tensions for them, as they themselves reveal, but in recognizing such tensions do we not also owe them the courtesy of taking them on their own terms, of acknowledging that there could be real conviction, real enjoyment, a positive attitude to life, and of trying with patience to understand that approach? Then again, much critical comment, even of major writers, dismisses the habit of sentiment out of hand. The evident influences of writers such as Mrs. Hemans or Longfellow or Tennyson are also reason for the quick brushing aside of work as derivative. Are either of these reactions entirely fair? Is Tennyson such a bad model after all? What might be more to the purpose is some fuller and more sympathetic study of the ways in which modes of feeling, and the reading of well-known authors who were available, affected how Canadian writers, major and minor, saw their world. Their eyes were not ours. What can also lead to dismissive words from critics is the strong and persuasive religious feeling that animated both women and men in nineteenth-century Canada. To turn away from it is to invite serious misunderstanding. Such feeling is deep and rich, for example, in Mrs. Traill as woman and author. It provides a motivating force just as real for Hannah Maynard (Thompson) Pickard (volume VII), though as a writer she cannot give her moral tales an equivalent strength.

As I have been implying throughout this paper, there are still many beckoning fields for exploration in the nineteenth century. Researchers might take the progression of the *DCB* volumes I to XII and see what relationships can now be studied beyond the cross-references which have been inserted as guides. All types of people can lead to rewarding explorations. What lies beyond the accumulating information? What was the true shape and form of the literary and social culture of their decades? Who knew whom? In what way? Who was related to whom? How did that matter? What did the smallness of social groups and their isolation from one another mean for literary interests? How did women writers fit into these groups and what did they know of one another or of men writers?[5] What books did readers have access to?[6] Where did the books come from? How did they circulate? What was the access to printers, to booksellers, to publishers? How did the book trade work? We have made only a tentative beginning in Canada with *histoire du livre*,[7] and more should be tried, daunting as the task may be. We need also much more work in descriptive bibliography,[8] which can always illuminate the book trade.

The nineteenth-century volumes of the *DCB*, created over twenty years of developing scholarship, represent individually a state of the art. Those more recently published have benefitted from the growth and complexity of scholarship. One hopes that the passion for modern figures so noticeable in Canadian studies will not prevent the detailed understanding that is now needed to give a fuller picture of the nineteenth century.

## NOTES

1.   A valuable article in this context is Brunet (1988).

2.   See Ewing (1983) and McDonald (1985).

3.   All the editions of the Centre for Editing Early Canadian Texts (CEETC), published by Carleton University Press, are adding interesting and important information about the careers of their authors.

4.   See Gerson (1983).

5.   Forthcoming in 1989 is Carole Gerson's *A Purer Taste: The Writing and Reading of Fiction in English in Nineteenth-Century Canada* (Univ. of Toronto Press).

6.   Research in related areas has been supported by the work of Yvan Lamonde and Daniel Olivier (1983).

7.   An important recent work is Parker (1985). See also Van der Bellen (1984, 1986).

8.   In this connection I commend the contribution of my colleague Patricia Fleming, whose *Upper Canadian Imprints, 1801–1841: A Bibliography* (Toronto: Univ. of Toronto Press, 1988) is the first comprehensive analytical bibliography of these imprints, located in more than forty collections in Canada, the United States, and Britain.

## WORKS CITED

Beavan, Emily Elizabeth. 1845. *Sketches and Tales Illustrative of Life in the Backwoods of New Brunswick*. London: G. Routledge.

Brunet, Manon. 1988. "Les femmes dans la production de la littérature francophone du début du XIX^e siècle québécois." *Livre et lecture au Québec (1800–1850)*. Ed. Claude Galarneau and Maurice Lemire. Quebec: Institut québécois de recherche sur la culture. 167–80.

Davies, Gwendolyn. 1980. "A Literary Study of Selected Periodicals from Maritime Canada, 1789–1872." Diss. York University, Toronto.

*Dictionary of Canadian Biography*: Vols. 5–12, 1801–1900. 1972–90. General eds., Francess G. Halpenny and Jean Hamelin. Toronto: Univ. of Toronto Press.

Ewing, Juliana Horatia. 1983. *Canada Home: Juliana Horatia Ewing's Fredericton Letters, 1867–1869*. Ed. Margaret Howard Blom and Thomas E. Blom. Vancouver: Univ. of British Columbia Press.

Gerson, Carole. 1983. "Three Writers of Victorian Canada: Rosanna Leprohon/James De Mille/Agnes Maule Machar." *Canadian Writers and Their Works*. Fiction series, vol. 1. Ed. Robert Lecker, Jack David, and Ellen Quigley. Toronto: ECW Press. 195–256.

Hart, Julia Beckwith. 1824. *St. Ursula's Convent, or The Nun of Canada*. Kingston, Upper Canada [Ont.]: H. C. Thomson.

Johnston, Elizabeth Lichtenstein. 1901. *Recollections of a Georgia Loyalist*. Ed. Arthur Wentworth Hamilton Eaton. New York: M. F. Mansfield.

Lamonde, Yvan, and Daniel Olivier. 1983. *Les bibliothèques personnelles au Quebec: inventaire analytique et préliminaire des sources*. Quebec: Bibliothèque nationale du Québec.

Leprohon, Rosanna. 1973. *Antoinette de Mirecourt*. 1864. Toronto: McClelland and Stewart.

*Literary History of Canada: Canadian Literature in English*. 1976. Ed. Carl F. Klinck et al. 2nd ed. 3 vols. Toronto: Univ. of Toronto Press.

McDonald, Donna. 1985. *Illustrated News: Juliana Horatia Ewing's Canadian Pictures, 1867-1869*. Saint John: New Brunswick Museum; Toronto: Dundurn Press.

Morgan, Henry J. 1867. *Bibliotheca Canadensis: or A Manual of Canadian Literature*. Ottawa: G. E. Desbarats; repr. Detroit, 1968.

Parker, George L. 1985. *The Beginnings of the Book Trade in Canada*. Toronto: Univ. of Toronto Press.

Traill, Catharine Parr. 1986. *Canadian Crusoes*. 1852. Ed. Rupert Schieder. Ottawa: Carleton Univ. Press.

Van der Bellen, Liana. 1984; 1986. ''A Checklist of Books and Articles in the Field of the History of the Book and Libraries.'' *Papers of the Bibliographical Society of Canada* 23 (1984): 84–99; 25 (1986): 139–52.

# Research—
# Problems and Solutions

Research in Nineteenth-Century
Canadian Women Writers: An Exercise
in Literary Detection

CARRIE MacMILLAN

**M**y research on nineteenth-century women writers in general and on New Brunswick author Maria Amelia Fytche (1844–1927) in particular has revealed that there are far fewer extant documents of women of this period than one would like. For various reasons, these women were not valued enough by their society for their letters, manuscripts, and other documents of their personal and writing lives to be preserved. The reasons for this probably include a hesitant, colonial mentality that doubted the value of Canadian literary achievement, and the frontier mentality that valued "practical" lives with "tangible" achievements, such as those of politicians and business figures rather than those of writers[1] (these attitudes operated, of course, against male as well as female authors). A third factor that tended to devalue women's writing was what recent feminist critics describe as the link between gender and judgement, the tendency to assess women's writing as trivial.[2] These conditions were exacerbated for all writers of the nineteenth century by the modernist movement in the 1920s, which tended to dismiss all writing that did not subscribe to its tenets. Not only are there few materials extant from the period, but many of the basic biographical "facts" of the authors' lives are inaccurate, particularly dates of death. This suggests that, even if a woman writer enjoyed some success during her active publishing career, she was rather quickly forgotten. One thinks particularly of Joanna E. Wood who, during her lifetime, was ranked with Charles G. D. Roberts and Gilbert Parker as one of the three major novelists of the day ("Judith Moore," 1898) but whose year of death is recorded erroneously in Watters (420) as 1919 (she in fact did not die until 1927), an error that was perpetuated until only the last several years. Mistakes in such vital statistics make it very difficult indeed to discover such basic background aids as obituaries and wills.

The nature, too, of the lives of many of the women writers of the period makes it difficult to reconstruct them. Many of these women had less "public" lives than their male counterparts and therefore there is less documentation. Frequently, women could not get the same education, have careers (beyond their writing), or belong to the same formal and informal clubs and associations (intellectual, literary, and social) as men. Hence, the kinds of records, subscriptions, minutes, and letters that might help to define the character, influences, and milieu of the male writer are less often available for the female.

The result of all this is that one does not walk into a library or an archive, consult a computer, card catalogue, or periodical index, and find much (or anything) on many of the women who wrote in Canada in the nineteenth century. In many cases, very primary and innovative searching has to be done.

My research on Maria Amelia Fytche illustrates the type of literary detection necessary in tracing the lives of nineteenth-century women writers. Fytche was a relatively minor writer, about whom I have found very little. She published only two novels in her lifetime, *Kerchiefs to Hunt Souls* (1895) and *The Rival Forts: or, The Velvet Siege of Beausejour* (1907). I became interested in her while I was doing my doctoral thesis on the artist in Canadian fiction and, in connection with the artist theme, saw two very brief references to *Kerchiefs* in *Literary History of Canada* (288, 327). A reading of the novel suggested that it is an important document, not so much on the artist during the period but, rather, on the condition of women, particularly working and travelling women, at this important time when women were entering the work force and becoming part of the "international" spirit of the day. The book also offers some critical analysis of women's education and of homes for working women. It does not seem necessary to mention more about the book here, except that it has been reprinted with an introduction which attempts to present something of the author's life, as well as to provide a critical analysis of the book.

I soon discovered that there was very little available on Fytche in the conventional sources: the references in *Literary History*, a listing of her titles in Watters, as cited, a brief reference in R. J. Long's *Nova Scotian Authors and Their Works* (84–85), and a sentence in O'Hagan's article, "Some Canadian Women Writers."

Luck and a very good archivist can be vital in searches of this kind. It occurred to me that Fytche might have corresponded with another contemporary Maritime woman writer, Margaret Marshall Saunders, and so I travelled to Acadia University to look at the Saunders Papers. Although these were unhelpful (I did find a letter in which Saunders offered to comment on *Kerchiefs*, but alas, if she did so, the letter is not at Acadia), the archivist, Pat Townsend, suggested that I should look at the Fitch family of Wolfville, a prominent Planter family. She recommended *The History of King's County, Nova Scotia*, which contains notes on the Fitches. Happily, not only was Maria Amelia to be found in notes on Nova Scotian authors (the note was very brief), but her father, Simon Fitch, was written up quite extensively as a prominent physician.

From these references I gleaned a wealth of information, including the fact that Fytche had changed the spelling of her family name for publishing purposes (to gain more autonomy?). There were references to medical encyclopedias which described her father's career, and in which I was able to trace Fytche's childhood years in Saint John, Portland, Maine, and New York, before the family finally settled in Halifax. References to her father's early studies in Europe, including Edinburgh, London, and Paris, suggested a fairly sophisticated family environment. City directories for Saint John and Halifax (which list not only the householder, but all inhabitants) told me exactly how long Fytche lived with her family.

I also discovered that Fytche's mother was a member of the Paddock family, a prominent Loyalist Saint John family which included several doctors, and I was able to trace her maternal genealogy in the archives of the Saint John Museum. Her father's distinguished career meant that it was not hard to date his death, and to obtain a copy of his will from the Court of Probate of Nova Scotia. This gave me an idea of the family circumstances, which were comfortable, judging from the extent of the estate, as well as the number and names of the surviving children (I had the names of the children as well from the *History*). The will also suggested that the disposition of the father towards his children was good, as the bequests are fair. I also learned that Fytche's mother had died and her father remarried, to be survived by his second wife.

I suspected that Fytche might have done some teaching (this was based on the heroine of *Kerchiefs*, who runs a private school for women), but a search in the New Brunswick and Nova Scotia education archives did not reveal evidence of this. I began to wonder whether she taught privately. A complete shot in the dark confirmed that she did. The Saint John Museum Archives contain the John Nicholson Estate papers, family papers which overlap chronologically with Fytche's time in Saint John (after her move from Halifax). Hoping to find something on the Saint John social and cultural milieu of the day, I went through these papers and discovered a receipt for a tuition bill for sixteen weeks of English instruction for one of the Nicholson children from M. A. Fitch, dated 1887.

There were gaps in Fytche's life from the late 1880s until after World War I, during which period the Saint John and Halifax City directories did not show her living in those cities. I had a hunch, again based on her novel, in which a Nova Scotia woman sells her private school and goes off to Europe, that Fytche herself probably lived abroad during the period. The novel's descriptions of Europe, of the experience of working there as a governess, of homes for working women and of inhabitants of those homes, are very realistic. I knew that her second novel, a historical romance, had been reprinted in *The Maritime*

*Advocate and Busy East* (1942), a result of the interest of the historian Clarence Webster. Again, the Webster Papers were at the Saint John Museum, and in them I found two letters from Fytche to Webster written late in her life, in 1927. In one letter she expresses very genuine astonishment that anyone remembers her and her books, and in the other she makes reference to having lived in England from the mid-1880s until after World War I.

At the Saint John Museum, I inquired whether there was anyone living today who might remember the elderly Maria Amelia Fytche, who lived with her unmarried sisters at 74 Coburg Street, in "The Cottages," just around the corner from Paddock Street, named after her maternal ancestors. The names of several people were given to me, one of whom provided me with some information. Miss Eileen Cushing, retired archivist of the Saint John Museum, recalled from her childhood the elderly Misses Fitch: Maria Amelia, Adelaide, Edith, and Margaret. By the 1920s, the family money was gone, but the sisters had a great deal of pride. Acts of assistance for the women (shovelling walkways, for example) had to be performed anonymously, under the cover of darkness, lest the women attempt repayment, a gesture they could ill afford. Before leaving Saint John, I took a picture of the house on Coburg Street, as I had of Fytche's father's house in Halifax, on Tobin Street. I also discovered (from her will) Fytche's grave with those of the other members of her family, in Wolfville, Nova Scotia.

And that is all I have been able to discover of the life of Maria Amelia Fytche. There are significant gaps. I know nothing of her education, although her books reveal that she was very familiar with the Bible and English literature. Her style of writing, which is assured though not polished or distinguished, the historical research she did for her second novel, and the evidence of her teaching suggest that she received a good education for a woman of her period. This certainly seems likely given her father's education and the family circumstances. From the chronology of her girlhood and the movements of her family, it is likely that she was educated in Portland, Maine, and possibly New York, probably at schools for young women. Another question that remains unanswered is that of her exact residence and occupation during the fairly extensive period of time she spent in Europe. One would like to know much more about her personal life and character: Why did she never marry? What were the exact experiences in the Maritimes and in Europe that led to her becoming interested in women's issues and in writing? What were her literary influences? Did she have literary friends? There are, of course, reviews and references to her writing in such contemporary Maritime publications as the *Evening Mail* (Halifax) and the *Truro News* and in national periodicals like *Canadian Magazine* and *The Week*, as well as in the American *Arena*. However, these are brief and indicate little about the author except to show that she did, for a short period, attract some literary attention.

Work on even an obscure or minor writer like Fytche can be rewarding. There is the fun of "the hunt," the pursuit of the first few meagre clues which may or may not open up new avenues of exploration, and there are also the disappointments (of course, I have not described the many dead-ends that accompanied the discovery of the few facts cited here). There is the excitement of "being the first," of exploring paths that have not been walked before. But most of all, there is the satisfaction of re-creating, albeit imperfectly, a literary life that surely deserves more than a few short, dry references in literary compendiums.

I must acknowledge here my indebtedness to the many patient and helpful librarians and archivists who have helped me with this project and with others, in this country and abroad. Without their direction to special collections and without their permission to use what are sometimes very fragile documents, this exercise would be impossible.

## NOTES

1. These attitudes in Canadian society have been observed by various critics, including Sara Jeannette Duncan in the nineteenth century (see, for example, her "Saunterings") and E. K. Brown in the twentieth (see, particularly, his "The Problem of Canadian Literature").
2. For example, Baym (1981).

## WORKS CITED

Baym, Nina. 1981. "Melodramas of Beset Manhood: How Theories of American Fiction Exclude Women Authors." *American Quarterly* 33, no. 2: 123–39.
Brown, E. K. 1973. "The Problem of Canadian Literature." In *On Canadian Poetry*. Ottawa: Tecumseh Press.
Duncan, Sara Jeannette. 1886. "Saunterings." *The Week* III (Sept. 30): 707–708.
Eaton, Arthur Wentworth Hamilton. 1910. *The History of King's County, Nova Scotia*. Salem, Mass.: Salem Press.
Fytche, Maria Amelia. 1980. *Kerchiefs to Hunt Souls*. 1895. Introd. Carrie MacMillan. Sackville: R. P. Bell Library, Mount Allison University.
John Nicholson Estate Papers. Pack #12, Box #5, Shelf 111.
"Judith Moore." 1898. *The Canadian Magazine* 10, no. 5: 460.
Klinck, Carl F., et al., eds. 1976. *Literary History of Canada*. 2nd ed. Toronto: Univ. of Toronto Press.
Long, R. J. 1918. *Nova Scotian Authors and Their Works*. East Orange, New Jersey: n.p.
O'Hagan, T. 1896. "Some Canadian Women Writers." *Catholic World* 63 (Sept.): 779–93.
Watters, R. E. 1972. *A Checklist of Canadian Literature*. Toronto: Univ. of Toronto Press.

# Anthologies and the Canon of Early Canadian Women Writers

## CAROLE GERSON

One of our current cultural myths is that women writers enjoy remarkable prominence in English Canada. In a spirit of smugness, naiveté, or optimism, we eagerly embrace the view recently expressed by an editor of several anthologies that "Canada has produced an unusual, even a predominant, number of women writers" (Sullivan, ix). Supporting evidence can be found without great difficulty. For example, there is *Books in Canada*'s recent readers' poll, in which seven of the top ten favourite authors were women: Alice Munro, Margaret Atwood, Margaret Laurence, Mavis Gallant, Janet Turner Hospital, Marian Engel, and Audrey Thomas outnumbered Timothy Findley, Robertson Davies, and Mordecai Richler (13). And there is Beryl Langer's study of the critical attention paid to Canadian and Australian women writers in selected academic periodicals of the late 1970s, which compares "the prominence of women writers in English Canada [with] their relative neglect in Australia" (133). Measuring the frequency of their appearance as the subjects of scholarly reviews and articles, Langer concludes that while "the critical attention accorded Canadian women is roughly proportional to their literary production, much of what Australian women write is simply not mentioned in critical journals" (170).[1]

Masked by these sanguine instances are other facets of the Canadian literary scene. Langer's Canadian figures are skewed by Atwood and Laurence, who enjoy a full 42 per cent of the total critical space given to female authors, leaving the remaining 58 per cent to be shared by another nineteen writers. This practice of conferring stardom on one or two representative women writers while neglecting the rest (see Nelson, 99) will become significant when we examine the practices of Canadian anthologists. Moreover, recent research behind the scenes of the Canadian literary establishment suggests that a woman who completes a manuscript has

> a one-in-four chance of getting it published compared to any man and after that a one-in-four chance of seeing it reviewed in a magazine. [Her] chances of getting newspaper coverage are even lower (80 per cent of that space is allotted to reviews of books written by men), and should [she] decide to apply for a teaching position in a creative writing department or a writer-in-residency at a university to help finance [her] next book, [she] is looking at a field that in 1980/81 hired women 20-29 per cent of the time (Crean, 30).[2]

As an emblem of the marginalization of women writers in the Canadian literary canon, I would like to suggest one of the teaching anthologies from the early 1970s, *The Evolution of Canadian Literature in English: 1914–1945* (George Parker, 1973). On the cover is a painting by Emily Carr, who won a Governor General's Award for *Klee Wyck* in 1941. Inside is the work of eighteen writers, three of them women, none of them Carr. (Mazo de la Roche, Dorothy Livesay, and Anne Marriott represent the period.)

"Literature," says Leslie Fiedler, "is effectively what we teach in departments of English; or conversely, what we teach in departments of English is literature" (73). What we teach in Canadian literature is largely determined by what appears in our anthologies, especially when we look at early writers who are otherwise out of print. For nearly two decades, feminist critics have been casting a scathing eye at the contents of general anthologies aimed at students in high school and first-year university. Tillie Olsen's finding that in the American literary institution of the 1970s the proportion of serious attention accorded women writers was one-twelfth of that given to men (209–16) concurs with Jean Mullen's 1972 analysis of American freshman English texts, which concludes that "the ratio of women writers to men [is] fairly constant: about 7% to 93%" (79). In Canada, Priscilla Galloway reported that during the 1970s the contents of Ontario high school English courses were 88 per cent male-authored and 86 per cent non-Canadian (10). These figures suggest that nascent editors of anthologies (and teachers who use them) have been unwittingly conditioned to regard literature as primarily a male preserve. Hence, the situation in the field of Canadian literature appears comparatively generous when a count of the contributors to thirty-five Canadian anthologies in common use from 1913 to 1980 concludes that a full 25 per cent are women (Dagg, 31; Nelson, 86).[3] As Margaret Atwood quipped, "Whether the glass is two-thirds empty or a third full depends upon how thirsty you are" (xxix).

Ostensibly the embodiment of a culture's objectively defined aesthetic achievement, a national literary canon is a malleable entity frequently reshaped by changes in taste and the appearance of new authors.[4] The values enshrined in a canon transcend aesthetic matters, reflecting the canon's identity as "a social construct'' and ''a means by which culture validates its social power'' (Lauter, 435, 452). In the literary world, less power is wielded by writers and readers than by what has been called ''invisible colleges.''[5] Comprised of publishers, the media, and the academy, they function as canonical ''gate-keepers,''[6] conferring status by deciding what gets published and reviewed and who gets onto course lists and into anthologies, reprint series, textbooks, and reference sources.

How this structure has operated in English Canada is demonstrated by *Canadian Writers/Ecrivains Canadiens. A Biographical Dictionary*, prepared by Guy Sylvestre, Brandon Conron, and Carl Klinck (1964, rev. 1966, rev. 1967, rpt. 1970). The editors' sole announced criterion for their selection of early and current authors is that those chosen ''have for the most part produced a notable first or second book and have thereafter embarked upon a literary career with repeated publications of generally acknowledged merit'' (1970, v). In English Canada, from the beginnings to 1950, women have represented 40 per cent of the authors of books of fiction and 37 per cent of the authors of books of poetry (Dagg, 28). In *Canadian Writers*, women account for fewer than 19 per cent of the entries. Sociologists L. M. Grayson and J. Paul Grayson, who have used this book as the research base for their work on Canadian authors, choose their words wisely when they describe their subject as the Canadian ''literary élite.'' Regarding the writers' occupations, they note that the English-Canadian male writer is most likely ''to have found a home in the school or the university'' (1978, 305). ''Generally acknowledged merit,'' the overt qualification for canonization, thus involves an unacknowledged component based on education, occupation, academic connections,[7] and therefore by extension, gender.

Hence, among the included male writers are people like John O. Robins, professor of German at Victoria College and author of several books of humour; lawyer W. H. Blake, who translated *Maria Chapdelaine* and wrote fishing books; cabinet minister and essayist Martin Burrell; and academic authors like E. K. Brown, Douglas Bush, Claude Bissell, James Cappon, and Pelham Edgar. The excluded female writers include Kathleen Coburn, the noted Coleridge scholar; Charlotte Whitton, Canada's first woman mayor as well as the author of five monographs; novelist and journalist Madge Macbeth, who was the first woman and only three-time president of the Canadian Authors' Association; and the three formerly significant poets and women of letters, Ethelwyn Wetherald, Susan Frances Harrison, and Agnes Maule Machar, who top the list of lost women poets in Table 2. R.A.D. Ford, who won the Governor General's Award for poetry in 1956 and was also Canada's Ambassador to Russia, is included, but not Marjorie Wilkins Campbell, who won the award twice, in 1950 for non-fiction and in 1954 for juvenile writing. Children's literature, largely a female domain, is less canonical than sporting literature or humour. Fortunately, information about Campbell can be found in Norah

Story's 1967 *Oxford Companion to Canadian Literature and History*, still the best reference source on earlier women authors. While the 1983 *Oxford Companion to Canadian Literature* adds eleven names to the roster of recognized female poets and fiction writers born before 1920, it drops another eighteen, many of them popular authors active during the first four decades of the twentieth century.

The canonizing process, while invoking "merit," clearly involves a complex web of institutional factors. Americans studying their country's decanonization of its early women authors have focused on several particular elements, beginning with Nathaniel Hawthorne's 1854 attack on the "damn'd mob of scribbling women" who were his competitors. Investigating why in 1977 the canon of pre-1940 American writers included only one woman poet (Emily Dickinson) and no women novelists, Nina Baym concludes from her reading of the critics who shaped that canon that the woman writer "entered [American] literary history as the enemy" (130). Paul Lauter finds the tendency to define "American" literature as "masculine culture" (449) solidifying in the 1920s, with "the academic institutionalization of reading choices." Under the control of a male professoriat, the activities of "choosing books to be remembered and read, building culture and taste" shifted from the woman-dominated family circle and local reading club to the male-dominated academy, which rejected female "gentility" (440–41).

The process by which women disappear from literary history, described as "the cycle of exclusion, the filtering out of women writers disproportionately to their numbers and the significance of their contributions," endures because " 'minor' women writers are perceived as *more* minor than their male counterparts" (Rosenfelt, 15, 16).[8] In Canada, this cycle has operated through reference books (like *Canadian Writers*) whose function is to "bestow not only accessibility but legitimacy" (Rosenfelt, 13), in honorific organizations like the Royal Society of Canada, whose literary section acquired its first woman member in 1947 with the admission of Gabrielle Roy, and in anthologies of Canadian literature.

The literary periodicals of nineteenth-century Canada reflect a high level of activity among women writers. A page count of work by identified authors shows that in *The Literary Garland* (1838–51) women produced 55 per cent of the poetry and 70 per cent of the fiction; in *The Canadian Monthly and National Review* and its successor, *Rose-Belford's Canadian Monthly* (1872–82), 52 per cent of the poetry and 30 per cent of the fiction; and in *The Week* (1883–96) 29 per cent of both poetry and fiction. Moreover, their participation in the production of books indicates that the numerical presence of women on the English-Canadian literary scene has altered much less over the course of this century than our current myth of female literary dominance would lead us to expect. In 1984–85, a count of all books published in Canada and listed in *Quill & Quire* shows that 31 per cent of the authors were women; they comprised 57 per cent of the writers for children and young adults, 29 per cent of the poets, and

26 per cent of the novelists (Dagg, 30). From Watters' *Checklist of Canadian Literature* (which does not distinguish between adult and juvenile literature), a count of works published up to and including 1905 reveals that women represented about 30.5 per cent of the total number of authors of monographs of poetry and fiction, and produced about 31 per cent of the titles. There is a clear distinction by genre: women were 24 per cent of the poets and wrote 19 per cent of the poetry titles, but were 41 per cent of the fiction writers and produced 45 per cent of the titles of fiction books. This generic difference in itself has presumably had some bearing on the visibility of early women authors: until recently, poetry has been viewed as more respectable than fiction, and it has also been more frequently and easily anthologized and thus kept in print. Early Canadian women fiction writers were therefore at a triple disadvantage as a marginalized sex working in a marginalized genre in a marginalized colonial culture.

When we turn to current (post-1970) anthologies to find out who our early women authors were and what they wrote, we find that the entire period is represented by a handful of names (see Table 3). Male writers born in or before 1875 are represented by seventy-two names, thirty of which appear in four or more recent anthologies. Women writers from the same period are represented by fifteen names, eight of which appear in four or more recent anthologies. To discover how the "cycle of exclusion" has operated in Canada, I have examined the contents of some sixty literary anthologies which claim to be national in scope (the word "Canadian" appears in the title) and include early Canadian writing; most of these are represented in Table 1. Writing in French and translations, while included in some anthologies, have been eliminated from all calculations. For manageability, I have defined early writers as those born in or before 1875. This category includes authors who spill over both ends of the nineteenth century: Frances Brooke at the early end and Nellie McClung, L. M. Montgomery, and Emily Carr at the later. However, they are balanced by their male counterparts—the explorers at the beginning, Stephen Leacock, Robert Service, and Ralph Connor in the early twentieth century—thus giving us a framed picture of the situation.

Arranging these anthologies chronologically allows us to see how the practices of editors have altered and what effect these changes have had on the visibility of women writers. The first group, from Dewart's 1864 *Selections from Canadian Poets* to Carman and Pierce's 1935 *Our Canadian Literature*, is generally characterized by a principle of inclusiveness. Eager to demonstrate that there was indeed a Canadian literature, nineteenth- and early twentieth-century editors cast a broad net and drew in a proportion of women authors (30 per cent) that roughly corresponded with their degree of publishing activity. Yet even here there begins the tendency, which will become especially pernicious during the mid-twentieth century, of giving women less space than men. In thirteen cases out of seventeen, the figure in column C, the percentage of pages given to women, is less than the figure in column B, the percentage of authors who are women. The most notorious example in this regard is J. E. Wetherell's *Later Canadian Poems* (1893). Wetherell originally intended to limit his selection to seven male poets. However, under pressure from Pauline Johnson, he added the "Supplement" at the back of the book representing "within somewhat narrow limits the notable work produced in recent years by some of our women writers" (preface). The six women share 27 pages, compared with 159 pages for the seven men.[9]

Agreeing with Louise Berkinow that "most women writers have gotten lost," Lynne Spender insists that "in each case *someone has lost them*" (108). As can be seen in Table 2, nearly a dozen previously important Canadian women poets were mislaid by the anthologists of the mid-twentieth century (although Harrison has been revived as a fiction writer with one story that appears in two recent short story anthologies). In Canada during the 1940s and 1950s, the concept of the national survey anthology underwent a transition most clearly seen in the anthologies of Ralph Gustafson and A.J.M. Smith. The old preservative notion of defining a literature as the sum of its practitioners yielded to the evaluative principle of choosing only the "best," thus replacing an "accessible canon" with a "selective canon," in the terminology of Alistair Fowler (Golding, 279–80[10]). As well, this period saw the birth of the pedagogical survey anthology intended for introductory university courses in Canadian literature. Together, the effect of the two trends was to limit the general representation of women writers and particularly narrow the canon of early female authors.[11]

In Gustafson's first major anthology, the 1942 Penguin/Pelican *Anthology of Canadian Poetry*, 23.5 per cent of the authors are women, six of whom (Isabella Valancy Crawford, Ethelwyn Wetherald, Helena Coleman, Isabel Ecclestone Mackay, Annie Charlotte Dalton, and Virna Sheard) were born in or before 1875. A seventh, Pauline Johnson, "was omitted because her publishers demanded too high a fee for her work" (Whiteman, n.p.). In this book's 1958 successor, *The Penguin Book of Canadian Verse*, the total representation of women authors has been reduced to 18 per cent, and the earlier period is represented by two: Crawford and Virna Sheard. At the same time, the number of male poets born in or before 1875 has increased, from fourteen to seventeen. The additions include Oliver Goldsmith, Charles Heavysege, Alexander McLachlan, Charles Sangster, Charles Mair, and John Frederic Herbin, who join such illustrious survivors from the first volume as George T. Lanigan, John McCrae, and Tom MacInnes (as well as the obligatory Confederation group). The net result is a nearly three-fold reduction in the proportional representation of early women writers. There are no changes to the selection of early writers in the 1967 and 1975 editions; in 1984, Pauline Johnson was finally added, along with Robert Service.

What occurred between 1942 and 1958 to cause a change of such magnitude was the publication of the three editions of A.J.M. Smith's *Book of Canadian Poetry* (1943, 1948, 1957) which culminated in his 1960 *Oxford Book of Canadian Verse*. In this series, the number of early women poets was reduced from seven (Susanna Moodie, Pamela Vining Yule, Crawford, Harrison, Helena Coleman, Johnson, Annie Charlotte Dalton) to two (Moodie and Crawford), and their proportional representation from 16.5 per cent to 10 per cent. While winnowing out the early women, Smith gradually established the sequence of Jonathan Odell, Joseph Stansbury, Oliver Goldsmith, Standish O'Grady, Joseph Howe, Thomas D'Arcy McGee, Charles Heavysege, Alexander McLachlan, Charles Sangster, and Charles Mair that precedes the Confederation poets in Klinck and Watters' *Canadian Anthology* and to some degree structures most subsequent teaching surveys of Canadian literature. This Canadian decanonization of early women writers paralleled the practice of anthologists of American literature during the same period (Lauter, 438–40, 450–51). In Canada, as in the United States, few women poets continued to appear in anthologies much past their date of death (Russ, 66–68).

During the 1940–69 decades, there were several survivors of the earlier type of popular omnibus anthology. *Canadian Poetry in English* (1954), Lorne Pierce and V. B. Rhodenizer's revision of Carman and Pierce's *Our Canadian Literature* (1935), was the last resting place of many early poets, including all but one of the lost women listed in Table 2. The next omnibus survey anthology, Gordon Green and Guy Sylvestre's centennial volume, *A Century of Canadian Literature* (1967), recognizes only four early women writers: two poets (Crawford and Johnson) and two prose writers (Sara Jeannette Duncan and L. M. Montgomery). In the last of the sampler anthologies, John Robert Colombo's *The Poets of Canada* (1978), of twenty-nine early English-language poets only two are women, again Crawford and Johnson.

As the popular anthologies discarded the early women writers, there was scant effort on the part of the academy to recover them. And it is in the third period, 1970–86, that the full effects of the narrowing process can be seen. Gustafson and Smith, the most influential anthology editors of the middle decades of this century, performed as modernists purging Canadian literature of its residue of Victorian sentimentality and patriotism. As practising poets, they exercised their licence to edit literary history to suit their taste (and their network of literary acquaintances), re-inventing the past in the light of "a contemporary and cosmopolitan literary consciousness" in Smith's well-known phrase (1943, 3). Their landmark anthologies, intended to educate a public readership that had been raised on a diet of what Smith once called "maple fudge" (1942, 458), remapped the contours of early Canadian poetry.

Since the 1970s, however, the intended audience for survey texts has been largely composed of students dependent upon the wisdom and booklists of their professors for their picture and understanding of the past. When we examine the representation of early women writers in the anthologies of the 1970s, we can see that the process of decanonization has been absolute. Even in the anthologies dealing specifically with the nineteenth century, there has been almost no effort to reconstruct the period and recover its lost women authors. A case in point is Douglas Lochhead and Raymond Souster's *One Hundred Poems of Nineteenth Century Canada* (1974), which includes the work of thirty-four poets, twenty-nine of whom are men. Of the twelve poems by women, seven are by Crawford. There are two poems by Johnson, one by Moodie, one by Rosanna Leprohon, and one by Duncan. An annotated bibliography describes this book as "an excellent anthology" whose "chief value lies in its inclusion of several minor writers" (Moyles, 34). So it is, if you define writers as male. David Arnason's *Nineteenth Century Canadian Stories* (1974), which revives Harriet Vining Cheney, gives us three women (all contributors to *The Literary Garland*), nine men (including Robert Barr), and three anonymous authors—not quite representative of the actual situation in the nineteenth century when women produced nearly half the fiction of English Canada.

As Table 3 makes clear, the recent academic anthologists have followed the practice of their immediate predecessors in limiting the canon of nineteenth-century women writers to six major figures from central Canada. Crawford functions as our Emily Dickinson, turning up in every possible anthology (with the surprising exception of Robert Weaver and William Toye's 1974 *Oxford Anthology of Canadian Literature*). Johnson may accompany her, especially when the editor is concerned about representing native peoples. Susanna Moodie and Catharine Parr Traill cover non-fictional prose, and selections from Duncan and Leprohon take care of fiction. Occasionally, Moodie, Duncan, and Leprohon have been seconded as poets and Crawford as a short story writer. Sheard survives only because of Gustafson's affection for her two humorous poems, "The Yak" and "Exile," which have remained in his Penguin anthologies. L. M. Montgomery and Nellie McClung, the most popular and successful Canadian women novelists of the early twentieth century, appear in the Canadian literature curriculum much less often than Ralph Connor, their male counterpart, who has been represented twice as frequently in post-1970 anthologies. Table 3 also shows that John McCrae and Oliver Goldsmith have each acquired canonical status on the strength of a single poem. Would the latter have done as well if his surname had not been Goldsmith and if his first name had been Olivia?

From the list of authors who now represent early Canadian literature, it is evident that importance has been granted on grounds other than aesthetic brilliance. Non-literary factors contribute substantially to the significance of the preserved male writer, whose cultural weight is enhanced by his historical public career as explorer, clergyman, educator, lawyer, newspaperman, or political figure, and by the personal connections fostered by his profession.[12]

Feminist historians argue that to re-inscribe women's history into national history it is necessary to alter old concepts of significance and to accord social and domestic life the attention previously devoted to military and political events.[13]

To re-inscribe women into the literary history represented by our anthologies, we can begin by considering journalists and diarists along with the explorers, by including temperance and suffragist writers with the political writers, and by accepting social and domestic topics into the early poetic canon in poems like Rosanna Leprohon's "Given and Taken." As well as valorizing the literary spheres favoured by women, such as juvenile literature, we need to rediscover their work in the areas we think of as distinctly Canadian. For example, Crawford was not the only early woman author of interesting narrative poems; in 1892, Ethelwyn Wetherald was judged to stand "in the front rank of Canadian sonnet writers" (Campbell, 177); Helen Mar Johnson's "The Watcher" (Dewart, 153–55) conveys a fine Frygian sense of terror on a winter night. Tired of being "cheated of recognition" (Shields, 18) by the literary establishment, the early Canadian woman poet has deviously begun to re-enter our literature in fictional form, in Carol Shields' Mary Swann (of *Swann: A Mystery*) and in Almeda Joynt Roth, heroine of Alice Munro's recent *New Yorker* story, "Meneseteung." These characters, elusive and intriguing, may have the effect of directing attention back to their quite "unobscure" historical counterparts like Wetherald, Machar, and Harrison, who all enjoyed long and prominent careers as poets, journalists, and vital members of their cultural community.

The self-replicating tendency of academic anthologies is a significant element in the process of canonization: "more people read these writers because their work is accessible in anthologies; these writers are included in anthologies because more people read them" (Nelson, 86). Hence, a contributing factor is the availability of the writers' work in reprint series. Of the eight women who top Table 3, only Crawford, Moodie, and Pauline Johnson appeared consistently in Canadian anthologies over the past century, during which time *Roughing It in the Bush* and Johnson's books remained more or less in print. The poetry of Rosanna Leprohon and Sara Jeannette Duncan was included in several late nineteenth-century anthologies but disappeared after 1900. Catharine Parr Traill's only early appearance is in one anthology from the 1920s. Frances Brooke, who makes her anthology debut in 1955 in the first edition of Klinck and Watters' *Canadian Anthology*, represents the pattern of recognition shared by the others. In the case of Brooke, Traill, Moodie, and Duncan, inclusion in the first or second edition of *Canadian Anthology* was soon followed by the reissue of a major prose work in the New Canadian Library (NCL) series, which was in turn followed by more anthology appearances. With Leprohon, recanonization was delayed until 1973, when Mary Jane Edwards included her in the first volume of *The Evolution of Canadian Literature* series and

*Antoinette de Mirecourt* was added to the NCL list. Anna Jameson, whose *Winter Studies and Summer Rambles in Canada* was reissued by both Coles and NCL (in an abridged edition), is the only early woman writer whose reputation has not benefitted from reprinting in the latter series.

The current ascendancy of fiction as our major literary genre is another factor that has significantly affected the visibility of early women writers and perhaps diverted attention from the poets. The formerly anthologized poetry of Moodie, Duncan, Leprohon, and L. M. Montgomery has been almost completely overshadowed by their prose, and Crawford's oeuvre has been combed for fiction suitable for inclusion in short story anthologies. Harrison may now be re-entering the canon through the door of fiction, a route that could be followed by some of the other writers in Table 2, particularly Isabel Ecclestone Mackay and Florence Randal Livesay.

The relation between the sex of the editor and the inclusion of women writers is a topic that bears consideration. Until recently, the few appearances of a female editor had little effect on the representation of women authors. Going back to the first period presented in Table 1, we can see that Edmund Kemper Broadus, identified on the title page as "Professor of English in the University of Alberta," and Eleanor Hammond Broadus (unaffiliated) anticipated the pattern of the future in their restriction of women writers in their first book to four (Crawford, Pauline Johnson, Moodie, and Marjorie Pickthall) and in their second to seven (adding Dalton, Mazo de la Roche, and Audrey Alexandra Brown). Susie Frances Harrison's popular *Canadian Birthday Book* was just slightly more generous. On the other hand, in Donalda Dickie's *The Canadian Poetry Book* (1924), which I omitted from Table 1 because it is a school text which its editor claimed "[was] not, in any sense of the word an 'Anthology of Canadian Verse' " (5), women are 33 per cent of the contributors and occupy 40 per cent of the text.[14] In contrast, there were no women editors of major national survey anthologies during the next period, 1940–69, when many previously important women poets disappeared permanently from sight.

In my tabulation of the post-1970 period, the anthologies compiled by Brita Mickleburgh, Mary Jane Edwards, and Donna Bennett certainly help raise the proportional representation of early women writers. Disappointing, therefore, is Margaret Atwood's *New Oxford Book of Canadian Verse*. While Atwood justifies her inclusion of early poets on the grounds of historical significance, she has stopped short of extending her "excavationism" (xxx) to her own sex. "In the nineteenth century," she jests, "a woman Canadian poet was the equivalent, say, of a white Anglo-Saxon Protestant Inuit shaman" (xxix), and then proves her point by including only two (Crawford and Johnson) in her selection of nineteen early writers. Women fare better in her recently co-edited (with Robert Weaver) *Oxford Book of Canadian Short Stories in English* (1986), where Crawford and Harrison almost balance Roberts, Scott, and

Leacock. Yet here too we can see the self-replicating process at work, for Atwood and Weaver's first two selections reproduce Rosemary Sullivan's Crawford and Harrison choices for *Stories by Canadian Women*, published two years earlier.

On the other hand, this duplication might be regarded as an example of what Elaine Showalter calls "mainstreaming" (19). One way to recover lost women authors is in anthologies devoted exclusively to women's work. These have not been plentiful in Canada. Rota Lister's substantial survey compilation of Canadian women's writing, which would help recover a broad range of fiction, non-fiction, and poetry, has been in search of a publisher for five years and now rests in the archives of the University of Waterloo. Rosemary Sullivan's historical anthology, *Poetry by Canadian Women*, was published by Oxford in 1989. Such books—when we have them—will be essential stages in the process of reconstructing the literary history of Canadian women, but they are only stages. Showalter cautions that unless this material can be integrated into a reconceived, broadened canon, all the archaeological work of feminist literary scholars may serve only to further marginalize women's writing. Using Harriet Beecher Stowe as her example, she describes the dilemma for American literature: "if we only teach Stowe in the women's courses, she remains ghettoized; if we simply squeeze in a lecture on Stowe, we have tokenism; if we drop *Moby Dick* to make room for *Uncle Tom's Cabin*, the sacrifice will be unacceptable to many, including feminists" (20). Showalter's tentative resolution is to recognize that the 1980s are a period of canonical uncertainty and to look forward hopefully to "the emergence of bold new paradigms" that will lead to a complete reassessment of literary history and values (21).

In Canada, while we cannot condense the issue into an epigrammatic contest between Uncle Tom and Moby Dick, we face the same problem of getting our early women writers into the canon and the curriculum. Once we have acknowledged that "what is commonly called literary history is actually a record of choices" (Berkinow, 3), we can start to exercise new options that would redesign the current picture of Canada's literary past. The task is large and multifaceted but not too daunting; women are accustomed to engaging in work that, in the words of the proverb, is "never done."

## NOTES

The research for this paper was assisted by a grant from the Social Sciences and Humanities Research Council of Canada's Women and Work strategic grants program.
1.  The percentage of women authors reviewed in mainstream newspapers and magazines is less; see Dagg, 35.
2.  In 1983–84 women occupied 36 per cent of short-term and 33 per cent of long-term writers-in-residence positions, and received 30 per cent of the funding (Dagg, 42). Crean's source is Nelson.

3.  The count of Canadian poets in American anthologies from 1890 to 1960, in A. R. Rogers, "American Recognition of Canadian Authors" (diss. Univ. of Michigan, 1964), reveals that women were 23.5 per cent of the Canadian poets recognized in the United States, but received only 16 per cent of the space.

4.  The major work on this subject is Jay B. Hubbell's *Who Are the Major American Writers?* (Durham, N.C.: Duke Univ. Press, 1972).

5.  Nelson takes this term from Coser, Kadushin, and Power, *Books: The Culture and Commerce of Publishing* (Basic Books, 1982), who in turn borrow it from Diana Crane, *Invisible Colleges: Diffusion of Knowledge in Scientific Communities* (Chicago: Univ. of Chicago Press, 1974).

6.  Nelson, 70, 79; from Spender, 186 and Smith, 287.

7.  For an assessment of the role of the university in contemporary Canadian literature, see Bruce W. Powe, "The University as the Hidden Ground of Canadian Literature," *Antigonish Review* 47 (1981): 11–15.

8.  See, for example, Moyles' classification of Frances Brooke, Pauline Johnson, Rosanna Leprohon and Catharine Parr Traill as "minor" and Charles W. Gordon and Ernest Thompson Seton as "major" (vii–viii).

9.  See Carole Gerson, "Some Notes Concerning Pauline Johnson," *Canadian Notes & Queries* 34 (1985): 16–19.

10.  Alastair Fowler, *Kinds of Literature: An Introduction to the Theory of Genres and Modes* (Cambridge, Mass., 1982): 213–16.

11.  We can draw a rosier picture of the representation of women poets by looking only at anthologies whose focus is *current* authors. From *New Provinces* (1936), which contains no women, the situation could only improve. In Gustafson's *A Little Anthology of Canadian Poets* (1943) 13.5 per cent of the poets are women, who occupy 7.7 per cent of the space. In A.J.M. Smith's *Modern Canadian Verse* (1967) 18 per cent of the poets are women; this figure rises to 35 per cent in Gary Geddes' and Phyllis Bruce's *Fifteen Canadian Poets Plus Five* (1978) and to 38 per cent in Dennis Lee's *The New Canadian Poets, 1970–1985* (1985).

12.  For an example of this kind of male literary/political power network, see the guest list of the 1897 banquet of *Canadian Magazine*, which mixed poets and fiction writers with newspaper magnates, political figures, academics, and businessmen. *Canadian Magazine* 8 (1897): 463–66.

13.  See, for example, Veronica Strong-Boag, "Raising Clio's Consciousness: Women's History and Archives in Canada," *Archivaria* 6 (1978): 70–82; Gerda Lerner, "Placing Women in History: Definitions and Challenges," *Feminist Studies* 3 (1975): 5–14.

14.  A higher representation of women appeared in anthologies of *current* poets, like the Toronto Women's Press Club's *Canadian Days* [1911], Ethel Hume Bennett's *New Harvesting. Contemporary Canadian Poetry, 1918–38* (1939), and Alan Creighton and Hilda Ridley, eds., *A New Canadian Anthology* (1938).

# WORKS CITED

"Advice and dissent." 1987. *Books in Canada* 16, no. 4 (May): 12–14.

Atwood, Margaret. 1982. Introduction. *The New Oxford Book of Canadian Verse in English.* Toronto: Oxford Univ. Press. xxvii–xxxix.

Baym, Nina. 1981. "Melodramas of Beset Manhood: How Theories of American Fiction Exclude Women Authors." *American Quarterly* 33: 123–39.

Berkinow, Louise. 1974. Introduction. *The World Split Open. Four Centuries of Women Poets in England and America, 1552–1950.* New York: Vintage. 3–47.

Campbell, Wilfred, et al. 1979. *At the Mermaid Inn.* Ed. Barrie Davies. Toronto: Univ. of Toronto Press.

Crean, Susan. 1984. "The Thirty Per Cent Solution." *This Magazine* 17: 26–31, 38.

Dagg, Anne Innis. 1986. *The 50% Solution: Why Should Women Pay for Men's Culture?* Waterloo, Ont.: Otter Press.

Fiedler, Leslie A. 1981. "Literature as an Institution: The View from 1980." *English Literature: Opening Up the Canon.* Ed. Leslie A. Fiedler and Houston A. Baker, Jr. Baltimore: Johns Hopkins Univ. Press.

Galloway, Priscilla. 1980. *What's Wrong with High School English?* Toronto: Ontario Institute for Studies in Education.

Golding, Alan C. 1984. "A History of American Poetry Anthologies." In *Canons.* Ed. Robert von Hallberg. Chicago: Univ. of Chicago Press. 279–308.

Grayson, J. Paul, and L. M. Grayson. 1980. "Canadian literary and other elites: the historical and institutional basis of shared realities." *Canadian Review of Sociology and Anthropology* 17: 338–55.

———. 1978. "The Canadian literary elite: a socio-historical perspective." *Canadian Journal of Sociology* 3: 291–308.

Langer, Beryl Donaldson. 1984. "Women and Literary Production: Canada and Australia." *Australian Canadian Studies* 2: 70–83. Rpt. in *Australian/Canadian Literatures in English: Comparative Perspectives.* Ed. Russell McDougall and Gillian Whitlock. Melbourne: Methuen Australia. 133–50.

Lauter, Paul. 1983. "Race and Gender in the Shaping of the American Literary Canon: A Case Study from the Twenties." *Feminist Studies* 9: 435–63.

Moyles, R. G. 1976. *English-Canadian Literature to 1900: A Guide to Information Sources.* Detroit: Gale Research.

Mullen, Jean S. 1972. "Freshman Texts. Part I: Women Writers in Freshman Textbooks." *College English* 34: 79–84.

Munro, Alice. 1988. "Meneseteung." *New Yorker* 11 (Jan.): 28–38.

Nelson, Sharon. 1982. "Bemused, Branded, and Belittled. Women and Writing in Canada." *Fireweed* 15: 65–102.

Olsen, Tillie. 1983. *Silences.* 1978. New York: Dell.

Parker, George, ed. 1973. *The Evolution of Canadian Literature in English: 1914–1945.* Toronto: Holt, Rinehart and Winston.

Rosenfelt, Deborah S. 1982. "The Politics of Bibliography. Women's Studies and the Literary Canon." In *Women in Print.* Ed. Joan E. Hartman and Ellen Messer-Davidow. New York: MLA. 11–35.

Russ, Joanna. 1983. *How to Suppress Women's Writing*. Austin: Univ. of Texas Press.

Shields, Carol. 1987. *Swann: A Mystery*. Toronto: Stoddart.

Showalter, Elaine. 1981. "Responsibilities and Realities: A Curriculum for the Eighties." *ADE Bulletin* 70: 17–21.

Smith, A.J.M. 1943. Introduction. *The Book of Canadian Poetry*. Chicago: Univ. of Chicago Press. 3–31.

———. 1942. "Canadian Anthologies, New and Old." *University of Toronto Quarterly* 2: 457–74.

Smith, Dorothy E. 1978. "A Peculiar Eclipsing: Women's Exclusion from Men's Culture." *Women's Studies International Quarterly* 1: 281–94.

Spender, Dale. 1981. "The Gatekeepers: a Feminist Critique of Academic Publishing." *Doing Feminist Research*. Ed. Helen Roberts. London: Routledge & Kegan Paul. 186–202.

Spender, Lynne. 1983. *Intruders on the Rights of Men. Women's Unpublished Heritage*. London: Pandora Press.

Story, Norah. 1967. *Oxford Companion to Canadian Literature and History*. Toronto: Oxford Univ. Press.

Sullivan, Rosemary, ed. 1984. *Stories by Canadian Women*. Toronto: Oxford Univ. Press.

Sylvestre, Guy, Brandon Conron, and Carl F. Klinck. 1970. *Canadian Writers/Ecrivains Canadiens. A Biographical Dictionary*. Toronto: Ryerson Press.

Toye, William, ed. 1983. *The Oxford Companion to Canadian Literature*. Toronto: Oxford Univ. Press.

Watters, Reginald Eyre. 1972. *A Checklist of Canadian Literature and Background Materials, 1628–1960*. Toronto: Univ. of Toronto Press.

Whiteman, Bruce. 1984. *A Literary Friendship. The Correspondence of Ralph Gustafson and W.W.E. Ross*. Toronto: ECW Press.

## ANTHOLOGIES CONSULTED

Arnason, David, ed. 1974. *Nineteenth Century Canadian Stories*. Toronto: Macmillan.

Atwood, Margaret, ed. 1982. *The New Oxford Book of Canadian Verse in English*. Toronto: Oxford Univ. Press.

Atwood, Margaret, and Robert Weaver, eds. 1986. *The Oxford Book of Canadian Short Stories in English*. Toronto: Oxford Univ. Press.

Bennett, Ethel Hume, ed. 1939. *New Harvesting. Contemporary Canadian Poetry, 1918–1938*. Toronto: Macmillan.

Birney, Earle, ed. 1953. *Twentieth Century Canadian Poetry*. Toronto: Ryerson Press.

Broadus, Edward Kemper, and Eleanor Hammond Broadus, eds. 1923. *A Book of Canadian Prose and Verse*. Rev. ed. 1934. Toronto: Macmillan.

Brown, Russell, and Donna Bennett, eds. 1982. *An Anthology of Canadian Literature in English*. 2 vols. Toronto: Oxford Univ. Press.

Burpee, Lawrence J., ed. 1910. *A Century of Canadian Sonnets*. Toronto: Musson.

———, ed. [1909?]. *Flowers from a Canadian Garden*. Toronto: Musson.

Campbell, W. W., ed. 1913. *The Oxford Book of Canadian Verse*. Toronto: Oxford Univ. Press.

Carman, Bliss, and Lorne Pierce, eds. 1935. *Our Canadian Literature. Representative Verse, English and French*. Toronto: Ryerson Press.

———, and V. B. Rhodenizer, eds. 1954. *Canadian Poetry in English*. Toronto: Ryerson Press.

Colombo, John Robert, ed. 1978. *The Poets of Canada*. Edmonton: Hurtig.

Creighton, Alan, and Hilda Ridley, eds. 1935. *A New Canadian Anthology*. Toronto: Crucible Press.

David, Jack, and Robert Lecker, eds. 1982. *Canadian Poetry*. 2 vols. Toronto: New Press.

Davis, N. Brian, ed. 1976. *The Poetry of the Canadian People, 1720–1920*. Toronto: NC Press.

Daymond, Douglas, and Leslie Monkman, eds. 1978. *Literature in Canada*. 2 vols. Toronto: Gage.

Dewart, Edward Hartley, ed. 1864. *Selections from Canadian Poets*. Montreal: Lovell.

Dickie, Donalda, ed. 1924. *The Canadian Poetry Book*. London and Toronto: Dent.

Dudek, Louis, and Irving Layton, eds. 1953. *Canadian Poems, 1850–1952*. 2nd ed. Toronto: Contact Press.

Edwards, Mary Jane, et al. 1973. *The Evolution of Canadian Literature in English: 1914–1945*. 4 vols. Toronto: Holt, Rinehart and Winston.

Garvin, John, ed. 1916. *Canadian Poets*. Rev. ed. 1926. Toronto: McClelland.

Grady, Wayne, ed. 1980. *The Penguin Book of Canadian Short Stories*. Harmondsworth: Penguin.

Gerson, Carole, and Kathy Mezei, eds. 1981. *The Prose of Life: Sketches from Victorian Canada*. Toronto: ECW Press.

Green, Gordon, and Guy Sylvestre, eds. 1967. *A Century of Canadian Literature/Un siècle de littérature canadienne*. Toronto: Ryerson; Montreal: HMH.

Gustafson, Ralph, ed. 1942. *Anthology of Canadian Poetry*. Harmondsworth: Penguin.

———, ed. 1958. *The Penguin Book of Canadian Verse*. 2nd ed. 1967; 3rd ed. 1975; 4th ed. 1984. Harmondsworth: Penguin.

Hardy, E. A., ed. 1920. *Selections from the Canadian Poets*. Toronto: Macmillan.

Harrison, Susan Frances, ed. 1887. *The Canadian Birthday Book*. Toronto: Blackett Robinson.

Klinck, Carl, and R. E. Watters, eds. 1955. *Canadian Anthology*. 2nd ed. 1966; 3rd ed. 1972. Toronto: Gage.

Lighthall, W. D., ed. 1889. *Songs of the Great Dominion*. London: Walter Scott.

Lochhead, Douglas, and Raymond Souster, eds. 1974. *One Hundred Poems of Nineteenth Century Canada*. Toronto: Macmillan.

Lucas, Alec. 1971. *Great Canadian Short Stories*. New York: Dell.

McLay, Catherine, ed. 1974. *Canadian Literature: The Beginnings to the 20th Century*. Toronto: McClelland and Stewart.

Mickleburgh, Brita, ed. 1973. *Canadian Literature: Two Centuries in Prose*. Toronto: McClelland and Stewart.

Pacey, Desmond, ed. 1950. *A Book of Canadian Stories*. 2nd ed. Toronto: Ryerson Press.

———, ed. 1974. *Selections from Major Canadian Writers: Poetry and Creative Prose in English*. Toronto: McGraw-Hill Ryerson.

Rand, Theodore H., ed. 1900. *A Treasury of Canadian Verse*. Toronto: Briggs.

Robins, John D., ed. 1946. *A Pocketful of Canada*. Toronto: Collins.

Ross, George W., ed. 1893. *Patriotic Recitations and Arbour Day Exercises*. Toronto: Warwick.

Ross, Malcolm, et al. 1960–72. *Poets of Canada*. New Canadian Library. 4 vols. Toronto: McClelland and Stewart.

Sinclair, David, ed. 1972. *Nineteenth-Century Narrative Poems*. Toronto: McClelland and Stewart.

Smith, A.J.M., ed. 1943. *The Book of Canadian Poetry*. Rev. ed. 1948; 1957. Chicago: Univ. of Chicago Press.

———, ed. 1965. *The Book of Canadian Prose. Early Beginnings to Confederation*. Toronto: Gage.

———, ed. 1973. *The Canadian Century*. Toronto: Gage.

———, ed. 1960. *The Oxford Book of Canadian Verse*. Toronto: Oxford Univ. Press.

Stephen, A. M., ed. 1928. *The Golden Treasury of Canadian Verse*. Toronto: Dent.

———, ed. 1926. *The Voice of Canada. Canadian Prose and Poetry*. Toronto: Dent.

Swayze, J. F., ed. 1946. *The Voice of Canada*. Toronto: Dent.

Watson, Albert Durrant, and Lorne Pierce, eds. 1923. *Our Canadian Literature. Representative Prose and Verse*. Toronto: Ryerson Press.

Weaver, Robert, and William Toye, eds. 1973. *The Oxford Anthology of Canadian Literature*. Toronto: Oxford Univ. Press.

Wetherell, James E., ed. 1893. *Later Canadian Poems*. Toronto: Copp Clark.

*Table 1*

*Representation of Women in Canadian Survey Anthologies*
*(English-language only)*

**Code**

A:  P = Poetry; M = Mixed Poetry and Prose; Pr = Prose
B:  total authors, % women
C:  total authors, % pages for women
D:  authors born ≤ 1875, % women
E:  authors born ≤ 1875, % pages for women
*:  woman editor

**Beginnings to 1935**

| A | Editor(s) | Pub. Date | B | C | D | E |
|---|-----------|-----------|---|---|---|---|
|   |           |           | per cent | | | |
| P | Dewart, *Selections from Can. Poets* | 1864 | 24 | 35.5 | 24 | 35.5 |
| P | *Harrison, *Can. Birthday Bk* | 1887 | 21 | 16.5 | 21 | 16.5 |
| P | Lighthall, *Songs of the Great Dominion* | 1889 | 28 | 18.5 | 28 | 18.5 |
| P | Wetherell, *Later Can. Poems* | 1893 | 46 | 15.5 | 46 | 15.5 |
| P | Rand, *Treasury of Can. Verse* | 1900 | 22.5 | 22 | 22.5 | 22 |
| P | Burpee, *Flowers from a Can. Garden* | 1909? | 50 | 33 | 50 | 33 |
| P | Burpee, *Century of Can. Sonnets* | 1910 | 16.5 | 18 | 16.5 | 18 |
| P | Campbell, *Oxford Bk of Can. Verse* | 1913 | 21 | 18 | 21 | 17.5 |
| P | Garvin, *Can. Poets* | 1916 | 40.5 | 34 | 33 | 30.5 |
| P | Hardy, *Selections from Can. Poets* | 1920 | 29 | 32.5 | 29 | 32.5 |
| M | Watson & Pierce, *Our Can. Lit.* | 1923 | 22.5 | 25.5 | 24 | 25.5 |
| M | *Broadus, *Bk of Can. Prose & Verse* | 1923 | 9.5 | 6 | 11 | 8 |
| P | Garvin, *Can. Poets* | 1926 | 38.5 | 34 | 33 | 30 |
| M | Stephen, *Voice of Canada* | 1926 | 30 | 26 | 27.5 | 20 |
| P | Stephen, *Golden Tr. of Can. Verse* | 1928 | 40 | 36 | 31 | 34 |
| M | *Broadus, *Bk of Can. Prose and Verse* | 1934 | 15 | 7.5 | 15 | 8 |
| P | Carman & Pierce, *Our Can. Lit.* | 1935 | 38.5 | 29 | 31 | 23 |
|   | AVERAGE: |   | 30 | 24 | 27.5 | 23 |

(*Table 1 cont'd.*)

**1940–69**

| A | Editor(s) | Pub. Date | B | C | D | E |
|---|---|---|---|---|---|---|
| | | | per cent | | | |
| P | Gustafson, *Anth. of Can. Poetry* | 1942 | 23.5 | 19.5 | 30 | 23.5 |
| P | Smith, *Bk of Can. Poetry* | 1943 | 28.5 | 19.5 | 16.5 | 11 |
| M | Swayze, *Voice of Canada* | 1946 | 15 | 13 | 14.5 | 17 |
| P | Smith, *Bk of Can. Poetry* | 1948 | 22.5 | 17.5 | 11.5 | 9 |
| Pr | Pacey, *Bk of Can. Stories* | 1950 | 22 | 18.5 | 10 | 12 |
| P | Dudek and Layton, *Can. Poems, 1850–1952* | 1953 | 26 | 19 | 7 | 6 |
| P | Carman, Pierce, Rhodenizer, *Can. Poetry* | 1954 | 35 | 27 | 25 | 22 |
| M | Klinck and Watters, *Can. Anth.* | 1955 | 23 | 18.5 | 21 | 15.5 |
| P | Smith, *Bk of Can. Poetry* | 1957 | 23.5 | 19.5 | 11.5 | 9.5 |
| P | Gustafson, *Penguin Bk of Can. Verse* | 1958 | 18 | 16.5 | 10.5 | 10.5 |
| P | Smith, *Oxford Bk of Can. Verse* | 1960 | 22 | 22 | 10 | 11.5 |
| Pr | Smith, *Bk of Can. Prose* | 1965 | 13.5 | 15.5 | 13.5 | 15.5 |
| M | Klinck and Watters, *Can. Anth.* | 1966 | 17 | 15 | 15 | 16.5 |
| M | Green and Sylvestre, *Cen. of Can. Lit.* | 1967 | 25 | 21 | 28.5 | 31 |
| P | Gustafson, *Penguin Bk of Can. Verse* | 1967 | 16.5 | 16.5 | 11 | 13 |
| P | Ross, *Poets of Canada* (NCL; 4 vols.) | 1960–72 | 20.5 | 17.5 | 0 | 0 |
| | AVERAGE: | | 20.5 | 18.5 | 14.5 | 14 |

**1970–86**

| A | Editor(s) | Pub. Date | B | C | D | E |
|---|-----------|-----------|---|---|---|---|
| | | | per cent | | | |
| Pr | Lucas, *Great Can. Short Stories* | 1971 | 17 | 17 | 0 | 0 |
| P | Sinclair, *19th-C. Narrative Poems* | 1972 | 17 | 17.5 | 17 | 17.5 |
| Pr | *Mickleburgh, *Can. Lit.* | 1973 | 30 | 28 | 45.5 | 44 |
| M | *Edwards et al., *Evol. of Can. Lit. to 1970* (4 vols.) | 1973 | 21.5 | 24.5 | 22 | 27.5 |
| M | Smith, *The Canadian Century* | 1973 | 14.5 | 11.5 | 18 | 16 |
| M | *McLay, *Can. Lit.* | 1974 | 17 | 20.5 | 17 | 20.5 |
| P | Lochhead and Souster, *100 Poems* | 1974 | 14.5 | 20.5 | 14.5 | 20.5 |
| Pr | Arnason, *19th-C. Can. Stories* | 1974 | 25 | 29 | 25 | 29 |
| M | Klinck and Watters, *Can. Anth.* | 1974 | 22.5 | 20.5 | 20.5 | 20.5 |
| M | Weaver and Toye, *Oxford Anth.* | 1974 | 26 | 24.5 | 23 | 23.5 |
| M | Pacey, *Selections from Can. Poets* | 1974 | 21 | 20.5 | 0 | 0 |
| P | Gustafson, *Penguin Bk of Can. Verse* | 1975 | 17 | 17 | 10.5 | 13 |
| M | Daymond and Monkman, *Lit. in Can.* (2 vols.) | 1978 | 23 | 26.5 | 21.5 | 27.5 |
| P | Colombo, *Poets of Canada* | 1978 | 16.5 | 16.5 | 7 | 8 |
| Pr | Grady, *Penguin Bk Can. Short Stories* | 1980 | 29 | 33 | 33.5 | 36 |
| P | David and Lecker, *Can. Poetry* (2 vols.) | 1982 | 24 | 22 | 14.5 | 15 |
| M | *Bennett and Brown, *Anth. of Can. Lit.* (2 vols.) | 1982 | 30 | 26.5 | 21 | 32 |
| P | *Atwood, *New Oxford Bk of Can. Verse* | 1982 | 24.5 | 22 | 10.5 | 15.5 |
| P | Gustafson, *Penguin Bk of Can. Verse* | 1984 | 16.5 | 17 | 14 | 12.5 |
| Pr | *Atwood and Weaver, *Oxford Bk of Can. Short Stories* | 1986 | 41.5 | 39 | 40 | 41 |
| | AVERAGE: | | 22.4 | 22.5 | 18.5 | 21 |

*Table 2*
*Lost Women Poets Born ≤ 1875*

**Code**
No.: No. of appearances in "Anthologies Consulted" (Appendix)
Dates: Years spanned by anthology appearances

| Name | Death | No. | Dates | Last Appearance |
|---|---|---|---|---|
| Ethelwyn Wetherald | 1940 | 15 | 1887–1954 | 1935, 1942, 1954 |
| Agnes Maule Machar | 1927 | 14 | 1887–1954 | 1935, 1946, 1964 |
| Susie Frances Harrison | 1935 | 13 | 1887–1954 | 1935, 1943, 1954 |
| Jean Blewett | 1934 | 13 | 1900–1954 | 1935, 1946, 1954 |
| Helena Coleman | 1953 | 13 | 1909–1954 | 1942, 1943, 1954 |
| Annie Charlotte Dalton | 1938 | 11 | 1926–1954 | 1946, 1953, 1954 |
| Isabel Ecclestone Mackay | 1928 | 11 | 1913–1954 | 1942, 1946, 1954 |
| Elizabeth Roberts MacDonald | 1922 | 8 | 1889–1954 | 1923, 1935, 1954 |
| Helen Merrill | 1951 | 7 | 1900–1954 | 1926, 1935, 1954 |
| Pamelia Vining Yule | 1897? | 7 | 1864–1943 | 1900, 1913, 1943 |
| Florence Randal Livesay | 1953 | 7 | 1916–1954 | 1935, 1939, 1954 |

*Table 3*

*Women Authors Born ≤ 1875 in Twenty Anthologies, published 1970–
(listed in Table 1)*

**Code**

No.: No. of appearances in twenty anthologies

| Author | Dates | No. | Last Appearance |
|--------|-------|-----|-----------------|
| Isabella Valancy Crawford | 1850–1887 | 14 | 1982(3), 1984, 1986 |
| Susanna Moodie | 1803–1885 | 9 | 1976, 1978, 1982, 1986 |
| Pauline Johnson | 1861–1913 | 8 | 1978(2), 1982, 1984 |
| Sara Jeannette Duncan | 1861–1922 | 7 | 1973(3), 1974(3), 1978 |
| Frances Brooke | 1723–1789 | 5 | 1974(2), 1978, 1982 |
| Catharine Parr Traill | 1802–1899 | 4 | 1978, 1982 |
| Rosanna Leprohon | 1829–1879 | 4 | 1973, 1974, 1976, 1978 |
| Emily Carr | 1871–1945 | 4 | 1973(2), 1974, 1978 |
| Virna Sheard | 1865–1943 | 2 | 1975, 1984 |
| Nellie McClung | 1873–1951 | 2 | 1973, 1978 |
| L. M. Montgomery | 1874–1942 | 2 | 1973(2) |
| Harriet Vaughan Cheney | 1796–1889 | 1 | 1973 |
| Anna Jameson | 1794–1860 | 1 | 1978 |
| Susie Frances Harrison | 1859–1937 | 1 | *1986 |
| Robina and Kathleen Lizars | d. 1918; 1931 | 1 | 1973 |

* also in *Stories by Canadian Women* (1984)

(*Table 3 cont'd.*)

*Male Authors Born ≤ 1875 in Twenty Anthologies, published 1970–*

| No. | Author |
|-----|--------|
| 19 | Roberts |
| 18 | D. C. Scott |
| 13 | Lampman |
| 13 | Carman |
| 12 | Sangster |
| 11 | Campbell, Leacock |
| 10 | Goldsmith, Haliburton, McLachlan |
| 9 | Heavysege, Mair |
| 7 | Drummond |
| 6 | Cameron, Howe, Kirby, Service, Stansbury |
| 5 | "Ralph Connor," McCrae, McCulloch, McGee, Richardson, F. G. Scott, E. W. Thomson |
| 4 | Dewart, De Mille, Tom MacInnes, Parker, Odell |
| 3 | Alline, Robert Hayman, Hearne, O'Grady |
| 2 | Levi Adams, Jacob Bailey, Adam Hood Burwell, Norman Duncan, John Frederic Herbin, Hunter-Duvar, G. T. Lanigan, Alex. Mackenzie, Goldwin Smith, David Thompson, Daniel Wilson |
| 1 | Adam Allan, Grant Allen, Isidore Ascher, Robert Barr, Samuel M. Baylis, Edward Blake, Sir Cavendish Boyle, John Burke, W. F. Butler, Edward John Chapman, Thomas Cary, John Gyles, Alexander Henry, Wilfrid Laurier, John Talon Lesperance, W. D. Lighthall, Evan MacColl, J. MacKay, Alexander Muir, John James Proctor, Theodore Harding Rand, Ernest Thompson Seton, George Vancouver, Arthur Weir, R. Stanley Weir |

Total: 72 names for men (83%), 15 names for women (17%)

# Separate Entrances: The First Generation of Canadian Women Journalists

MARJORY LANG

It was exactly a century ago that two young Canadian women set off on a journey around the world. In late Victorian Canada, the departure of two unmarried women travelling without escort was unconventional if not positively scandalous. But these were not ordinary women, nor ordinary tourists. The two female adventurers meant to make their trip as unorthodox as possible because they were journalists. Both they and their newspapers intended the voyage to be a news event full of public interest. How two attractive and unchaperoned women encountered the newly opened West, the dangerously exotic Orient, and the old civilizations of the Mediterranean would make remarkable reading and sell newspapers.

One of these young newspaper women was already quite well known as Garth Grafton to the readers of the Toronto *Globe* and the Montreal *Star*. Serious readers of *The Week* might also recognize her real name, Sara Jeannette Duncan. Her companion, Lily Lewis, also wrote for the Montreal *Star* and *The Week*, signing herself Louis Lloyd. Although both assumed masculine pseudonyms, they wore their disguises lightly, more as daring accessories than as veils. Theirs was not the dilemma of female talent forced to parade itself as male in order to get an audience. When, on a few occasions, Sara Jeannette Duncan had to correct the misapprehension of less-than-discerning readers, she firmly identified herself as a woman. Correspondents to her Woman's World department in the *Globe* addressed Garth Grafton as "Dear Madam." (Nor did Louis Lloyd make any attempt to camouflage her female identity in her travelling articles for *The Week*.)

Duncan was keenly alert to the latest trends in newspaper fashion and knew how to exploit her assets in the literary marketplace. Having served her apprenticeship in the United States where journalistic innovations set the pace for the rest of the English-speaking world, she knew that a woman doing unusual things and expressing audacious opinions held an intrinsic interest for the late nineteenth-century newspaper reading public. She also assumed, correctly as it turns out, that enterprising newspaper proprietors would take risks backing a woman journalist who showed some flair. For her around-the-world journey, she gained the sponsorship of the most controversial and successful of American newspaper tycoons, Joseph Pulitzer, and his nearest equivalent in Canada, Sir Hugh Graham of the Montreal *Star* (Godwin, 48; Mahaffey, 10–11). It is a testament to Duncan's remarkable originality that her escapade predated by a year the much more famous around-the-world journey in less than eighty days of Nelly Bly, an American who was also backed by Pulitzer. One of the most shrewdly entrepreneurial newspaper publishers of the day observed of these intrepid women journalists: "once launched upon the sea of adventure, trifles such as would hardly be read if written by a man become thrilling or picturesque as an episode in the life of a woman" (Sheppard, 1).

Sara Jeannette Duncan was among the few women in Canada who were able to make a living in journalism because they wrote what a large number of people wanted to read. With her talent and ingenuity, Duncan stood out in the contemporary press, but she was not the only woman to write for newspapers in Canada. The imprecision of contemporary surveys, combined with the anonymity and pseudonymity of newspaper writing, bedevils attempts to pinpoint exactly how many women were practising journalists in late nineteenth-century Canada. The first census for which any estimates are available, 1891, recorded thirty-five women editors, reporters, and journalists. A few years later, the National Council of Women of Canada described the careers of fifty-five editors, contributors, and correspondents (73–77). The former estimate probably excluded the many women labouring for family newspapers; the latter embraced a range extending from the enthusiastic contributor of small-town gossip to the owner-operator of a country weekly. Both enumerations acknowledged the lively cluster of francophone women journalists who were subject to newspaper conventions quite distinct from those developing in English Canada (see Boivin and Landry; Trofimenkoff). Conversely, both estimates excluded those who were working as journalists in the pioneering communities of the West. The opportunities and obstacles for women in the fluid society of the newly settled territories were quite different from those facing women in the more conventional urban society of eastern Canada, and again constitute a separate chapter in the story of women's experience in Canadian journalism (see Gorham).

The purpose of this study is to explore the historical milieu of women's entry into journalism in Canada: why newspapers began to hire women writers and why women were attracted to newspaper work. Thus, only those writers who were regularly employed as reporters, correspondents, contributors, or editors on a daily or weekly anglophone journal will be considered here.

As with so many areas of female achievement, the history of women in journalism is strewn with firsts. Alice Lemmon Keeler wrote for and then ran her husband's paper in Brantford in the 1830s; Agnes Maule Machar was writing articles under the *nom de plume* of Fidelis in the 1870s (see Chenier); Kate Massiah was covering the House of Commons for the Montreal *Herald* in 1879 (see Canadian Women's Press Club). Other women engaged in journalism as part of a family enterprise. But the fact that women had written for newspapers before them in no way diminished the novelty of what the late nineteenth-century newspaper women accomplished. They carved out new fields in journalism and attracted a new kind of newspaper subscriber. The most famous among these pioneers won their renown by creating and projecting literary personae which attracted enormous followings. Newspaper owners could not fail to be impressed by the volume of mail that arrived at the desk of Garth Grafton, Pharos in the *Globe*'s "Circle of Young Canada," or Kit of the Mail.

Strange as it may now seem, the press had not always been so solicitous of mass popularity. Earlier Canadian newspapers served as organs of special interest groups, defined most often by political party but also by religion and ethnicity, and were dependent upon their specific constituency in a closed circle of concurring opinion. In an era of what was called "personal journalism," the newspaper was the product of the owner-editor who often wrote most of it himself, sometimes with the help of female family members. Even on the largest papers, staffs were small and not likely to include regular female employees.

Women journalists owed their presence in the newspaper world to major structural changes in the ownership and operation of the press which took place in Canada in the last decades of the nineteenth century (Rutherford). In the 1880s, the big city dailies multiplied and began to take on a distinctly popular style in their bid to attract a mass readership. Unlike the earlier party papers, the urban dailies aimed for political independence. In lieu of party coffers, they turned for revenue to advertising and large circulations, and they competed murderously with each other to secure the largest share of both. As the contest for the pennies and loyalty of the customer grew intense, it began to dawn on some newspaper editors, especially when prodded by the business department, that a female readership could be a crucial element in the forecast of financial success. Not only would the female subscriber boost raw sales; her allegiance was especially attractive to advertisers who recognized women's increasing power as consumers. The newspaper that could direct women's attention to the advertisements for household goods, fashions, or patent medicines by displaying them in a section "of interest to women" would certainly have an advantage in the battle for revenue.

Thus, the emergence of the women's page in the popular daily newspaper was a direct result of commercial pressure on newspaper owners and editors. At the same time, in those last decades of the century, the nature of journalism and what the press deemed suitably "newsworthy" changed in the favour of the woman journalist. In the earlier newspapers, parliamentary debates, reported verbatim, and editorial infighting based on political differences had provided the main substance of news, which was directed at an élite who managed commerce and politics. In contrast, the popular press of the late nineteenth century was more local than national and more personal than political. It pitched its contents at ordinary people who were not vitally concerned about distant affairs over which they had no control; they were interested instead in events in their street, neighbourhood, and community. They wanted their newspapers to entertain them, not merely to harangue them, and to serve women and children as well as the male head of household.

The effort of late nineteenth-century Canadian newspapers to reach a family audience established the métier of the aspiring female reporter who could specialize in community affairs and human interest stories. As one newspaper historian has argued, papers for the people tended to enhance the importance of everyday life by focusing attention on matters close at hand (Schudson, 26). According to prejudices of the time, women writers were supposed to be better at seeing life through the microscope rather than the telescope, at detailing the minutiae of personality and relationship rather than enlarging on grand themes.[1] The woman reporter could be expected to take a sympathetic view of her community, to enhance local colour and elevate the pitch of drama of ordinary events.

The general trend towards entertainment and popular appeal in newspapers created a climate in which a few women journalists could flourish. Opportunities for female reporters arose more directly as a result of the increasing visibility of women in the public life of the local community. The women's club movement was beginning to develop in Canada, and the activities of such organizations as the Women's Christian Temperance Union, the National Council of Women of Canada, and various church auxiliaries were regularly reported in the press. "Temperance and Social Reform" was a daily column in the *Globe*, a paper whose upright moral tone had earned it a reputation as "The Scotsman's Bible." The women who led these organizations were venturing into the limelight for the first time and were understandably reluctant to undergo the glare of publicity. Ejecting male reporters sent to scrutinize their opening addresses might temporarily ease the speakers' minds, but it would not win favourable reception for their causes. But who was to know that the serious young lady taking notes at the Elm Street Methodist annual mission meeting was Garth Grafton of the *Globe*? The real Miss Duncan squirmed a little in her disguise when a kindly soul beside her praised her dedication to mission work. Perhaps to compensate for her subterfuge, in her write-up in the *Globe* on October 1, 1886, Garth Grafton only gently lampooned and, in the main, applauded the conduct of the women-only meeting[2] (Duncan). This, and other more serious accounts from writers less mischievous than Duncan, could only serve to increase the confidence of women's club leaders and, ultimately, their co-operation with female journalists.

Reporting the civic reform activities of strong-minded women provided one portal through which a number of women journalists entered their chosen profession. Recording the more frivolous goings-on in the homes of social leaders furnished a much wider point of entry. Society gossip columns were an innovation in late nineteenth-century newspapers, which proved to be enormously popular both with the select circles whose names were recorded and with the less exalted reading public who liked their daily fare spiced with gossip about the rich and famous. Thus, most newspapers had some kind of society column by the end of the century. Since society reporting was a specialty male journalists were not eager to embrace, most newspapers hired at least one woman to cover the local balls, teas, and weddings. On smaller newspapers, the society reporter might be the only woman on staff. It became virtually imperative that newspapers carry some sort of information about High Society, but those papers with a reputation for seriousness participated in trading social trivia only with reluctance. The Ottawa *Journal* kept a close rein on the freedom of its first society columnist, Florence Randal, confining her to mere lists and chronicles of the débutantes and dowagers of the capital (Gwyn, 371–79). The *Globe* had similar reservations about the inauguration of its first society column in 1893. As Melville Hammond recalled, "At first there were wry faces against such 'horrid vulgar stuff' in the newspaper office and indignant protests from High Society matrons unused to the publicizing of private life" (196). Gradually and tactfully, the first editor, Mrs. Willoughby Cummings, expanded her empire at the *Globe* from weekly personal notes culled from cities around Ontario to a daily column in 1896.

Because women's entry into journalism coincided with the overturning of old conventions and the introduction of new departments, features, and even new ways of telling news stories, the new women journalists became symbols of the changing face of journalism in the late nineteenth century. On one hand, proprietors and managing editors tolerated them because their names or their topics drew readers. On the other hand, conservative critics of the new trends in the newspaper industry disparaged the female contribution to the news and views of the day.

It was the most enterprising of late nineteenth-century newspaper entrepreneurs who were most favourably disposed towards the woman journalist. E. E. Sheppard, the most flamboyant of this group, boasted of the number of successful female journalists he had launched. When a certain young lady from Brantford applied to him, however, he gently scotched her ambitions, much to his chagrin later on when he realized that he had missed hiring the great Sara Jeannette Duncan (1). His *Saturday Night* had an unusually brilliant society page under the direction of Grace Denison, also known as Lady Gay, and featured the pointed commentary on Ottawa social life of Amaryllis, in real life Agnes Scott. To edit his women's page, Sheppard recruited Elmina Elliott, who established a brilliant reputation as Madge Merton, although she also wrote under the *noms de plume* of Clip Carew and Frances Burton Clare. Kate Westlake gained her first experience as sub-editor of a country weekly, the St. Thomas *Journal*, but it was Sheppard who gave her the chance to edit a family magazine, his *Fireside Weekly* (Charlesworth, 95; Willard and Livermore, 761).

Sheppard could also claim to have given a start to the greatest of all nineteenth-century Canadian women journalists, Kathleen Blake Watkins, later Coleman. Even though she had no experience in journalism and previously had written only for her own amusement, Sheppard published a couple of her essays. These in turn attracted the attention of Christopher Bunting of the *Mail*, who offered her a staff position editing the women's page. This was in 1890 at a time when the *Mail* was attempting to extricate itself from direct dependence on the Conservative party. The inauguration of a women's page was, no doubt, part of the strategy to gain independence by establishing commercial viability. In the end, the *Mail* did not succeed in its bid for freedom. It had to merge with the *Empire*, the Conservative party organ John A. Macdonald launched to compete with the recalcitrant *Mail*. But Bunting would never have cause to regret hiring the woman who became famous as Kit of the Mail.

Kit's weekly pages in the *Mail* became one of the most widely read features in the whole newspaper industry. Households where political loyalties would normally prohibit the purchase of a Conservative paper overcame their scruples on Saturday for the sake of Kit's "Woman's Kingdom" (Charlesworth, 95). Liberal fans included the Prime Minister. She in turn expressed her admiration for Laurier, although she wrote for the politically hostile *Mail and Empire*.[3] Kit also won the heart of the woman the *Globe* hired to compete with her. Jean Blewett christened Kit "The Queen of Hearts" in recognition of her popularity and her unrivalled rule in the land of the lovelorn (Ferguson, 11).

Although the selling power of women's features, such as the society column or romantic advice correspondence, was unassailable, there were many critics who resented the changes taking place in the newspapers of their day and associated women journalists with the decline of newspaper traditions and the degradation of public taste. Few would go so far as an American editor who fumed:

> As a rule, women are either dilettanti in journalism or professional panderers to an unhealthy literary appetite . . . . A careful examination of the "great dailies" will demonstrate that at least half the intellectual slime that is befouling the land is fished out of the gutter by females (Brann, 13).

But even Edmund Sheppard, whose bread was buttered by the efforts of Lady Gay and Amaryllis, when asked why he tolerated "society chatter" in *Saturday Night* replied sardonically, "Well you'll notice that if pink teas are popular on the inside, they don't cut much of a figure on the front page'' (Bridle, 21). Sheppard knew very well that the ''feminine departments'' were essential to his publication's viability, but his tone suggested that newspaper women must be quarantined in their own sphere lest their influence emasculate the whole newspaper.

The grudging acceptance and truncated opportunities offered women in the newspaper field inevitably coloured the way that they saw their work. Mary McOuat, a Canadian journalist who gained wide experience on the New York *Recorder and Tribune* before returning to Canada to work for the Ottawa *Journal*, railed against her confinement in the women's section:

> I have ''chopped copy,'' conducted a cooking column, book reviews, inter-
> views, answered in a correspondence column, and reported everything from
> an afternoon tea to a political meeting. This has all been done for the
> Woman's Page, however, and as a consequence I am unspeakably weary
> of everything connected with the sex. The one thing I most wish is that I
> had had the good fortune to be born a man for then I would not have been
> obliged to write about women (Sanford Papers).

Similarly, Sara Jeannette Duncan, although she had no reason to be ashamed of the work she had done for the press and, in any case, would not have denigrated the task of writing for women, lamented the highly circum-scribed realm women journalists inhabited in Canada:

> Here in Canada nothing, comparatively speaking, has been accomplished
> by women in journalism, partly because the Canadian newspaper world is
> so small as to be easily occupied by some half dozen influential journals,
> partly because it is a very conservative world indeed, and we know what
> conservatism means in relation to the scope of women's work.

She ended her editorial on women's opportunities in journalism by referring to difficulties ''which look insuperable at first and can only be surmounted by the exercise of the divinest kind of patience'' (Tausky, 49–50).

Tracing Duncan's mobility during the four or so years she worked as a journalist as she moved from Brantford to Washington to Toronto to Montreal to Ottawa and then around the world, it would seem that restlessness and bril-liance rather than patience characterized her progress. Within that short span she had exhausted the best opportunities open to a woman in Canadian news-paper work and even some chances that men would envy, such as the prestig-ious post of parliamentary correspondent for the Montreal *Star*. During those years, she was feverishly productive, writing regular columns for *The Week* both as Garth Grafton and Sara Jeannette Duncan, in addition to her daily work for the *Globe* and the Montreal *Star*. Before routine could dull the piquancy of her writing, she had dropped out of Canadian journalism.

Duncan seemed quite self-consciously to be using her adventures in jour-nalism as an apprenticeship for her more serious literary aspirations.[4] Having found her literary footing writing about things that happened to her or that she observed first hand, she set out to gather as much of that sort of experience as possible to draw upon in later years. Newspaper work gave Duncan the opportunity to investigate all sorts and conditions of people in the course of her daily round, the discipline of production deadlines, and almost instantaneous audience response to what she wrote. Although her autobiographical heroine, Margery Blunt in "How an American Girl Became a Journalist," traded her immature "Secret Purpose" to distinguish herself in literature for the more practical ambition of writing a political leader, the alacrity with which the real Sara Jeannette Duncan abandoned the work-a-day world of journalism suggests that she never relinquished her dream of the higher flight (Tausky, 6–13).

If Sara Jeannette Duncan intended to use her experience in journalism as an entrance into a literary career, she was not unique. Almost all the women who achieved some prominence in Canada as journalists harboured literary aspirations which they realized in writing stories, poetry, or novels in addition to their regular newspaper or magazine responsibilities. Ethelwyn Wetherald, who took over the Woman's World department of the *Globe* after Duncan's departure and subsequently became principal editorial writer of the London *Advertiser* and co-editor of the woman's magazine, *Wives and Daughters*, saw herself as a poet rather than a newspaper woman. Thus, even when she seemed headed for striking success as the verse and book review editor of the prestigious *Ladies' Home Journal* in Philadelphia, she yearned for the contemplative life. "I shall be rather glad to go back to Fenwick and the sweet realities of life away from the bubbles and baubles of journalism," she confessed to W. W. Campbell (see letter to Campbell, 1896). Later she recalled why journalism frustrated her: "it was a lasting dissatisfaction to feel, at the end of each day, that I was too tired to do any creative work of my own" (Wetherald, xvi). Keeping her vision fixed on her ultimate goal and limiting her forays into journalism, Wetherald was able to achieve the kind of reputation her talents warranted. One critic pronounced her *House of Trees* the best collection of poetry ever written by a Canadian woman (O'Hagan, 793).

Conversely, the professor who summed up the career of Grace Blackburn warned readers that her literary reputation had better rest, not on "the efforts inspired by journalistic demands," but on the few poems which reflect her lyrical nature (Roberts and Tunnell, vol. 2, 34–35). Blackburn aspired to join Canada's nascent literary community. She had a fine critical sense, which writers like Arthur Stringer appreciated (see his letter to Lorne Pierce, 1924). But in her newspaper persona of FanFan, she was responsible for the social notes and women's news, as well as literary and dramatic criticism, in *The London Free Press*, which her family owned.[5] Like so many Canadian women journalists, she must have found that the enormous appetite of the periodical press for articles, reports, and chit chat devoured creativity and channelled output towards the easily digestible piece which would satisfy and soon be forgotten.

For Florence Randal, the realization that her literary longings could not find satisfaction in the daily grind of newspaper work translated into a sense of personal failure. In her diary for September 15, 1904, she wrote:

> It's so tiresome to have a little literary ability that will never amount to any-
> thing and yet hounds one out of laissez faire. I never had any pretension
> to ability above the usual one of people "with" a gift for that sort of thing
> and yet there comes so often the sense of failure . . . .

For similar reasons, Mary McOuat abandoned the literary ambition of her younger days. Writing to Mary Sanford, another Canadian woman journalist who was writing a novel, McOuat demurred: "I attempt nothing outside of my work for the paper, for that takes all my strength and if I tried to write things I want to write they would turn out to be trash, and there is enough of that on the market now."

It would seem that the great Kit Coleman drew the same conclusion, that newspaper work and literary achievement were ultimately incompatible, much to the disappointment of her friends and admirers. Her friend Eve Brodlique, a Canadian who won great success as a journalist in the United States, urged Coleman "not to waste herself in journalism but to write the novel that she could write which would bring her more permanent fame" (MacMurchy[6]). But Kit Coleman did not proceed with her novel: "There seems to be so little time for anything outside the daily routine—that is the worst of journalism" (1897). When she died, the newspapers across the country were full of lamentations that Coleman had not made a permanent contribution to Canadian literature. On May 21, 1915, the Edmonton *Journal* published these sentiments in her obituary:

> It is one of the tragedies of newspaper work that a great deal that deserves
> to live appears in the daily press, makes a strong impression for a day or
> a week and then is forgotten . . . . It isn't right that one who for more than
> a generation brightened and stimulated so many lives and who provided such
> faithful pictures of so many different phases of the Canadian life of her time
> should pass out of the public memory.

Given the popular aims of their proprietors, the daily or weekly news-paper was probably the best possible forum for Jean Blewett's poetry and stories. Her homespun philosophizing and maudlin tales were enormously successful with her audience and earned her much praise from critics (O'Hagan, 793; Coleman, 1896, 35–38). Her colleague on the *Globe*, Laura Durand, however, was witheringly contemptuous of Blewett's abilities. In a letter to Mary Sanford, she wrote: "[Blewett] writes poor prose and worse verse and is entirely medio-cre in range and sentiment; yet there seems to be conspiracy abroad to foist her into Canadian literature."

Laura Bradshaw Durand was a hard-working, talented, and conscientious journalist, but her passionate nature was not easily contained in the humdrum routine of newspaper work. Her correspondence with Mary Sanford and John Willison reveals a trail of personal animosities and resentments: her arrogant dismissal of the *Globe* society editor, Mrs. Willoughby Cummings; her battles with editor John Willison over her autonomy in the book review department; her wounded pride at being omitted from the cast of Canadian women writers. She had unusually liberal opportunities—she initiated the book review department and the "Circle of Young Canada" section in the *Globe*— but she would not brook interference nor bend her individuality to the omnipotent editorial authority. In 1910, she had her final showdown with an editor less tolerant than Willison and resigned from the *Globe*. In a letter to Ethelwyn Wetherald in 1911, E. W. Thomson, a former *Globe* editor, applauded Durand's fighting spirit and suggested that editors habitually bullied women. Thomson's approval notwithstanding, Laura Durand, with her ardently held convictions and artistic temperament, would have done well to heed the warnings a practical newspaper woman issued to the over-sensitive aspirant: "I seriously advise any cultivated woman determined to do only the finer kind of journalistic work to choose some other mode of bread-winning, if she would not find herself in middle age doomed to hack work and a poverty very close to destitution" (Low, 3).

It was not surprising that young women with poetic yearnings and a passion for scribbling should want to enter journalism. It would seem to the novice to be an exciting opportunity to practise her craft and to be taken seriously as a writer. To be one of the first generation of women accepted in the press world may have had a certain cachet, but the gloss soon wore off. For many, there were irreconcilable contradictions between their aspirations to be writers and the reality of their lives as journalists. Unless they had the freedom to make a quick entrance and exit, like Sara Jeannette Duncan, journalism impeded their literary ambitions.

Many of them did not have the luxury of choice. Contrary to the contemporary prejudice that women journalists were only earning their "pin money," most of them had urgent financial need for a regular salary.[7] Jean Blewett's husband was often ill; Grace Denison of *Saturday Night* was separated from her husband; Agnes Scott's family, part of the "impoverished gentility" class, required its daughters to earn their bread. After her father's death, Florence Randal contributed to the maintenance of her family. Kathleen Blake Watkins was in desperate need of a secure situation, having been married twice and with two young children to support. But like so many literary women, she had mixed feelings about her motives for writing, as if there was something base about earning money by the pen. Thus, in the *Mail* on December 27, 1890, she rebuked herself when musing about the old days when women were not "always so alive to dollars and cents as now-a-days": "Why are you writing for, my friend, quoth I to myself, if not for those same greasy, stained, ragged but inexpressibly powerful greenbacks?''

This generation of women writers marketed their literary abilities in order to earn a living; in turn, their employers profited by the promotion of their female "personalities." That Kit's column enlarged the circulation of the *Mail and Empire* by at least a third was widely acknowledged, yet she was treated, on occasion, with unnecessary meanness (MacAree, 296).[8] It was when she refused to write a daily column in addition to her weekly pages with no extra pay, that Coleman finally left the *Mail and Empire* in 1911. Yet at the height of her fame, when she became the world's first female war correspondent covering the Spanish American war in Cuba, the *Mail and Empire* capitalized on her personal fame. Her reports were not given the respectably objective anonymity accorded male correspondents; rather the headlines blazoned: "Kit's Experiences at Tampa Amidst a Hail of Bullets" (June 11, 1898) or "Kit's Description of the Embarcation of Troops at Santiago" (June 18, 1898). "Hard" news of the war appeared daily on the front page and featured the anonymous reports of the correspondent the *Mail and Empire* shared with the New York *Herald*. In contrast, Kit's articles usually adorned the Saturday edition somewhere in the middle with the "soft" human interest and entertainment stories. Moreover, she starred in her own stories; how she felt and how she went about discovering her information was an integral part of her news. Indeed, simply by being there, Kit made herself into news, just as a decade earlier in less heroic times, Sara Jeannette Duncan did the same.

The fact that editors and proprietors were willing to feature their female contributors did not necessarily mean that the authors were taken seriously as writers or as journalists. From his experience as the editor of a women's magazine in London, Arnold Bennett sneered, "In Fleet Street . . . there are, not two sexes, but two species: journalists and women-journalists . . ." (Bennett, 11). On the whole, the press world treated its female recruits as anomalies. If the public wanted "the woman's point of view" and advertisers wanted the public, then newspapers would supply it and even encourage their women writers to express their "womanliness." For instance, when Mary Bouchier Sanford suggested a series written under the pen name of Tabitha Twitters, her editor enthusiastically agreed: " 'Views' of any kind are accepted or laughed at from a woman that would be considered silly or impertinent from a man . . . " (Croly). While male news writers were to hone their facts and write crisp copy, women journalists could indulge in "fine writing," a term of abuse in the news-room. It was extremely rare for a male journalist to have a by-line; in contrast, newspapers promoted their women journalists' names.

Within their "Woman's Kingdom" or "World" or "Sphere," the most successful of this generation reigned as queens, each one alone in her contained domain. So long as they did not overstep their borders, as Laura Durand did, they were given remarkable latitude. But they could not advance, nor could they branch out. They could do no more than exploit the personalities they created for the newspaper, be it the spirited "new woman," the "fine lady," or the oracle of worldly wisdom.

But through the legends they created about themselves and about their careers as journalists, they transcended the limits of their compartments. No one was better than Kit Coleman at personal myth-making. For generations, women journalists continued to worship at her shrine. Peggy Balmer Watt, who met Kit as a tyro reporter and went on to a career spanning half a century, remembered the peerless Kit Coleman as the mother of them all: "Kit made it possible that we were even recognized. Behind her skirts we crept gropingly forward. What a fighter she was! What a Leader! The Romantic days of women in journalism are no more."

## NOTES

Research for this paper was made possible by a grant from the Social Sciences and Humanities Research Council of Canada, Strategic Grants Program.
1.   See, for example, the judgement of the *London Review* (1860), "On Female Novelists": "The most successful female authors are those who have drawn upon the topics that lay closest at hand, and submitted them to the investigation of the microscope. There is no generalization, or reasoning, of a practical kind in these books; but they contain an abundance of quiet and vivid surface observation, acute guesses at profounder truths, and heaps of conventional commonplaces which men generally overlook, or are incapable of appreciating."
2.   On another occasion a less sympathetic Duncan took exception to the florid emotionalism of a temperance meeting. Her column in the *Globe*, July 15, 1885 is cited by Tausky (1980, 6).
3.   Coleman and Laurier corresponded and she shared his coach at Queen Victoria's Diamond Jubilee in 1897. In one letter, she wrote: "I know, Sir Wilfrid, that I write on what is called 'the Opposition' paper, but I have always been well treated by the *Mail and Empire* and allowed to pay tribute to you" (Kathleen Blake Coleman Papers).
4.   Schudson describes how the development of the ethos of objectivity in journalism combined with the movement towards literary realism made newspaper work a logical preparation for would-be novelists, a path chosen by many American writers, including Willa Cather, Jack London and Theodore Dreiser. Tausky, in *Sara Jeannette Duncan: Novelist of Empire*, traces how Duncan's journalism foreshadows themes she developed in her novels.
5.   Blackburn seems to have kept her two identities separate. In a letter to Madge Macbeth, she explains that "Grace Blackburn the poetess and Grace Blackburn the newspaper woman are one and the same person" (Madge Macbeth Papers, vol. 1. Grace Blackburn to Macbeth, July 30, 1917).
6.   MacMurchy does not name the encouraging friend but it was almost certainly Eve Brodlique who so frequently praised Kit's work in the Chicago *Times-Journal*.

Significantly, Eve Brodlique wanted to be a poet more than a journalist. See Bayard (517).

7.   See, for instance, the editorial in the Manitoba *Free Press*, Feb. 28, 1890, which described the new "fad" among women in need of pin money to become journalists.

8.   See also Coleman's indignant letter to Amelia Warnock about how the managing editor refused to give her any advance when she returned penniless from her harrowing trip to cover the Spanish American war in Cuba. NAC. Kathleen Blake Coleman papers, vol. 3.

## WORKS CITED

Bayard, Mary Temple. 1896. "Eve Brodlique." *Canadian Magazine* 7.

Bennett, E. A. 1898. *Journalism for Women: A Practical Guide*. London: The Bodley Head; New York: John Lane.

Boivin, A., and K. Landry. 1978. "Françoise et Madeleine: pionnières du journalisme féminin au Québec." *Atlantis* 4, no. 4: 63–74.

Brann, W. C. 1932. "Women in Journalism." *The Iconoclast* n.d. (c.1894–98). Reprinted in *The Matrix* 17, no. 6 (Aug.): 13.

Bridle, Augustus. 1916. "One of the Oddest of Editors." *The Courier* 20, no. 17 (Sept. 23): 21.

Canada. 1929. *Sixth Census of Canada, 1921*. Vol. IV, Table 1: Occupations of the Population . . . by Sex, for Canada, 1891. Ottawa: King's Printer.

Canadian Women's Press Club. 1938. *Newspacket* 4, no. 2 (Mar. 1).

Charlesworth, Hector. 1925. *Candid Chronicles: Leaves from the Notebook of a Canadian Journalist*. Toronto: Macmillan.

Chenier, Nancy Miller. 1977. "Agnes Maule Machar: Her Life, Her Social Concerns and a Preliminary Bibliography of her Writing." M. A. research paper, Carleton University, Ottawa.

Coleman, Katherine Blake [Kit]. 1896. "Jean Blewett." *Our Monthly* 1, no. 1 (May): 35–38.

———. 1897. Letter to Mary Bouchier Sanford, March 22. M. B. Sanford Papers. Public Archives of Ontario, Toronto.

———. [1898]. Letter to Sir Wilfrid Laurier. Katherine Blake Coleman Papers. Public Archives of Canada, Ottawa.

Croly, J. C. Letter to Mary Bouchier Sanford, Feb. 8, 1891. M. B. Sanford Papers. Public Archives of Ontario, Toronto.

Duncan, Sara Jeannette. 1886. Woman's World. Toronto *Globe*, Oct. 21.

Durand, Laura. Letter to Mary Bouchier Sanford, n.d. M. B. Sanford Papers. Public Archives of Ontario, Toronto.

———. Letter to John Willison. John Willison Papers. Public Archives of Canada, Ottawa.

Edmonton *Journal*. 1915. Coleman Obituary. May 21. Katherine Blake Coleman Papers. Public Archives of Canada, Ottawa.

Goodwin, Rae. 1964. "The Early Journalism of Sara Jeannette Duncan: with a chapter of Biography." M.A. thesis, University of Toronto.

Gorham, Deborah. 1978. "Pen and Buckskin: Women Journalists in the West Who Knew Wheat and Justice." *Content*, May: 22–23.

Gwyn, Sandra. 1984. *The Private Capital: Ambition and Love in the Age of Macdonald and Laurier*. Toronto: McClelland and Stewart.

Hammond, M. O. "Ninety Years of the *Globe*." M. O. Hammond Papers. Box 2. Public Archives of Ontario, Toronto.

Livesay, Florence Randal. 1904. Diary. Folder 3, Sept. 15. Florence Randal Livesay Papers. Public Archives of Manitoba, Winnipeg.

Low, Frances H. 1904. *Press Work for Women: A Text Book for the Young Woman Journalist*. London: L. Upcott Gill; New York: Charles Scribner's Sons.

MacAree, J. V. 1934. *The Fourth Column*. Toronto: Macmillan.

Mahaffey, R. V. 1960. "The Tradition Makers: Colorful Moments in Canadian Journalism, Pt. 6." *The Canadian Journalist and Press Photographer*, Jan.-Feb.: 10–11.

MacMurchy, Marjory. 1915. *The News*. May 17.

McOuat, Mary Elizabeth. Letters to Mary Bouchier Sanford. M. B. Sanford Papers. Public Archives of Ontario, Toronto.

National Council of Women of Canada. 1975. *Women of Canada: Their Life and Work*. 1900. Rpt. The National Council of Women of Canada, Ottawa.

O'Hagan, Thomas. 1896. "Some Canadian Women Writers." *Catholic World* 54, no. 5 (Sept.).

Roberts, C., and H. Tunnell, eds. 1938. *A Standard Dictionary of Canadian Biography*. 2 vols. Toronto: Trans Canada Press.

Rutherford, Paul. 1982. *A Victorian Authority: The Daily Press in Late Nineteenth-Century Canada*. Toronto: Univ. of Toronto Press.

Schudson, Michael. 1978. *Discovering the News: A Social History of American Newspapers*. New York: Basic Books.

Sheppard, E. E. 1890. "Around Town." *Saturday Night*, Sept. 6.

Stringer, Arthur. 1924. Letter to Lorne Pierce. Feb. 10. Lorne Pierce Collection. Box 001, File 011. Queen's University Archives, Kingston.

Tausky, Thomas E. 1980. *Sara Jeannette Duncan: Novelist of Empire*. Port Credit, Ont.: P. D. Meaney.

———— , ed. 1978. *Sara Jeannette Duncan: Selected Journalism*. Ottawa: Tecumseh Press.

Thomson, E. W. 1911. Letter to Ethelwyn Wetherald. Jan. 27. E. W. Thomson Papers. Queen's University Archives, Kingston.

Trofimenkoff, Susan Mann. 1986. "Feminism, Nationalism and the Clerical Defensive." In *Rethinking Canada: The Promise of Women's History*, edited by Veronica Strong-Boag and Anita Clair Fellman, 123–36. Toronto: Copp Clark Pitman.

Watt, Peggy Balmer. Letter to Katherine (Hale), n.d. Katherine Blake Coleman Papers. Vol. 3. Public Archives of Canada, Ottawa.

Wetherald, Ethelwyn. 1896. Letter to W. W. Campbell. Feb. 10. W. W. Campbell Papers. Box 9, File 003. Queen's University Archives, Kingston.

———— . 1931. "Reminiscences of the Poet." *Lyrics and Sonnets*. Toronto: Nelson.

Willard, F., and M. A. Livermore. 1973. *American Women*. 1897. Detroit: Gale Research.

# Breaking the "Cake of Custom": The Atlantic Crossing as a Rubicon for Female Emigrants to Canada?

D.M.R. BENTLEY

*For Anne Bolgan—humanist, feminist, fighter, friend*

*. . . . I witnessed the interesting spectacle of the disembarkation of a number of British emigrants. The greater part were from Scotland . . . and a seven weeks passage across the Atlantic did not appear to have divested them of a single national peculiarity . . . .*

> JOHN HOWISON, *Sketches of Upper Canada*

*The sight of the Canadian shores had changed [some of our steerage passengers] into persons of great consequence. The poorest and worst-dressed, the least-deserving and the most repulsive in mind and morals exhibited most disgusting habits of self-importance.*

> SUSANNA MOODIE, *Roughing It in the Bush*

Ford Madox Brown, *The Last of England*.

Some time ago, Alfred G. Bailey drew my attention to Arnold Toynbee's remarks on "The Stimulus of Migration Overseas" in *A Study of History*, particularly to Toynbee's richly metaphorical and allusive suggestion that the " 'sea change' " involved in such a migration can shatter the " 'cake of custom' " to produce in "long-imprisoned and suddenly liberated souls" a strong new awareness of the self and of social issues (93). According to Toynbee, the "stimulating effect of crossing the sea" resides in "one . . . simple fact":

*. . . you're riding high and mighty/In a gale that's pushing ninety . . . . And you've got along for comfort/All the world there ever shall be, was, and is. —Jay Macpherson,* The Boatman *(1957).*

> In transmarine migration, the social apparatus of the migrants has to be packed on board ship before they can leave the shores of the old country and then unpacked again at the end of the voyage before they can make themselves at home on new ground. All kinds of apparatus—persons and property, techniques and institutions and ideas—are equally subject to this law. Anything that cannot stand the sea voyage at all has simply to be left behind; and many things—and these not only material objects—which the migrants do manage to take with them can only be shipped after they have been taken to pieces—never, perhaps, to be reassembled in their original form (88).

*After moving: recon-structions. Once again to set new conditions. Choosing details; the apartment with the bay windows, the court-yard, the city by the ocean. For the first time living by the ocean. —Rhea Tregebov,* Remembering History *(1982).*

In Toynbee's view, the ocean voyage itself, the fact of being contained in what A. B. Lubbock likens to "a hermeti-cally sealed box" during a transmarine migration (3), was a major stimulus to the creation of new social configura-tions: "Having co-operated at sea as men do co-operate when they are 'all in the same boat' in the midst of the perils of the deep," Toynbee writes, "[the emigrants] would continue to feel and act in the same way ashore . . ." (97).

These and other remarks of Toynbee's seemed to me to have obvious application to some recent works of popular Australian culture such as the television series "Against the Wind," where the basis for a new social con-tract in the form of a sort of honour among thieves is seen developing in the steerage of a transport vessel bound for Botany Bay. But his remarks rang almost no bells at all in regard to the writings of (or literature about) Canada's early emigrants, some of whom might be expected to have commented on similar or parallel phenomena if they had occurred in vessels crossing the Atlantic from Britain to

North America. Since many of the better-known authors of Canadian emigrant accounts were women, I especially wondered whether an examination of several emigrant accounts by Catharine Parr Traill, Susanna Moodie, Anne Langton, and others might not reveal a common—or at least interestingly diverse—pattern of response to the trans-Atlantic voyage.

The first thing to emerge from this line of enquiry was a recognition that every bit as important as the trans-Atlantic voyage itself as a site of stimulus and potential transformation for female emigrants were the moments of departure from Britain and arrival in Canada (or at the coast of the United States), for at these points of stress and tension in emigration's larger and more open-ended process of displacement and replacement,[1] the emotions evoked by leaving a familiar place and arriving at a strange one were at their most acute and plangent. In the terms of Anthony Wilden's *System and Structure*, the complex moments of an emigrant's departure and arrival resemble boundaries,[2] each being both a site of differentiation (what lies ahead is not the same as what lies behind) and a site of communication (a necessary stage in getting from what lies behind to what lies ahead). A preliminary sense of the complexity of such boundary moments can be gained from the Reverend William Bell's account of the behaviour of his fellow passengers as their boat drew away from the coast of Scotland: "some appeared lively and cheerful—some thoughtful and serious—while a few, by the tears which they shed, showed that they were not leaving their country and their friends without a struggle" (2). This essay examines a variety of significant responses, some by men but most by women, to the three stages of the trans-Atlantic crossing—the departure, the voyage itself, and the arrival—in the hope of revealing at each stage some of the personal, social, and cultural ramifications of the emigrant experience, especially the implications, for female identity and writing, of emigration to Canada in the nineteenth century.

Before proceeding to specific details and individual personalities, the general and obvious point needs to be made that at the archetypal or mythic level a transmarine journey of emigration is incompatible with most of the patterns that are usually attached to such voyages. It is not

*It is a fact that to one person a voyage may mean only a departure and an arrival, an expense incurred, only a happy lapse of coloured time, only an embarking and a disembarking —the distance between two places on a map which may be pink or even blue; but to Ellen the voyage was a shaking and transforming experience . . . .* —Ethel Wilson, Love and Salt Water *(1957).*

a journey of excursion and return, but an intermediate (and mediating) stage in a process of frequently reluctant removal from a cherished home and usually arduous relocation in an unfamiliar place. Unlike Homer's Odysseus or Jason and the Argonauts or most of the adventurous knights of medieval romance (whose quests are circular)—unlike even Tennyson's Ulysses (who voluntarily undertakes his westering journey)—the typical nineteenth-century emigrant to Canada was more or less driven across the ocean to a place of permanent exile and new beginning. Nor does the experience of emigration from Britain to Canada find an entirely satisfactory analogue in the biblical stories of the Exodus and the Expulsion,[3] or in Virgil's epic of the founding of Rome; for, in contrast to more southerly regions of North America, the continent's attic was only sporadically perceived as a refuge from captivity or as a Promised Land, let alone as a New Rome. A possibly useful way of coming to terms with the experience of emigration to Canada in the nineteenth century is to imagine it, for the time being (and further metaphorical possibilities will be advanced in due course), as a combination of the biblical pattern of permanent removal, exodus, or expulsion to a remote land (Goshen, Canaan), and the classical myth of Hercules, the Greek hero who unwillingly undertakes great and unpleasant labours in distant and inhospitable places and, as a result, was held by the Greeks themselves to be "almost the ideal embodiment of the . . . settler."[4]

With the recognition of an affinity between the labours of Hercules and the experience of a Canadian emigrant comes a realization that, on the basis of mere physical strength alone, the Herculean analogue seems to deny heroic stature to women, especially to those women who because of their class were sufficiently exempted from manual labour to warrant being described as the "gentler sex." As will be seen, just such a realization is implicit in the opening sketch of *Roughing It in the Bush*, where Moodie gives narrative force to her argument that Canada offers no prospects for gentlefolk like herself and her husband. Yet a form of Herculean heroism was achieved by several female emigrants to Canada, including, it could be argued, Moodie herself—women who, by performing such traditionally masculine labours as ploughing, sowing, and

*Pique had gone away. She must have left during the night . . . . I've got too damn much work in hand to fret over Pique . . . . If I hadn't been a writer, I might have been a first-rate mess at this point.*
—Margaret Laurence, The Diviners *(1974)*.

harvesting, blurred the conventional distinctions between the sexes. In the process, they forged in their lives and in their writings a new role model for Canadian women in the pioneering and post-pioneering periods: the powerful figure at the centre of what should be recognized as a *topos* in Canadian women's writing, the *topos* of the woman who, either through widowhood or through a temporary absence of the male members of her family, finds herself control-ling all aspects, both domestic and agricultural, of an iso-lated homestead.[5] Drawn as they were by necessity, and occasionally by temperament, to create and embody the gender-blurring *topos* of the female Crusoe (as it might be called in honour of one of its obvious literary anteced-ents),[6] most pioneering women felt a contrary need to remain feminine in the conventional terms of their day—to paint and write and sew as well as to sow and plant and reap.[7] The resulting tension is described explicitly by Anne Langton in her journal:

> perhaps you would think my feminine manners in danger if you were to see me steering a boat for my gentlemen rowers, or maybe handling the ropes a little in sailing, but don't be alarmed; though such things do occur occasionally, they are rather infrequent, and my woman's avocations will always, I think, more than counterbalance them. I have caught myself wish-ing an old long-forgotten wish that I had been born of the rougher sex (Langton 1950, 72–73).[8]

To indicate that a tension between the "masculine" and the "feminine," the necessary and the conventional, can be found in many of the writings of pioneering Canadian women is already to anticipate a later stage of the discus-sion and, to an extent, to move beyond the limits of the present essay. For the time being, it is sufficient to recog-nize that the *topos* of the female Crusoe constitutes one pos-sible goal of the trans-Atlantic journey for the nineteenth-century female emigrant to Canada, and with this possibility in mind, to begin at the beginning, with the departure of the emigrants from Britain.

I

*The Departure*

*Dearest Mother, and
all/On board all right
and children and lug-
gage. A large ship,
crowded with people.
We have got a berth
to ourselves. Found a
gentleman who helped
us with everything,
so kind. So is every-
body . . . . Love to all
and farewells. Children
are happy.—Anna
Leveridge, Your
Loving Anna
(1972).*

The earliest account of the emigrant experience by a
woman writer appears in the opening pages of Frances
Brooke's *The History of Emily Montague*, where Edward
Rivers is given a double focus of vision, a Janus-like quality of looking both forward to the future and back to the
past, which, as already intimated by the quotation from
William Bell, finds echoes in much nineteenth-century
writing about the Atlantic crossing. As his "vessel is
unmoor'd" at Cowes on the Isle of Wight en route to
Quebec, Rivers writes to John Temple in Paris that he is
going to Canada "with all the eager hopes of a warm imagination; yet friendship casts a lingering look behind" (4).
This "lingering look," either directly or in the mind's eye,
at "the land of . . . nativity, friends, and former home"
is a nearly ubiquitous feature of the moment of departure
in emigrant writing (Pickering, 2).[9] It is most intense,
prolonged, and emphatic in the case of emigrants who were
least happy about leaving Britain and most intense in
the case of women who, in following their husbands to the
New World, had to leave behind family, friends, and
what Moodie calls "congenial minds" (138). Indeed, for
Moodie, the experience of leaving England was enduringly
numbing and dehumanizing: "like Lot's wife," she says,
"I still turned and looked back, and clung with all my
strength to the land I was leaving" (138).[10] For Langton,
the distress of "embarking on [her] awful voyage" to North
America was compounded by the middle-class necessity
of keeping up the appearance of being unmoved:

*. . . they were leaving
behind them all the
familiar safe things that
had for so long com-
posed their lives . . .
happiness of familiar
loves, dear places, and
ordered ways.—Ethel
Wilson,* The Inno-
cent Traveller
*(1949).*

> I wish . . . to banish what is past from my thoughts,
> and, if I could, the feelings of my last sight and touch
> of my first-born, but the stunning sensation can never
> be forgotten, and my feeling when the ship cleared
> the pier-head must ever remain as long as memory
> lasts. It was a call on all my energy and resolution to
> support an appearance of composure. What a relief
> would tears have been! (12).

The obvious parallel between Langton's departure and a
bereavement suggests that, by refusing to give way to her
sorrow at the time of leaving, she merely ensured the

repression and indefinite extension of her sadness, perhaps to the detriment of her ability to embrace life fully in the New World. It may even be that the melancholia evident at various points in Langton's later letters is traceable in part to the repression of her emotions on leaving England.[11]

In marked and understandable contrast to unwilling and unhappy emigrants such as Moodie and Langton, eager and forward-looking emigrants like Traill apparently indulged only briefly, if at all, in a "lingering look behind." Allowing merely that she was "much pleased with the scenery of the Clyde" as the *Laurel* sailed downriver from Greenock, Traill describes her last sight of the British Isles in her characteristically (and, as *The Backwoods of Canada* proceeds, somewhat cloyingly) cheerful terms: "The morning light found our vessel dashing gallantly along, with a favourable breeze, through the North Channel; that day we saw the last of the Hebrides, and before night lost sight of the north coast of Ireland. A wide expanse of water and sky is now our only prospect . . . ." At the boundary between her old life and her new prospects, an optimistically hinterland-oriented Traill barely notices the curtain of night falling on the British Isles. Instead, she places the emphasis of her description on aspects of the scene that reflect her sense of going to a land of new, positive, and expansive possibilities: the "morning light," a "favourable breeze," and the "wide expanse of water and sky."

*It is possible that the effect of the seamen's singing was so powerful because the passengers did not understand the words. What were the words? There was no meaning for the passengers, and no meaning was needed, only the passion and vigour and the sound of the singing in unison in that cave of the sea. —Ethel Wilson,* Love and Salt Water *(1957).*

Even more eager and cheery than Traill at the moment of departure is the irrepressible Mary (Gapper) O'Brien, who takes a few moments away from admiring the handsome and capable crew of her emigrant vessel, a "British trader" (3) called the *Warrior*, to notice the coast of Britain passing rapidly by and to observe: "I must bid farewell to Charlinch [her home] without one more look. The water is dancing gaily under the breeze and gives a gently cradling motion" (3). Notable here in the word "cradling" and later in Gapper's child-like and child-centred account of the Atlantic crossing (3), and indeed in Langton's determination to greet the New World like a "dutiful child . . . greet[ing] . . . mother earth after [a] long separation" (1904, 26), is the implication that for some emigrant women a new start involved, if not a regression to infancy or childhood, then a return to the material realm, with a consequent feeling of security, familiarity, and burgeoning potential. Equally evident in Gapper's account of her departure is a repression of the "lingering look behind," which in her case turns out to be merely a postponement of the experience until her exit from the "cradling" nursery of the ship: "After coming to anchor and making arrangements with the customs house," she says of her arrival in New York, "we left the 'Warrior' with feelings of regret . . . . I now felt for the first time that I was far away from home and all that makes home dear" (9). For Gapper, travelling in the relative luxury and privilege of a cabin, the emigrant vessel was more than a maternal realm in the personal sense. It was an extension of the mother country, a floating microcosm of British society, with all its familiar comforts, hierarchies, customs, and associations. Since even New York seems to Gapper to be a continuation in miniature of what, in her child-like way, she knows and loves—a town "very like [a] children's plaything city" in which "everything and everybody" looks "perfectly English" (9–11)—she could hardly have felt other than a minimal sense of displacement at either the beginning or the end of her trans-Atlantic journey.

*So it was. Far ahead, in the midst of an ocean of darkness, two small jets of light stood out like candle flames braving the night. Why it should be so, I cannot say, but those wavering jets of yellow light marked a division of time for the little girl at her father's feet. From that moment her little thoughts and starry impressions were distinctly individual, and she herself no longer just the little girl who existed as a small, obedient extension of her mother. —Laura Goodman Salverson,* Confessions of an Immigrant's Daughter *(1939).*

In a sense, Gapper left England and arrived in North America as a child-woman, with all the openness and adaptability that, viewed positively, such a state brings with it. As a consequence, she was able to grow with relative ease into her real adulthood as a Canadian pioneer woman, accepting almost naively the hardships and compensations that settler life in Canada afforded women— herculean labour, of course, but also the increased dignity of working women,[12] and as regards property, the greater rights of married women.[13] No doubt Gapper possessed to an extraordinary degree "the qualities required of the ideal pioneer wife" (285); perhaps one of these qualities was the ability to enter again a child-like state and a maternal realm as she embarked on a new life in the New World whose "woods and plains" were, in the words of Isabella Valancy Crawford, another nineteenth-century female emigrant to Canada, "bounteous mothers . . . mellowing the earth,/That she may yield her increase willingly" (37–38).

One of the most poignant and complex renditions of the emigrant's "lingering look behind" is Ford Madox Brown's *The Last of England*, a painting of "voyaging consciousness" (Auerbach, 45) which was executed at the time of the departure for Australia of the pre-Raphaelite sculptor Thomas Woolner. Despite the antipodean destination of its subjects, *The Last of England* warrants consideration here for what it can tell us about the burdens and possibilities bestowed upon women by the emigrant experience. Although ostensibly about Brown's friend in art, the painting, as Nina Auerbach has shown, actually subordinates Woolner to his wife, giving her almost iconic importance at the centre of a series of concentric circles consisting of her hair, her bonnet, her umbrella, and the circular shape of the canvas as a whole. As she looks wanly back towards England, placing temporarily behind her what lies in the future (and observe how the obvious coarseness of the men at the rear of the picture space indicates the chimerical nature of the "El Dorado" inscribed on the ship's lifeboat),[14] Woolner's wife is burdened to a remarkable extent with the expectations of her male painter and patriarchal culture. Clasping the hands of both her husband and her nearly hidden and very young child (another aspect of her future), she "alone unites" (Auerbach, 45) her family as it travels out past those resonant symbols of England, the white cliffs of Dover, into and towards a largely unknown world. Placed with her child in her arms near the centre of a circular canvas, Brown's emigrant woman clearly recalls Raphael's *Madonna della Sidia* and thus takes with her to the New World, as did Moodie, Traill, and others, enormous expectations concerning the moral and spiritual function of the wife and mother in a pioneer society.

Here in embryo, it might be said, is the saintly woman who occupies the familial and ethical centre of so much male writing about European women in early Canada, from Thomas Cary's *Abram's Plains*[15] to the fiction of Ralph Connor.[16] A telling indication of the sort of religious and social apparatus (to use Toynbee's word) that was placed or taken on board vessels bound for the New World, *The Last of England* embodies a male fantasy about the emigrant wife and mother which became a component of emigrant women's view of themselves—a model of spiritual strength which could be entrapping certainly, but also empowering. As different as conventionally conceived femininity and masculinity, the Madonna and Hercules archetypes can be understood as the extremes that lay to the right and left of women when they emigrated to Canada in the nineteenth century. However, they can also be understood as representative of the choices that confronted emigrant women—options that could be chosen fairly straightforwardly or combined in complex, exciting, and genuinely liberating ways. As will now be seen, the voyage itself to Canada was for many emigrants a site of fascinating choices in the realms of individual identity and social organization.

## II
### *The Voyage*

The literature of the Atlantic crossing contains many indications that, especially for the comparatively well-off travelling as families in cabins, the sea passage tended both to reinforce the unity of the family and to affirm the transportability of a traditional social apparatus, thus ensuring, as in the case of Mary Gapper, a high degree of continuity between the Old and New Worlds, a relatively minor crumbling of "the cake of custom." For those less (or perhaps more) fortunate, however, the circumstances of travel on emigrant ships in which men and women, often regardless of family ties, were separated on sexual lines could and did lead during the lengthy voyage to the crumbling of the "cake of custom" (sometimes in ways startling to modest observers)[17] and to the formation of units of loyalty other than the family. Writing of the "hard-favored . . . , poorly and insufficiently clad" wives of soldiers going to join their regiments in Canada, George Warburton observes in *Hochelaga*: "I saw during the voyage many traits in [these poor women] of good and tender feeling: the anxious care of their little ones . . . ; their kindness to each other, sharing their scanty covering and scantier meals" (I, 2). Whether this feeling of generosity and co-operation, perhaps even of sisterhood, endured beyond the women's experience of being " 'all in the same boat' " cannot be known, but the suspicion is that, particularly in the case of soldiers' wives, there would be a continuity of behaviour between ship and shore, with perhaps some permanent reapportioning of value from "kin" to "comradeship."[18] In the "ladies cabins" of more privileged passengers, a sense of sorority was likely to be established less through the sharing of creature comforts than through the exchanges of conversation and sympathy (not least during bouts of seasickness, a far from negligible aspect of trans-Atlantic voyages), with the resultant establishment of what today would be called a "network" of female friends in the New World. Much emphasis has traditionally been placed by critics of North American culture on the bonds between and among men that develop on rafts on the Mississippi and elsewhere, but in Warburton's slightly surprised account of female mutuality en route to Canada, and—to give just one more example—Langton's engaging account of the "transatlantic ladies" in her cabin on the *Independence* (1904, 177)—there is more than a suggestion of a parallel phenomenon among women on at least some of the vessels that brought emigrants to Canada.

Since most of the readable journals and letters written on nineteenth-century emigrant vessels are post-Romantic in nature, the light that they cast tends to be most sharply and most illuminatingly directed towards the individual's own experience of the trans-Atlantic voyage. Thus—to turn for a moment to a less well-known writer—Mrs. William Radcliff is especially expansive and engaging when she leaves off counselling future emigrants about the inadvisability of bringing their own servants and provisions on board ship and turns instead to chronicle her own experiences en route to the New World, including her not insignificant participation in the traditionally masculine activity of ocean fishing: "*We fished* (observe how I identify myself with the sport) . . ." (Talman, 35), she says in a parenthetical remark that shows none of Langton's misgivings about the gender-blurring aspects of the emigrant experience. Quite as open-minded and cheerful as Traill, Radcliff proclaims the "sudden alterations of a sea voyage" between frightening storms and relaxing calm proof of her belief in the benefits of a "mind easily amused" (37) and capable of ensuring the eclipse of present discomforts by inevitable turns for the better. As she ascends the St. Lawrence, Radcliff shows herself fully to be the spiritual heiress of Kent and Gonzalo by proclaiming the Canadian landscape remarkable for its "exquisite beauty and luxuriance" and for pastures whose verdure could "not be rivalled, even by the Emerald Isle of [her] nativity" (40). So positive is Radcliff about Canada that, in an intriguing

*Was it madness after all, Mama?/—bringing your Russian shtetl to America,/smuggled into Canada safely in your head/deposited in Montreal/replanted in our flat/in the kitchen . . . .*
*—Gertrude Katz,*
Duet *(1982).*

reversal of the nostalgic emigrant's habit of bringing with them "old country" (Guillet, 40) plants and "song-birds," she wishes to see "a miniature silver fir tree" which she is given on her arrival "transplanted into our shrubbery" (28) back in Ireland.

Probably the most engaging and complex account by an emigrant woman of the crossing to Canada is contained in "The Ocean Voyage" and "Majestic and Mighty River" sections of *The Backwoods of Canada* where, among other things, Traill uses the wild and domesticated bird life that she encounters to define herself in relation both to the external world and to the men travelling with her. In the first instance, she identifies herself by an unstated analogy with the "sea-fowl" which she sees on the Atlantic —"wanderers of the ocean" who are guided by providence from the " 'zone to zone' " (28) of William Cullen Bryant's poem. In the second, she takes a traditional emblem of the circumscribed female, a caged song bird (in this instance, a male goldfinch called Harry which belongs to the ship's captain) and applies it to men generally, featherless bipeds who, in her view, tolerate being "confined to a small space" much less readily than women, who always have "their needle as a resource against the overwhelming weariness of an idle life" (29). Neither denying nor accepting the inevitability of female circumscription (but leaning towards the latter because ultimately she is confined to the ship as the "water-fowl" are not), Traill is here highlighting traditionally feminine accomplishments which, if positively understood and undertaken, will stand women in good stead as pioneers to Canada.[19] Of course, Traill knew firsthand that the "hardships and difficulties of the settler's life . . . were felt peculiarly by the female part of the family" (25), and *The Backwoods of Canada* as a whole is an attempt to mitigate the "hardships and difficulties" of the female emigrants who constituted a major part of her intended audience by fostering "female ingenuity . . . expediency . . . [and] high-spirited cheerfulness" (25). No propagandist on behalf of emigration, Traill nevertheless had much to gain by encouraging women to become successful pioneers, to participate in an expanding and sustaining community of settlers' wives and daughters who were fully equal, if not to their husbands and fathers, then certainly to the pioneering life and the Canadian environ-

*Next day the ship began its insidious assuagement. Frank and Ellen walked round and round the deck . . . , and the wind whipped them and rain stung their faces and the great grey waves came slowly toward the ship from as far west as one could see . . . .*
*—Ethel Wilson,* Love and Salt Water *(1957).*

*Saint Catharine! Where are you now that we need you? C.P.T.: I am waiting. —Margaret Laurence, The Diviners (1974).*

ment. By presenting the "facts [of emigration to Canada] in their real and true light, that the female part of the emigrant's family may be able to look them firmly in the face" (25), Traill was thus attempting to give future female settlers what is abundantly evident even in the departure and voyage sections of her book: a forward-looking vision that is realistic and optimistic, that places the "facts" within the context of the ability of women to cope with them, to triumph in adversity, and to participate in the creation of a viable community.

Less obviously female in their orientation than Traill's comments on sewing in the opening section of *The Backwoods of Canada* are the remarks on genre that occur at the beginning of her two chapters on the voyage to Canada. Addressing her "dear[est] mother" in both places, Traill justifies her decision to write as "inclination prompts [her]," but neither in the form of "short letters" nor in the form of a daily diary or "log," a species of composition that she associates with the ship's mate and dismisses as not sufficiently "amusing" (27, 31). By setting up as a foil for her own generic choice "the mate's log" (which provided the format for the writings of most of the early explorers and fur-traders), Traill throws into relief the gender-dimension of the long letter home to mother, a type of writing that affirms a female connectiveness of the blood and heart across enormous geographical barriers,[20] and, for both daughter and mother, mitigates the feeling of separation—the post-partum depression (?)—that follows the removal of the child from home and family. Moreover, Traill's reference in "The Ocean Voyage" to the "old novels and musty romances" in the "ship's library" (29) points towards the fictive components and romance elements in *The Backwoods of Canada*, where the long letters are seldom mere summaries of activities or day-to-day accounts but, rather, carefully elaborated and patterned accounts of occurrences in the life of a new and definitely not musty hero: the pioneer woman (or female Crusoe) whose genesis in the work of Traill and whose presence in the fiction of Sara Jeannette Duncan, Margaret Laurence, and others has recently been placed on view by Elizabeth Thompson.[21]

For many emigrants, the Atlantic crossing provided time to think and talk and dream about their future life in Canada—to expand upon Rivers' "eager hopes of a warm imagination." Traill gives an indication of this when she writes of pacing the deck with her husband, "talk[ing] over plans for the future, which in all probability will never be realized" (29).[22] One emigrant guide even suggests that such planning could take a more practical form through such activities as the construction of "a mimic log house" on the way to Canada (Guillet, 78). But as this suggestion indicates and as most accounts of the trans-Atlantic voyage confirm, the most common feature of the crossing (with the possible exception of seasickness and other illnesses) was boredom. As day followed day with crushing monotony, "schooling" the religious-minded "to patience" (Guillet, 104), most emigrants wiled away their time with occupations like gambling, sewing, and writing. The ultimate effect of the boredom and monotony of the voyage, however, was to make the emigrants ecstatically happy when at last land was sighted (or, frequently, smelled).[23] "Baltimore, with its white buildings . . . had a most exhilarating effect on one whose vision had been confined to the monotonous rolling of the unstable waters for sixty five days . . ." wrote one male emigrant (Pickering, 8), and Radcliff agreed that the sight of land was indeed "very agreeable and soothing to the eye that had so long rested on a waste of water" (Talman, 43). Insofar as they heightened the emigrants' feeling of exhilaration and pleasure at the first sight of the New World, the monotony, boredom, and other unpleasantnesses of the voyage obviously contributed significantly to the "change in attitude" from despair to hope in "the hearts of all but the most miserable" (138), which Edwin G. Guillet saw as a major feature of the last days of the Atlantic crossing.

Whatever its direct or indirect causes, a "change of attitude" is certainly noted or evident in most writing by emigrants about the final stages of the voyage to North America. In some cases, the impending arrival in the New World is treated as both a fresh beginning in *terra incognita* and as a return to *terra firma*. Anne Langton wrote:

> Land . . . was now visibly not far, and I determined to be up with the dawn, like a dutiful child, to greet my mother earth after a long separation . . . . The bay [of New York] I had, unluckily, been told several times was equal to the Bay of Naples, and my first

*Like migrating birds delayed, the passengers twittered and became fidgety. The voyage had lasted too long—Ethel Wilson,* Love and Salt Water *(1957).*

*On the last day of open ocean the seeming and delusive eternity of the voyage vanished. "Tomorrow we enter the St. Lawrence River!" . . . Even the Grandmother, who lived neither in the present nor the past nor the future, not in Time at all but in a constant moment of Eternity, felt the approaching change. —Ethel Wilson,* The Innocent Traveller *(1949).*

impressions were therefore those of disappointment. But it is very beautiful in its own way, and so totally different from the one it was compared with that the comparison was absurd (1904, 26–27).

In other instances, the actual arrival in the New World after a long and stressful voyage seems to have produced what Toynbee calls a "dynamic effect" on the emigrant (II, 88), liberating or crystallizing attitudes that were not previously evident. This is certainly apparent from Moodie's descriptions of the behaviour of Irish and Scottish emigrants on their arrival in Canada (more of which later). Nor can the effect of being again on land after an unpleasant Atlantic crossing be accorded less than catalytic importance in the behaviour of Mary Murray in Lucy Maud Montgomery's partly autobiographical *Emily of New Moon*. Emily's cousin Jimmy explains how her ancestors came to be on Prince Edward Island:

*The bloody captain . . . landed all of them at the wrong place, now, the name escapes me at the moment . . . . So Piper Gunn . . . he says to his woman Morag,* Here we are and by the holy Jesus here we will remain. *And then didn't his woman strap onto her back the few blankets and suchlike they had, and her thick with their unborn first-born, and follow.* —Margaret Laurence, The Diviners *(1974).*

*By naming them [the Glass House Mountains] he made them./ They were there/before he came/but they were not the same./It was his gaze/that glazed each one.* —P. K. Page, The Glass Air *(1985).*

"They were bound for Quebec—hadn't any notion of coming to P.E.I. They had a long rough voyage and water got scarce, so the captain of the *New Moon* put in here to get some. Mary Murray had nearly died of seasickness coming out—never seemed to get her sealegs—so the captain, being sorry for her, told her she could go ashore with the men and feel solid ground under her for an hour or so. Very gladly she went and when she got to shore she said, 'Here I stay.' And stay she did; nothing could budge her; old Hugh—he was young Hugh then, of course—coaxed and stormed and raged and argued—and even cried, I've been told —but Mary wouldn't be moved. In the end he gave in and had his belongings landed and stayed, too. So that is how the Murrays came to P.E. Island."

"I'm glad it happened like that," said Emily (73).

There is an element of female fantasy in this description of a stubborn and powerful matriarch establishing the location, and effectively the name, of her family's new home in the New World. But given the autobiographical component of *Emily of New Moon*, there may well be an element of truth to Mary Murray's story that justifies a second look at its depiction of a sexual role reversal on the arrival of the *New Moon* in Canada. Once Mary Murray has been permitted by the captain to go ashore with the men (a rare privilege), she begins to behave like a man, becoming the master, not merely of her own destiny, but also of her family's future. For his (castrated?) part, Hugh mimics the weather that is partly responsible for the "sea change" in his wife (he "stormed and raged") and "even," when arguing and coaxing have failed to shake her resolve, resorts to a traditional weapon in the feminine arsenal and cries. While Emily is glad to hear that her ancestors' putting down roots on P.E.I. occurred in the manner described by her cousin Jimmy, "old Hugh," the deposed patriarch, never quite forgives his wife's behaviour. The " 'Here I stay' " that he has engraved on her tombstone is thus a double text: a testament both to a female will discovered or exercised after a tempestuous Atlantic crossing and to the refusal of patriarchy either to forgive or to forget such a transgression.

## III

*The Arrival*

The Aristotelian elegance of assigning a distinct beginning, middle, and end to the Atlantic crossing has already been transgressed in the present discussion. It is destined to be transgressed even more by the fact, long ago recognized by Northrop Frye, that for emigrants entering British North America at almost any place other than the Maritimes there was no distinct moment of arrival but, rather, the sensation of gradually entering "an alien continent" (824). An attempt must nevertheless now be made to concentrate exclusively on the arrival of emigrants in Canada, to come to terms with a blurry border that comprises the prime site of communication between the emigrant's old "apparatus" (insofar as it has remained intact on the ship and in the mind) and the realities of the New World. In order better to show in some detail the complexities contingent upon arrival in Canada for female emigrants, the discussion will focus in this final stage on two very well-known accounts of the journey up the St. Lawrence to Quebec and beyond: that of Traill in the second and third letters in *The Backwoods of Canada* and that of Moodie in the opening sketch of *Roughing It in the Bush.*

In the manner characteristic of "all but the most

*. . . for now she is content to wander on the beach foraging for food and naming everything she sees in the new words which come so freely to her tongue.— Anne Szumigalski,* Instar *(1985).*

miserable'' of emigrants, Traill greeted the appearance of the Newfoundland coast after a long and monotonous voyage with ''rapture'' and a distinct feeling of renovation: ''Never did anything seem so refreshing and delicious to me,'' she writes, ''as the land breeze that came to us bearing health and gladness on its wings. I had become very weak but soon revived as I felt the air from the land reaching us and some winged insects came to us—a welcome sight'' (32). As an amateur scientist with a keen and sustaining interest in insects, plants, and birds, Traill had noticed the ''restless activity'' of the captain's caged bird prior to the sighting of land, and as the *Laurel* made its tedious way up the Gulf of St. Lawrence, she spent hours poring over the ship's ''great chart,'' which was ''constantly being rolled and unrolled by [her] husband to gratify [her] desire of learning the names of the distant shores and islands which [they] pass[ed]'' (32). An analogy with Adam on the naming day recommends itself as a gloss on this passage (Frye, 824), but as an ensuing event makes clear, Traill intended a closer parallel between her own experience of making landfall and a biblical story which seems also (though more pessimistically) to have recommended itself to her sister Susanna as an analogy for the transAtlantic crossing:[24] the story of Noah and the Ark. In the entry in her letter for August 7, Traill writes: ''We were visited this morning by a beautiful little bird, not much larger than our gold-crested wren. I hailed it as a bird of good omen—a little messenger sent to bid us welcome to the New World, and I felt almost a childish joy at the sight of our little visitor'' (32–33). Not only does this passage indicate that Traill perceived herself as a latter-day Noah on the brink of a world of fresh possibilities (and the ''little bird'' as evidence of the providential nature of her journey), but it also shows that, on the threshold of the ''New World,'' she conceived herself as being—if not, strictly speaking, reborn—then, like Gapper and Langton, in the process of starting life anew, with all the enthusiasm of a Romantic child.

Whereas Coleridge's Burke found himself, ''as it were, in a Noah's ark, with a very few men and a great many beasts'' (Hughes, 19), Traill found herself on a vessel in which the few men that she mentions seem to her to resemble the captain's caged bird Harry. True to this anal-

*Outward the fresh shores gleam/Clear in new-washed eyes./Fare well./From your dream/ I [the Ark] only shall not rise.—Jay Macpherson,* The Boatman *(1957).*

ogy, the men on the *Laurel* soon begin to evince the "rest-less activity" earlier displayed by the goldfinch: "The captain . . . [grows] quite talkative. [Her] husband [is] more than usually animated, and even [a] thoughtful young Scotchman [who had struck Traill earlier as 'too much wrapped up in his own affairs to be very communicative to others' (28)] became an entertaining person" (33). As if to cement the connection between the feathered and featherless bipeds on the *Laurel*, Traill observes that in sight of land the "crew displayed the most lively zeal in the per-formance of their duty, and the goldfinch sang cheerily from dawn till sunset" (33). Amid all this pleasant garru-lity and animation, the female presence at the centre of Traill's narrative apparently exercised a firm captaincy over potentially distressing feelings: "As for me," says Traill, "hope was busy in my heart, chasing from it all feelings of doubt or regret [the 'lingering look behind'] that might sadden the present or cloud the future" (33). As she moves ever further into the region of new light and new life that she wants Canada to be, Traill keeps her heart and her eyes firmly fixed on the positive aspects of what she sees, finding happy (rather than wistful) memories of the Scottish Highlands in the shapes of "fantastic clouds" in the St. Lawrence estuary and becoming weary only of what she purports to admire the most: the sublimity of the water and mountain scenery of "the majestic and mighty river" (33).

No Mary Murray, willing to transgress sexual and social hierarchies in order to get her own way, Traill allows her "longing desire to set [her] foot on Canadian ground" (36) to be chivalrically denied by the captain and her hus-band. She finds in the "foggy" weather, and in the men's description of the Isle of Bic as "swampy," ample "reason to be thankful" that she has not followed her "own way-ward will" (36) but has contented herself with continuing to admire the land from afar. Thus, while the men in the party are busy making forays onto the islands and shores of the St. Lawrence, indulging in foreplay, as it were, before penetrating what Rupert Brooke would later call the "unseizable virginity" of Canada,[25] Traill allows herself to be born(e) along the St. Lawrence, entering the New World as through a birth canal.

At this stage of the journey, it would appear that

Traill is less and less the "wandering water-fowl" and more
and more the caged bird, the traditional woman who had
shown at least the potential for radical modification and
liberation in mid-Atlantic. If the "cake of custom" could
be crumbled en route to the New World, so apparently
could it be reconstituted as actual arrival—treated by Traill
as a return "once more" and "again" to "*terra firma*" (54)
—became imminent. Or at least partly reconstituted. For
everywhere in the later letters in *The Backwoods of Canada*
and elsewhere, there is evidence that, while she allowed
herself to remain within the confines of the traditional
model of femininity which she brought with her across the
Atlantic (thus avoiding the accusation of compromising too
far what Langton calls her "feminine manners" and
"woman's avocations"), Traill nevertheless played a pioneering role both in her personal life and in her writing
in expanding and dignifying the spheres of activity and
influence normally inhabited by nineteenth-century women
of her background. To Traill, Canada was a nearly Edenic
New World (the first Canadian flowers that she saw while
still on the *Laurel* in the St. Lawrence were "red roses . . .
with . . . few if any thorns" (36)), but it was a nearly
Edenic New World in which women were to exercise their
powers according to the known rules of matrimony. It is
within this traditional context that in *The Backwoods of
Canada* Traill shows herself commanding and receiving the
respect of her husband, the man who brought back from
the Isle of Bic—so that she "might not regret not accompanying him"—a "delightful bouquet" containing those
virtually thornless roses (36). Nor, if the figure of the caged
bird is being read correctly, did Traill fail to command the
chivalric attention of men other than her husband on this
side of the Atlantic. "The steward [on the *Laurel*] furnished
me with a china jar and fresh water, so that I shall have
the pleasure of a bouquet during the rest of the voyage,"
she notes, adding, with perhaps a trace of amusement at
her own self-created situation, that the "sailors had not
forgotten a green bough or two to adorn the ship, and the
bird-cage was soon as bowery as leaves could make it" (37).
In Traill's case, it would appear that—to borrow Langton's
words again—"feminine manners" as traditionally conceived did more than "counterbalance" the tendency of
the female emigrant to assume conventionally masculine
characteristics.

For over a week after her husband's visit to the Isle of Bic, Traill continued to feel what she now describes as a "longing desire . . . *to be allowed* to land and explore" the Canadian terrain (41).[26] And, once again, the pattern of male refusal and chivalric gesture is repeated: "to all my entreaties [to be allowed to go ashore at Grosse Isle], the visiting surgeon . . . returned a decided negative," she explains, but "[a] few hours after his visit . . . an Indian basket, containing strawberries and raspberries, with a large bunch of wild flowers, was sent on board for me with the surgeon's compliments" (41). During her long wait for permission to go ashore, Traill amused herself by sketching the "surrounding scenery or watching the groups of emigrants on shore" (41). She also indulged in what previous quotations from Gapper and Langton already have indicated was a characteristic pastime of emigrants in sight of the New World—fitting, or attempting to fit, an unknown landscape into moulds constituted by memories of similar shapes and patterns in the Old World. Since memory is a major component of this process, older people were perhaps more likely than younger ones to manifest the sorrows and pleasures of attempting to match old and new. "I observed several grandfathers and grandmothers, who . . . had accompanied their offspring . . . to the *terra incognita* of Upper Canada," writes John Howison. "They looked round with disconsolate and inquiring eyes, and if any feature in the appearance of the town chanced to resemble some part of their native village or city, it caused a joyful exclamation, and was eagerly pointed out . . . "(4).

*They [the comfortable farms and broad meadows of Ontario] had a look of home. Here were elms. Here were sheep and cattle. Here was lazy smoke rising from chimneys of white farms. The sheep grazed in an international manner.—Ethel Wilson,* The Innocent Traveller *(1949).*

For younger and more educated emigrants such as Traill, especially those who took pains to disabuse future emigrants of their illusions about Canada (as did both the Strickland sisters for different reasons), the activity of fitting frequently took the aesthetic form of a recognition of the contrast between picturesque expectations and a less attractive reality. At Grosse Isle, Traill's husband is informed by an officer from the fort that, though the scene at the quarantine station has a "picturesque appearance" when viewed from afar, at close quarters the groups of people that he considers "picturesque" will be seen to resemble the subjects of William Hogarth's pictures and George Crabbe's poems (42). To Traill herself, the heights of Point Levis opposite Quebec are "highly picturesque," but they do not quite fit the expectations generated by her previous

*112*

*Her mother's hands have scrubbed a patina onto every surface of the house. Daria shows it to her visitor . . . . A wooden crucifix is hanging above the sink. The visitor believes it a token of the old country. —Rhea Tregebov,* Remembering History *(1982).*

experience of landscapes: "How lovely would such a spot be rendered in England or Scotland! Nature here has done all, and man but little, except sticking up some ugly wooden cottages, as mean as they are tasteless" (45). Similarly, the log houses along the banks of the St. Lawrence between Quebec and Montreal do not fit Traill's preconceptions of rural cottages: "In Britain even the peasant has taste enough to plant a few roses or honeysuckles about his door or his casement, and there is the little bit of garden enclosed and neatly kept; but here no such attempt is made to ornament the cottages" (49–50). From these and other passages, the reader easily deduces that, when Traill herself has the opportunity to build and adorn a house, she will do so in accordance with her picturesque preconceptions, thus attempting to create in Canada at least a domestic environment that fulfils expectations frustrated on arrival. As Traill's example makes clear, accommodation in both its senses of housing and adaptation is a nodal point at which the domestic and aesthetic concerns of many of Canada's female emigrants met as part of an overall attempt to reconcile imported assumptions with new realities, and vice versa. It is hardly surprising, then, that accommodation, both as an entity (cottages, log houses) and as a process (fitting), figures prominently in accounts by women of their early impressions and subsequent activities in the New World.

Traill's eventual disembarkation at Montreal was an occasion of not "unmixed delight and admiration" (52). On the one hand, she was happy to be "on *terra firma* . . . [and] free from the motion of the heaving water, to which [she is] . . . , in truth, glad to bid farewell" (54). On the other hand, she was "greatly disappointed" with Montreal, a town which, in addition to being in the midst of a cholera epidemic, failed dismally to meet the expectations built up by travellers' accounts (especially, perhaps, by Howison's account[27]): "I could compare it," says Traill, "only to the fruits of the Dead Sea, which are said to be fair and tempting to look upon, but yield only ashes and bitterness when tasted by the thirsty traveller" (55). The comparison with the "fruits of the Dead Sea" is more apt than Traill may have envisaged, for in some ways Montreal, despite its location on terra firma, functions for her as the sea (or ocean) did for many emigrants: as a site of mingled discomfort and anticipation, despair and hope, en route to a new life. In Montreal, Traill found houses that corresponded in their architectural structure (though not in their lack of picturesque adornment) to the houses of her childhood dreams (56). In Montreal, she also fell ill with cholera, a potentially fatal disease through which she was courageously nursed by "the females of the house" in which she and her husband were staying (63). The description of these women can be read as a depiction of female heroism and sisterhood encountered both in the New World and on the way to a new life:

> Instead of fleeing affrighted from the chamber of sickness, the two Irish girls almost quarrelled which should be my attendant; while Jane Taylor . . . never left me from the time I grew so alarmingly ill till a change for the better had come over me, but, at the peril of her own life, supported me in her arms, and held me on her bosom when I was struggling with mortal agony, alternately speaking peace to me and striving to soothe the anguish of my poor afflicted partner (63).

Both the Madonna-like strength of Jane Taylor and the relative ineffectualness of Thomas Traill are remarkable in this passage, and both contribute to the sense that Traill is being helped through a dangerous stage of her journey towards a new life by a compassionate female support system which, like a nurse or a midwife, assists in bringing about a recovery or rebirth. (That the sympathy of Traill's doctor increases when he learns that she is the wife of a British officer only serves to highlight the fact that the women who help her apparently value her for her own sake.) Between Montreal and finally reaching the location of her new home across the "tempest-tost sea" of Lake Ontario (77), Traill went through various other experiences which are part of the attenuated process of arrival described in *The Backwoods of Canada*. Enough of this process and what preceded it has probably now been seen, however, to establish that in Traill's case, it involved a crumbling and reconstitution of the "cake of custom," a negotiation of various possibilities for the female emigrant that ended neither in entirely fresh territory nor exactly as it began but in a considerable rethinking and reorganization of accepted ideas about women's strengths, relationships, and roles in a relatively new society.

Like her sister, Moodie arrived in the St. Lawrence estuary in the midst of a cholera epidemic; unlike Traill, however, the author of *Roughing It in the Bush* lacked a cheerful and sustaining optimism about the Canadian emigrant experience and wrote her book, not to advise "the wives and daughters of emigrants of the higher class" on how best to cope with pioneer life (Traill, 21), but to dissuade gentlemen and their families from "sinking their property, and shipwrecking all their hopes, by going to reside in the backwoods of Canada . . ." (Moodie, 237). While many emigrants used the idea of a shipwreck, often with reference to Robinson Crusoe, as a metaphor for the difficult creation of a workable society in a distant realm,[28] Moodie uses the figure to image forth the nearly unmitigated disaster that she conceives emigration to be for people of the "higher class." For the "industrious and ever-to-be-honoured [and patronized] sons of honest poverty" (xviii), however, Moodie predicts a bright and, indeed, heroic future in Canada. The poor are the chosen people of the "great tide of emigration" (xvi) from Britain to North America in the mid-nineteenth century, a fact Moodie is certain of because she understands the workings of Providence:

> The Great Father of the souls and bodies of men knows the arm which wholesome labour from infancy has made strong, the nerves which have become iron by patient endurance . . . and He chooses such, to send forth into the forest to hew out the rough paths for the advance of civilization. These men become wealthy and prosperous, and form the bones and sinews of a great rising country (xvii–xviii).

Such men (and clearly Moodie does not mean men and women) are herculean, not only in their strength and endurance, but also in their identification with the advance of civilization and with the emergence of what Charles G. D. Roberts would later call a "Child of Nations, giant-limbed . . ." (29). Their representative in the opening sketch of *Roughing It in the Bush* is a poor Irishman who resembles Hercules both in his size and in his possession of the equivalent of the large club that identifies the Greek hero: "One fellow, of gigantic proportions . . . leaped upon the rocks, and flourishing aloft his shilelagh, bounded and capered like a wild goat from his native mountains.

'Whurrah! my boys!' he cried. 'Shure we'll all be jintle-men!' " (27).

Excluded by both class and sex from the herculean brand of heroism that she sees as a prerequisite for suc-cessful pioneering in Canada, Moodie depicts herself on arrival at the portals of the New World as facing what can be seen as a female version of the "Choice of Hercules." (The young Hercules was faced at a crossroads with a choice between two paths as represented by two women, one young and beautiful—the path of pleasure—and the other old and stern—the path of heroic virtue, the path of course chosen by Hercules.) The allegorical figures encountered by Moodie on her arrival off Grosse Isle are not women but men—"health officers sent aboard the vessel to check for the presence of disease":

> One of these gentlemen—a little, shrivelled-up French-man—from his solemn aspect and attenuated figure, would have made no bad representative of him who sat upon the pale horse . . . . His companion—a fine-looking, fair-haired Scotchman—though a little con-sequential in his manners, looked like one who in his own person could combat and vanquish all the evils which flesh is heir to. Such was the contrast between these doctors that they would have formed very good emblems, one, of vigorous health, the other, of hope-less decay (19).

*All through the long/ third week of August, the* Prince of Wales/*crept south [towards James Bay] . . . . John Scarth could not get near me with his eyes/ and we slept apart. I had become a man.*— Stephen Scobie, The Ballad of Isabel Gunn *(1987).*

Although death and "hopeless decay" are recurring spec-tres in *Roughing It in the Bush*, Moodie's character and ambi-tion gave her no real option but to follow a path of heroic, masculine virtue for which, on the basis of mere physical strength, she was ill-equipped. As unpalatable as this choice was for Moodie at the time of her arrival in Canada, it resulted in due time in her painful but ultimately trium-phant acquisition and exercising of the strength and self-reliance that permitted her to become a female Crusoe and, in effect, a feminine version of the Herculean hero.

As well as encountering and re-engendering a "Choice of Hercules" on her arrival in Canada, Moodie had to contend in the St. Lawrence with a ship's captain who clearly represents another aspect of Canadian life— its lack of the graces and accents of the hierarchical English society in which the Moodie and Strickland families held a relatively privileged place. Compared, significantly, with a "bear," a North American creature proverbially renowned for its gruffness and roughness, Moodie's captain is a "rude, blunt north-country sailor" who receives the "Frenchman" and "Scotchman" "with very little courtesy, [and] abruptly [bids] them follow him down to his cabin," where he teasingly introduces the two doctors to three "babies" born during the Atlantic crossing: a litter of "fat, chuckle-headed [and male] bull terriers" (19–20). When the "Frenchman" bestows a "savage kick on one of [these] unoffending pups" (20), it is as if someone on the *Laurel* had wrung the neck of the "little bird" that seemed to Traill such a "good omen" when it joined the vessel off Newfoundland. (As Moodie's puppies and Traill's bird make evident, emblematic events and symbolic acts are a common feature of accounts of arrival in the New World; on another vessel, "the sand from the first soundings off the Grand Banks was placed under a baby's feet 'so that she might be the first who stepped on American soil' " (Guillet, 101). Both the reference to the ship's captain as a "bear" and the behaviour of the French doctor towards the bull-terrier puppy speak loudly of Moodie's conviction that Canada is a place hostile to all but men of a fairly brutal disposition.

A further indication that Moodie regards the New World as hostile to civilization, as she conceives it, can be gleaned from her rendition of the speech of the captain and the "Frenchman." In the utterances of the former are "commonly expunged all the connective links" (19)—that is, such words as "and," which can indicate the connection and addition of words in the same class or type, and "the," which can make crucial distinctions of the sort valued by people of Moodie's background, the distinction, for example, between "a house" and "the house." In the utterances of the latter—" 'You tink us dog . . . . Joke! me no understand such joke. Bete' "—violence is done both to articles and to words and phrases such as "I" and "we are" that are indicative of individual and collective identity. The very speech of the men whom Moodie describes on arrival in Canada thus reflects her fearful sense of a social and personal disintegration, a disconcerting shattering of the "cake of custom," during the transition from the hierarchical civilization that she cherishes to the independent or republican culture that she knows to exist in North America. Later in the opening sketch of *Roughing It in the Bush*, this feeling of fear (and consequent alienation) is again expressed in terms of language as Moodie describes emigrants newly arrived on Grosse Isle: "The confusion of Babel was among them. All talkers and no hearers—each shouting and yelling in his or her uncouth dialect, and all accompanying their vociferations with violent and extraordinary gestures, quite incomprehensible to the uninitiated. We were literally stunned by the strife of tongues" (20). Both men and women are included in this comment, and no more than the former do the latter give Moodie grounds for believing that her conception of civilization, and of femininity, can survive the shattering of the "cake of custom." "I shrank, with feelings almost akin to fear," she writes, "from the hard-featured, sunburnt women as they elbowed rudely past me" (25).

While the opening sketches in *Roughing It in the Bush* do contain some positive first impressions of Canada, particularly of the sublime and picturesque sights on the St. Lawrence, the dominant mood of these pieces is that of an outsider being unpleasantly initiated into a reality that is far removed from the "perfect paradise" (25) created either by propagandistic emigrant literature or, as in Traill, by the distance that lends enchantment. With hindsight, Moodie can exhort "British mothers of Canadian sons" to teach their offspring "to love Canada—to look upon her as the first, the happiest, the most independent country in the world!" (24); she can even look back and see Grosse Isle and its "sister group" of islands "[c]radled in the arms of the St. Lawrence, and basking in the bright rays of the morning sun, . . . [as] a second Eden just emerged from the waters of chaos" (30). But these expressions of a child-like belonging to a new maternal realm and a fresh sister-hood serve merely to counterpoint the dominant notes of alienation and disenchantment, isolation and homesick-ness, in Moodie's opening sketches. And nowhere is Moodie's dismay at the crumbling of the "cake of custom" on arrival in Canada more poignantly evident than in her account of the behaviour at Grosse Isle of the normally reliable Scots, both two- and four-legged. On the arrival of the *Anne* off the island, Moodie is left "alone with [her] baby in the otherwise empty vessel. Even Oscar, the captain's Scotch terrier, who had formed a devoted attachment to me during the voyage, forgot his allegiance, became possessed of the land mania, and was away with the rest'' (28). When later she has the opportunity to go ashore at Grosse Isle, she notices that even Oscar's countrymen are not immune to the republican spirit of the New World: ''our passengers, who were chiefly honest Scotch labourers and mechanics from the vicinity of Edinburgh, and who while on board ship conducted themselves with the greatest propriety, and appeared the most quiet, orderly set of people in the world, no sooner set foot upon the island than they became infected by the same spirit of insubordination and misrule, and were just as insolent and noisy as the rest'' (21–22). As this passage makes very clear, those who had most to resent as the ''cake of custom'' crumbled were men and women who, like Moodie, would have preferred to retain their status as icing on the cake rather than become part of a new mixture.

Yet Moodie's response to her loss of social privilege and its contingent identity in Canada was to create for herself in *Roughing It in the Bush* and elsewhere a new sense of self and purpose which was and still is of more consequence than what she would have done had she remained in England. When he arrived at the Pacific coast, where neither he nor his guide could anymore understand the local Indian languages, Alexander Mackenzie famously affirmed his achievement and his identity by inscribing his name ''in large characters'' on the ''face of [a] rock'' (25). Being emigrants rather than explorers and women rather than men, Moodie, Traill, and others were denied such grandiose gestures, but on their farms and in their books they nevertheless inscribed a part of themselves that endures and, even as it does so, reveals something of the complex process of retention and modification, disintegration and reassembly, that must always have been an aspect of great migrations, especially those involving long journeys across oceans. In ''The Stimulus of Migration Overseas,'' Toynbee holds the experience of transmarine colonization directly responsible for the creation of the Homeric epics and the Icelandic sagas, as well as for other major artistic achievements and innovations, observing as he does so the greater creativity of emigrants in relation to those who are left behind. Why no corresponding artistic achievements and innovations took place in the circumstances of emi-

[On our arrival at Montreal] travelling companion cast off travelling companion and the unity of the ship was gone. —Ethel Wilson, The Innocent Traveller (1949).

Crossing the Atlantic they doubtless suffered some dilution; but all that was possible to conserve them under very adverse conditions Mrs. Milburn and Miss Filkin made it their duty to do. Nor were these ideas opposed, contested, or much traversed in Elgin. —Sara Jeannette Duncan, The Imperialist (1904).

gration to Canada in the nineteenth century is not difficult to fathom: by the nineteenth century, removal to British North America meant, not the severing of communication with the mother culture and a consequent need to tell all the stories again, but a movement from the centre to the periphery with a consequence that is characteristic of all minor (which is to say, deterritorialized) literature[29]: the need to explain life on the periphery to those at the centre.

That the writing of women about being women in the colonies is twice marginalized—once by being distant from the centre and once again by being of "the second sex"—gives it, for many contemporary readers, a double interest. Certainly, and with a double sense on both words, it is writing of skill and power—able and energetic writing about the abilities and strengths that were expanded or discovered, often with considerable pain and effort, when women were forced by emigration to Canada to rethink their relations with men, with themselves, and with a New World. No great social and literary consequences are traceable to emigration to Canada in the nineteenth century, but *The Backwoods of Canada, Roughing It in the Bush*, and other works by emigrant women are of enduring interest for a variety of reasons, not least as records of the process of adjustment to a new place and as testaments, by their very existence, to "The Stimulus of Migration Overseas."

## NOTES

In addition to Alfred G. Bailey, I am grateful to several people, particularly J. M. Zezulka, Elizabeth Thompson, A. M. Young, and Susan Bentley, for discussing and sharing with me ideas and books that have been important in the development of this essay.

1.    Beyond the stages of packing and unpacking described by Toynbee in the indented quotation above, are obviously the processes of deciding to emigrate and, on the other side of the Atlantic, reaching and settling (into) the new home. See Edwin C. Guillet (*passim*) for an account of the entire process of emigration that has been very helpful in the present study, not least in calling my attention to pertinent primary and secondary sources.

2.    See Wilden (183–88).

3.    See Toynbee (84).

4.    C. M. Bowra, *Greek Poetry*, cited by Galinsky (20). See my "Large Stature and Larger Soul: Notes on the Herculean Hero and Narrative in Canadian Litera-

ture," *Journal of Canadian Poetry* 2 (1987), 1–21, for further discussion of the importance of the Hercules myth in Canadian writing of the pioneering and post-pioneering periods.

5. See Curtius (70, 79–105) for the classic definition and discussion of *topoi*. The first, frustrated inkling of the *topos* of the female Crusoe in Canadian writing is found in the depiction of Madame Des Roches in Frances Brooke's *The History of Emily Montague*. Although a beneficiary of Edward Rivers' help, Madame Des Roches lives in "absolute solitude" on an "estate" that she apparently runs herself (see Brooke (72–90)). More fully developed examples of the *topos* can be found, for example, in Moodie (212–19) and in O'Brien (164–68).

6. See Thompson (*passim*) for a discussion of the pre-eminent part played by Traill in establishing the characteristics of the pioneer-woman-as-heroine and, by extension, of the *topos* described above.

7. See Moodie (212–16) on her writing for *The Literary Garland* and "painting birds and butterflies upon . . . white, velvety . . . fungi" during her husband's absence.

8. Langton proceeds to lament the fact that in Canada "women are very dependent . . . [and] feel our weakness more than anywhere else."

9. Pickering's account of his departure from England is also indicative of the emotional complexity of the moment: "We left Gravesend with a fair wind, and pretty good spirits, my thoughts ranging through the New World . . . and then returning again [to the Old] . . . which, at times, would cause an involuntary sigh; but the hopes and prospect ever-cheating fancy presented to my mind, dissipated all gloom, and I bade adieu to Old England without much regret."

10. See also Moodie (37) for a description of her homesickness.

11. See Langton (1950, 29; 1904, 65).

12. See O'Brien (17–18).

13. See O'Brien (33–34). Constance Backhouse of the Faculty of Law at the University of Western Ontario has confirmed for me that Canadian women did enjoy some advantages relative to English women in the area of married women's property rights.

14. See also the quotation from Joseph Pickering in note 9.

15. See the reference to Lady Dorchester in Cary (16, lines 484–91).

16. See Thompson (151–81).

17. See Guillet (77n).

18. On a darker note, see Guillet (86) for evidence that women were frequently assaulted sexually during the trans-Atlantic crossing.

19. See also Langton (1904, 18) on the value of needle "work" as a "resource."

20. Dahlie, *Varieties of Exile: The Canadian Experience* (Vancouver: University of British Columbia Press, 1986), p. 13 sees the letters of exiles as constituting a "tangible link . . . with their homeland."

21. See Thompson (*passim*).

22. By way of contrast, see the supplement to Guillet (11) for an emigrant thinking of home and the past during the voyage. Quoted by Guillet (78).

23. See, for example, O'Brien (7).

24. This inference could be drawn from Moodie's characterization of the scene

on her arrival in Lower Canada as a "Babel," a reference to events that follow the story of Noah in Genesis.

25.   Quoted by Frye (826) from Waterston (363). I would like to express a general debt here to Kolodny's two books (1975, 1984), which have helped to alert me to similar and different patterns and possibilities in early writing about Canada.

26.   Emphasis added. Cholera was, of course, a major cause of the refusal to allow Traill to go ashore.

27.   Howison's book is mentioned by Traill (72). See Howison (2–3).

28.   See, for example, Cary (5, lines 64–75).

29.   MacKenzie (349).


# WORKS CITED

Auerbach, Nina. 1982. *Woman and the Demon: The Life of a Victorian Myth.* Cambridge, Mass.: Harvard Univ. Press.

Bell, William. 1824. *Hints to Emigrants: in a Series of Letters from Upper Canada.* Edinburgh: Waugh and Innes.

Brooke, Frances. 1985. *The History of Emily Montague.* Ed. Mary Jane Edwards. Ottawa: Carleton Univ. Press.

Cary, Thomas. 1986. *Abram's Plains: A Poem.* Ed. D.M.R. Bentley. London, Ont.: Canadian Poetry Press.

Crawford, Isabella Valancy. 1987. *Malcolm's Katie: A Love Story.* Ed. D.M.R. Bentley. London, Ont.: Canadian Poetry Press.

Curtius, Ernst Robert. 1953. *European Literature and the Latin Middle Ages.* Trans. William R. Trask. Bollingen Series 36. Princeton: Princeton Univ. Press.

Dahlie, Hallvard. 1986. *Varieties of Exile: The Canadian Experience.* Vancouver: Univ. of British Columbia Press.

Frye, Northrop. 1973. Conclusion. In *Literary History of Canada.* 1965. Ed. Carl F. Klinck. Toronto: Univ. of Toronto Press.

Galinsky, G. Karl. 1972. *The Herakles Theme: The Adaptations of the Hero in Literature from Homer to the Twentieth Century.* Oxford: Basil Blackwell.

Guillet, Edwin C. 1967. *The Great Migration: The Atlantic Crossing by Sailing-Ship Since 1770.* 1963. Repr. Toronto: Univ. of Toronto Press.

Howison, Joan. 1965. *Sketches of Upper Canada: Domestic, Local, and Characteristic.* 1821. S. R. Publishers.

Hughes, M. D. 1921. *Edmund Burke: Selections, with Essays by Hazlitt, Arnold and Others.* Oxford: Clarendon.

Kolodny, Annette. 1984. *The Land Before Her: Fantasy and Experience of the American Frontiers, 1630–1860.* Chapel Hill, N.C. and London: Univ. of North Carolina Press.

————. 1975. *The Lay of the Land: Metaphors as Experience and History in American Life and Letters.* Chapel Hill, N.C.: Univ. of North Carolina Press.

Langton, Anne. 1950. *A Gentlewoman in Upper Canada: The Journals of Anne Langton.* Ed. H. H. Langton. Toronto: Clarke, Irwin.

————. 1904. *Langton Records: Journals and Letters from Canada 1837–1846*. Edinburgh: R. and R. Clark.

Lubbock, A. B. 1921. *The Colonial Clippers*. Glasgow: J. Brown and Son.

MacKenzie, Alexander. 1971. *Voyages From Montreal on the River St. Lawrence through the Continent of North America to the Frozen and Pacific Oceans in the Years 1789 and 1793*. 1801. Edmonton: Hurtig.

Montgomery, Lucy Maud. 1986. *Emily of New Moon*. 1925. Toronto: Seal Books.

Moodie, Susanna. 1962. *Roughing It in the Bush*. New Canadian Library, 31. Toronto: McClelland and Stewart.

O'Brien, Mary (Gapper). 1968. *The Journals of Mary O'Brien*. Ed. Audrey Saunders Miller. Toronto: Macmillan.

Pickering, Joseph. 1831. *Inquiries of an Emigrant*. New ed. London: Effingham Wilson.

Roberts, Charles G. D. 1974. "Canada." *Selected Poetry and Critical Prose*. Ed. W. J. Keith. Literature of Canada: Poetry and Prose in Reprint. Toronto: Univ. of Toronto Press.

Talman, James John, ed. 1953. *Authentic Letters from Upper Canada*. Toronto: Macmillan.

Thompson, Elizabeth Helen. 1987. "The Pioneer Woman: A Canadian Character Type." Diss. University of Western Ontario, London.

Toynbee, Arnold. 1955. *A Study of History*. 1939. London: Oxford Univ. Press.

Traill, Catharine Parr. 1929. *The Backwoods of Canada*. Introduction. Edward S. Caswell. Toronto: McClelland and Stewart.

Warburton, George. 1846. *Hochelaga; or, England in the New World*. Ed. Eliot Warburton. 2 vols. London: Henry Colburn.

Waterston, Elizabeth. 1973. "Travel Books 1880–1920." In *Literary History of Canada*. 1965. Ed. Carl F. Klinck. Toronto: Univ. of Toronto Press.

Wilden, Anthony. 1980. *System and Structure: Essays in Communication and Exchange*. 2nd ed. New York: Tavistock.

# Women and the Garrison Mentality: Pioneer Women Autobiographers and their Relation to the Land

HELEN M. BUSS

The idea that the garrison mentality is a significant force in the development of the Canadian imagination was first suggested by Northrop Frye in his conclusion to *Literary History of Canada*:

> Small and isolated communities surrounded with a physical or psychological "frontier" separated from one another and from their American and British cultural sources: communities that provide all that their members have in the way of distinctively human values, and that are compelled to feel a great respect for the law and order that holds them together, yet confronted with a huge, unthinking, menacing, and formidable physical setting—such communities are bound to develop what we may provisionally call a garrison mentality (830).

Since its publication in 1965, this passage has acquired the power of a biblical authority, informing the work of critics of Canadian literature in the last twenty years. These twenty years have been an important period of growth and consolidation in the history of Canadian literary criticism. In this essay, the nature of that consolidation will be briefly examined in order to show how it excludes female voices that are important to the understanding of Canadian literature.

In his *Butterfly on Rock*, published in 1970, D. G. Jones sets out consciously to extend "Frye's metaphor" (6).[1] Choosing to see Canadian literature in the "perspective, the pattern of the Old Testament" (15), Jones finds that Canadians "must live by the law and not by love" (57) in a culture "garrisoned against nature" (87–88). Under such a dictum, the "major" or relevant writers may well be seen as those who work at removing the garrison, at letting nature in. However, to do this writers must first affirm the reality of the garrison recoil from nature; anything else is labelled as an oversimplification of the relationship of human beings to the environment. In the works of prairie writers, for instance, Laurence Ricou expects to find the "single human figure amidst the vast flatness of landscape" (14). In *Vertical Man/Horizontal World*, Ricou dismisses Robert Stead's work as "shallow," because his reaction to the land does not include an initial extreme recoiling from the natural world; it does not assume a prairie that is "dismissive of man," a "hated . . . foreign and vertical thing" (37).[2] For Ricou, more positive attitudes towards the human/natural interrelationship lack "a balance, comprehension and imaginative validity" (37) which he finds in a more suitably garrisoned imagination, such as that of Frederick Philip Grove.

The tracing of the map of the garrison mentality continues in John Moss' 1974 study, *Patterns of Isolation*; with such chapter titles as "Garrison Exile," "Frontier Exile," "Colonial Exile," Moss' exploration of Canadian fiction seems to have been fully informed by Frye's text. Although Moss describes Frye's "epithet" as "facile" (15), he does not argue against its basic correctness. Instead, Moss develops the theory of "Geophysical Imagination" (109), by which Canadian writers' overwhelming consciousness of Canada's "immense northern landscape, its aggressive climate" leads them to a moral vision in which the "geophysical presence [is] inseparable from the isolation of individual experience and that of the community" (127).

While Moss is primarily concerned with tracing a pattern of moral vision, Margot Northey, in *The Haunted Wilderness*, maps an image pattern, characterized by the gothic and grotesque that grows from the "terror and horror" (1976, 6) of confronting the Canadian wilderness. Such a view leads Canadian writers, in Northey's words, to a vision of "the dark side of the soul, the night side of life or the impulses of the id," which allows them to seek "a truth beyond the accepted surface of life." In such writing "sin and death are the dominant themes" (8). Though these critics offer imaginative and painstaking elaborations of Frye's garrison mentality, they do not move us very far from his view of the nature of human reaction in the Canadian landscape.

Perhaps the most complete elaboration of Frye's text is Gaile McGregor's 1985 study, *The Wacousta Syndrome*.[3] McGregor claims that our "recoil [from the land] was so extreme [that] nature became . . . demythicized, invisible," thus creating a landscape that is a "tabula rasa, neutralized to a degree that has been impossible since the primitive first projected the spirits of his ancestors in the trees: usable again" (71–72). In a mere twenty years, Frye's "provisional" naming, expressing the limitation of our reaction to our landscape, has become the documentation of a Canadian virtue: our ability to imaginatively erase the environment and like Adam, to name the universe in our own image. McGregor takes pains to condemn any other than the "tabula rasa" reaction as "Circum Locutions" (27), romantic or realistic lies we tell ourselves when we are afraid to take the imaginative leap to erasing the environment. She is particularly hard on "circum locutors" like Catharine

Parr Traill, who "takes refuge in the cheerful, short-range, domesticated view of the wilderness" (43).

The elaboration of Frye's garrison mentality has also become, with McGregor's study, a big stick critics may wield to beat any writer whose reaction to the Canadian landscape is anything less than traumatic. As well, a kind of second generation of "garrisoned" critical commentary has begun to emerge in which Frye's garrison mentality is assumed and internalized. Critics now propose that various postmodern writers can rescue us from its doom and gloom. Such writers are seen as self-engendered (or at least foreign-engendered) white knights, puncturing with their postmodern comic shafts the heavy "realism" of earlier writers. In his article "Current Prairie Fiction: Openings/Beginnings," Wayne Tefs proposes that Robert Kroetsch is such a writer. The same works that have been lauded for their sensitive representation of our garrisoned mentality by formerly mentioned critics, works by Frederick Philip Grove, Sinclair Ross, Rudy Wiebe, Margaret Laurence, Tefs now sees as part of a bygone realist world where "geography imposed a . . . variation of the Immanent Will," a world "appropriate" to a pre–World War II mentality (245).

The great problem with this kind of criticism is that by not being able to see anything except the garrison mentality he has been taught to see, and never having had occasion to examine literature outside the garrison-defined canon, Tefs ends by making a case for Kroetsch's being the writer who "begins to transform the landscape rather than [being] molded by it" (246). I cannot accept the implied view that Robert Kroetsch does not, at least in part, grow out of a native Canadian tradition, that he is some exotic creature found by critics like Tefs under a metaphorical cabbage leaf. In fact, Robert Kroetsch, like the rest of us, was born of woman, or the womanly side of our tradition. From that "woman," that tradition, spring present-day writers who wish to ungarrison our literature and our criticism.

I have no root quarrel with this activity of elaboration, except in some of its extreme conclusions. Nor do I intend to dismiss past critical research as "paraphrase" and suggest that critics should now move on to a more up-to-date post-structuralist world and reject the past as "thematic criticism."[4] My real complaint about the work of such critics as Ricou, Moss, Northey, and McGregor, is that it only tells a portion of the structuralist story, a valid and important portion, but one that, once accepted as the only valid one, misleads and misdirects the act of reading. My own endeavour here is, like Moss' and McGregor's, to elaborate on a text. The passage that informs my own discussion is, coincidentally, taken from Robert Kroetsch. In *Labyrinths of Voice*, Kroetsch muses on his archaeological research for his novel *Badlands*:

> When I did the study of the paleontologists in southern Alberta, I was amazed
> that they didn't pick up the small bones—small animals—because everybody

was into finding bigger bones—the biggest bones were the most important. Their simple rule was that a still bigger dinosaur was better. And now they have to go back and go through the destroyed sites looking for seashells or whatever that would tell them a great deal (15).

That simple "going back" to the site again to look for those "seashells or whatever," now that all the "big bones" of Canadian literature and criticism have been examined and assembled, is an appropriate metaphor for a new exploration. This work is already underway. For my own search, two studies have been particularly helpful.[5]

Carol Fairbanks' *Prairie Women: Images in American and Canadian Fiction* and many of the essays in *A Mazing Space: Writing Canadian Women Writing* point to a radical difference in the way women encounter the land. Fairbanks claims that women writing on the prairies show a very optimistic view of the land and woman's place in it compared with the women portrayed in fiction written by men. In *A Mazing Space*, even the titles of the essays propose this "different" reaction. For example, an essay on Anna Jameson is entitled "Femininely speaking," one on Native women's oral histories is called "Voicing difference"; Caroline Hlus contributes "Writing womanly" and France Théoret, "Writing in the feminine."

These accounts of "difference" confirm a vision of women and the Canadian land that I have found in autobiographical accounts by women. By foregrounding autobiographical works rather than traditional fiction or poetry, I am recommending not only that we go through the archaeological site of the Canadian tradition again, but that we expand the perimeters and, indeed, even change our definition of territory. Elizabeth Meese argues in her article "The Languages of Oral Testimony and Women's Literature" that, through broadening our idea of the literary canon, we "generate both the unwritten historical and literary records," which allows us to answer such questions as: "Do women speak and write out of a different experience of culture? Are their uses of language and their observations on the world different from those of men?" (26). These questions in turn enlarge our vision of our entire tradition. Although I do not intend to examine oral testimony here, that pursuit, like the examination of unpublished archival materials, is a valid part of the effort to create a female tradition in literature. Along with autobiographical accounts, they are generally considered to be outside the mainstream (or "malestream") of literary canon.[6]

All the women autobiographers examined in this essay react to the strangeness of the Canadian landscape by merging their own identity, in some imaginative way, with the new land.[7] They arrive at this point in two ways: through a relationship with significant others and through some creative activity that discovers each woman's unique relation to the land.

Diarist Elizabeth Simcoe is the earliest illustration of this.[8] As wife of Ontario's first governor and as an accomplished landscape painter, Simcoe had a unique opportunity to encounter wilderness Canada. One of her first acts after arriving at the military fort at Niagara was to get out of the "garrison" and into the countryside. For her young son's health in the summer heat and for her own recreation, she had her tents set up on Queenston Heights. There she experienced lightning storms and summer downpours but remained enthusiastic about her new location. She writes: "A wet day . . . is very dismal in a Tent but to see the light again and feel the air dry is such a pleasure that none can judge but those who have felt the reverse" (99).

Many of the adventures she describes take place in the company of Thomas Talbot, her husband's aide and later Colonel Talbot, lord of the great estate on Lake Erie. In his company, she reaches out in various ways to touch the Canadian landscape. Simcoe, who came to Canada fearing the natural environment, is calmly able to allow "a green Caterpillar with tufts like fur on its back [to touch her] face" (106), and despite its painful sting, she continued her firsthand experimentation with her environment.

The degree to which she makes the natural world part of her self is indicated by the fact that, after Talbot leaves Canada, Simcoe makes her young son Francis her companion in her adventures. It is in his name that she and her husband claim land and build the open air "Castle Frank" on the Don River in York. A parthenon-type wooden structure, where she and Francis camped while she pursued her painting and sketching, Castle Frank symbolizes in its style and materials Simcoe's desire to bring her old-world self and her new-world experience together.

Marian Fowler, in *The Embroidered Tent*, sees Simcoe's art changing with her increasing adaptation to Canada. It shows a movement from a rational eighteenth-century picturesque concept of "sense to sensuality . . . all her senses newly awakened, in the rich texture of the land itself" (28).[9] Perhaps an even greater indication of the degree to which Canada has entered Simcoe's sense of herself is revealed when she is told that she must finally return to England after four years in Canada. She "cried all the day" (189), she writes, and upon arrival in her homeland, she mourns:

> The weather is damp raw & unpleasant. I could not but observe as we passed many good Houses that those Mansions appeared very comfortable in which people might live very happily, but it could not be supposed they could ever be induced to go out of them in such a damp climate for the fields looked so cold, so damp, so cheerless, so uncomfortable from the want of our bright Canadian Sun that the effect was striking & the contrast unfavorable to the English climate (207–208).

For Simcoe, at least for that moment in her life, what is alienating is not Canada but England.

It could easily be argued that Simcoe was only a "visitor" to Canada, a privileged visitor with servants and luxuries in tow. A settler's life is a very different experience. It offers a fuller and deeper knowledge of women's expe-

rience in the Canadian wilderness. Mary O'Brien was an Ontario settler whose
*Journals*, written from 1828 to 1838, document her movement from a genteel
English maiden of thirty to a Canadian pioneer and mother of several children. Integral to O'Brien's discovery of herself in Canada are her growth in
competence as she becomes a wife, a mother, and the chatelaine of a large farm
estate on Lake Simcoe and the fact that throughout the experience she sent
her journal entries home to her beloved sister. Her writing reveals her development moving from a lighthearted, humorous attitude towards the colonial
world, which has her observing that the locals are "making such rapid strides
in civilization as to have had two murderers tried and condemned at the same
assizes" (22), through an enchanted discovery of the Lake Simcoe area where
she will settle with her new husband, to her single-handed management of a
large farm while her husband spends an increasing amount of time engaged
in political activities in Toronto.

One of the more revealing incidents in O'Brien's journals involves a
woman named Mrs. Monck. O'Brien, by this point not only a wilderness wife,
mother, farmer, teacher, hostess, and gentlewoman, but also country midwife,
attends Mrs. Monck who is in a state of nervous collapse and physical exhaus-
tion. She takes Mrs. Monck home, nurses her, delivers her baby, restores her
to health. After returning home, the woman suffers another mental collapse
and runs away into the woods. The search party brings the woman to O'Brien
who observes that, although Mrs. Monck refuses to see her husband, she con-
fesses that her wandering in the woods left a "comparatively comfortable
impression on her mind" (244). Mrs. Monck is not the only woman who seems
to prefer the company of the wilderness to that of her husband. O'Brien's diary
reveals that, as the years go by, her own husband is either in Toronto or at
home in poor health. This does not lessen O'Brien's own enthusiasm for country
life.

The key to O'Brien's positive and radical adjustment is her relationships. Each role—wife, mother, community resource—allows her to grow. Like
many women, she finds that the wilderness frees her from the strictures the
old life put on women. She would have agreed with Anne Langton, a settler
in the Peterborough area, who writes: "As long as the lady is necessarily the
most active member of her household she keeps her ground from her utility;
but when the state of semi-civilization arrives . . . then she must fall, and just
be contented to be looked upon as belonging merely to the decorative department of the establishment and valued accordingly" (127–28). A garrison mentality becomes impossible in circumstances where each role increases a woman's
awareness of her ability to encompass the wilderness world in her own identity.

As well, O'Brien's self-dramatization in the *Journals* contributes to her
sense of self as a capable Canadian wilderness pioneer. That the *Journals* are
addressed to the intimate audience of sister and family only reinforces the conviction that it is through a woman's relationships to significant others, includ-

ing the reading others, that she makes a positive adjustment to the wilderness. The *Journals* as *bildungsroman* end abruptly in 1838, and the editor speculates that, since the primary purpose of the writing was to stay in touch with and later to convince O'Brien's sister Lucy to emigrate, her aim must have been accomplished by 1838 (280). Thus, writing, self-growth, and the wilderness experience are motivated and enlarged by the same desire, the desire to remain connected.[10]

That desire to connect, especially to connect with the Canadian land, through a relationship is nowhere more clearly illustrated than in the experience of Anna Jameson. Her *Winter Studies and Summer Rambles in Canada* would seem to begin with the worst attack of recoil from the new land in all Canadian literature. She almost sobs out her disappointment with Canada as she writes:

> What Toronto may be in summer, I cannot tell; they say it is a pretty place. At present its appearance to me, a stranger, is most strangely mean and melancholy. A little ill-built town on low land, at the bottom of a frozen bay, with one very ugly church, without tower or steeple; some government offices, built of staring red brick, the most tasteless, vulgar style imaginable; three feet of snow all around, and the grey sullen, wintry lake, and the dark gloom of the pine forest bounding the prospect; such seems Toronto to me now'' (I, 2).

In fact, it is not really Canada or even the winter that Jameson objects to; rather, it is the garrison represented by the "little ill-built town" of Toronto. The town is connected with a failed relationship, Jameson's soon-to-end marriage to Robert Jameson, a colonial official.[11] Throughout the *Studies*, Jameson seeks more positive relationships that will connect her to the country, and she finds them in such experiences as visits to a farm family on the Credit River and to Colonel Talbot at Port Talbot.

But it is in the *Rambles* that we see her connection with the land reach its fruition through relationships. In the Upper Lakes, Jameson finds an Indian woman, Mrs. Johnson, and her two half-breed daughters, and although each of these women has an identity as the wife of a white man, each has important connections with her Indian heritage as well as with the life of the land. Through them, Jameson makes a positive exploration of Canada on both an intellectual and a personal level. Knowledge of these women and their Indian traditions lead Jameson to a comparison of women's lives in Indian and white cultures. Unlike a white woman, she concludes, "however hard the lot of woman [in Indian society] she is in no *false* position. The two sexes are in their natural and true position relatively to the state of society; and the means of subsistence" (III, 303–304).

More important for her personal development than her realization of the hypocrisy of the white world's attitudes towards women is Jameson's ability to make a connection with Canada in a very personal way through Mrs. Johnson, who becomes her spiritual mother. Jameson writes of Mrs. Johnson comforting her during an illness: "[she] took me in her arms, laid me down on a couch, and began to rub my feet, soothing and caressing me. She called me Nindannis, daughter, and I called her Neengai, mother" (III, 185). Later, Jameson is baptized into wilderness life by successfully shooting the falls at Sault Ste. Marie. Neengai "embraced me several times," she writes. "I was declared duly initiated and adopted into the family and henceforth to be known as 'the woman of the bright foam' . . . among the Chippewas" (III, 200). Evidence offered by Fowler indicates that the baptism may have been partially staged by Jameson (166). If this is true, it only furthers my argument about women's desire to enter into a communion with the Canadian scene, since it indicates not only instinctive attraction, but intentionality as well.

Simcoe achieved her merging with the wilderness through art, O'Brien through nurturing, Jameson through intellectual activity. But they all achieved realization of self in the wilderness through significant relationships and the act of writing to an intimate audience: Simcoe to her daughters, O'Brien to her sister, and Jameson to her friend Ottilie von Goethe.[12] Relationships, and the opportunity they offer for a greater appreciation of the land, also figure prominently in the writings of Sarah Ellen Roberts, an American immigrant and author of *Alberta Homestead*. Lacking the advantages of youth, money, and situation which Simcoe, O'Brien, and Jameson enjoyed, Roberts nevertheless expresses a similar imaginative merging of her own sense of self with the land.

Arriving in southern Alberta at the age of fifty-four, her husband still recovering from a serious illness and bankruptcy, Sarah Roberts brings with her a fear of open spaces, migraine headaches, and a fragile physical constitution. She writes of her first days in the new land:

> How shall I describe the feeling that then settled down upon me? I had never had it before . . . . It wasn't exactly homesickness or fear or loneliness or awe, although I think that all of these may have entered into it . . . . I felt as though I were absolutely alone in the world, and my sense of littleness and helplessness overwhelmed me (21–22).

Despite the incredible hardships of her homesteading experience, the disadvantages she brought with her, and the fact that farm life never did get easier for Roberts (neither did the migraines in southern Alberta's changeable climate), she does not succumb to "garrison recoil." Her reaction is one in which relationships and the land are integrally united. She writes of her first spring in Alberta:

> The snow disappeared, the crocuses challenged the frost with their purple blossoms all over the prairie, and the ice melted in the ponds, which were once more alive with water fowl. It was like greeting old friends to hear the "honk, honk" of the geese as they flew northward, or to hear the musical note of the meadow lark. The men say that the best of all days is that when the frost has left the ground and the work in the fields has begun. And I

am sure that only one who has plowed early in the spring, when it seems so good to be out of doors, can know how it feels to walk out over a great breezy field, down the long, black, straight furrows. Lathrop [her son] says that when he first plows in the spring he rests under a sort of illusion, for it seems that it is he and not the team ahead that is forcing the plowshares through the stubborn soil. The grasp of the plow seems to give him a sense of power.

I used to go out to where the men were plowing. It fascinated me to watch the moist earth roll up on the moldboard and turn over, black and cool and sweet-smelling. There is nothing quite like that odor. It has in it all the essence of the spring, all the promise of the summer. It is as though the very clods had language and spoke to us of the wealth that lay latent in them (102–103).

What intrigues me about this description is the way Roberts incorporates many voices into her own consciousness: the active voice of the prairie's emerging spring, the voice of the wildlife, the voice of the men's work (in which, ironically, they perceive the soil as a "stubborn" entity into which they must "force" the plowshares), and her own voice which becomes identified with the voice of the land as the "clods" of earth are given "language" to speak to her of their latent wealth.

I have found that an imaginative identification of self-development with the experience of the land is always present in Canadian women's autobiographical writing throughout the nineteenth century and into our own. Susan Allison, who wrote *A Pioneer Gentlewoman in British Columbia* when she was over eighty, survived floods, fires, and fourteen childbirths in the interior of British Columbia in the 1860s and 1870s. She writes that the day she married John Farr Allison at the age of twenty-three and left Hope for the interior was the beginning of "my camping days and the wild, free life I ever loved till age and infirmity put an end to it" (21). Reading the actual record with our own garrisoned eyes, we might well find Allison's life anything but "free"; rather, her life seems full of risk, inconvenience, dreadfully hard work, and danger. But what is important is that Allison perceived it as freeing. Her need, like Sarah Roberts', to mythologize the difficult reality of her life into the "freedom" of her written account is the opposite of the garrison mentality.[13] This ungarrisoned, mythopoeic imagination also runs through the writings of Georgina Binnie-Clark, a prairie farmer who speaks of Canada as her "virgin mother," and of Martha Black, who sought her "lodestar" in the Yukon, and of other settler women confronted with accommodating their sense of self to the new land.

How does the fact that women's writing offers a different vision of the Canadian experience than the one traced in the garrison-mentality tradition change our view of the more established "canon" of Canadian writing? The first and most practical result would be the restoration of the missing text of women's writing. Books that are out of print, such as Lily Dougall's oeuvre—out of print perhaps because they express a view of Canada that the garrison mentality might call facile, in Ricou's word "shallow," or in McGregor's words "short-ranged, domestic"—might once again be seen as valuable.[14] With such a change in values, McClelland and Stewart might restore to its paperback edition of Moodie's *Roughing It in the Bush* the full text, including the chapter entitled "The Walk to Dummer," which narrates an important part of Moodie's own adjustment to the Canadian wilderness nurtured by her significant female other, her servant Jenny.[15] This new perspective on Canadian literature could make us recognize that our group of four founding poets is really a group of five and includes Isabella Valancy Crawford. Her work, viewed in the context of a female tradition, might well show us unrealized aspects of the "confederation poets." Our idea of canon might well expand to include the works examined in this paper.

In viewing the tradition through ungarrisoned eyes, we might begin to reconsider works such as Martha Ostenso's *Wild Geese*, which Ricou sees as affirming the "total nothingness . . . [of] a completely exhausted world" (74). We might find that this undervalued novel also celebrates a natural world that can be seen, not through the eyes of Caleb the father, but only through the eyes of his daughter Judith, as she stretches her naked body against the earth:

> Oh, how knowing the bare earth was, as if it might have a heart and a mind hidden here in the woods. The fields that Caleb had tilled had no tenderness, she knew. But here was something forbiddenly beautiful, secret as one's own body. And there was something beyond this. She could feel it in the freeness of the air, in the depth of the earth. Under the body there were, she had been taught, eight thousand miles of earth. On the other side, what? Above her body there were leagues of air, leading like wings—to what? The marvelous confusion and complexity of the world had singled her out from the rest of the Gares. She was no longer one of them. Lind Archer had come and her delicate fingers had sprung a secret lock in Jude's being. She had opened like a tight bud. There was no going back now into the darkness (53).

This is the same interconnection of self, other, and land that can be found in autobiographical accounts, as a female vision of the land grows from the touch of another, realized through the felt connection with the earth itself. Revisioning the tradition through this alternative view might allow us to establish the wholeness of our tradition.

In such a wholeness, we would know something of the nineteenth-century origins of what Shirley Neuman calls (in a twentieth-century context) "the many bodies; mothering bodies, erotic bodies" of women's writing (400). Female bodies are inscribed on the landscape of Canadian literature from our beginnings, and if the active verbs of Sarah Roberts' description of the earth's language or Ostenso's "knowing" earth are any indication, the land inscribes itself on the women who encounter it in their writing.

In that same "conclusion" which I quoted at the beginning of this essay, Northrop Frye describes the entry of the stranger into Canada as the experience of "being silently swallowed by an alien continent" (824). Women's experience of Canada indicates that being enclosed by the land is a somewhat more positive experience, one which demands metaphors of a more erotic and maternal nature. Their optimism verifies the belief that survival and success here, in life as well as in literature, depends not on our ability to mount garrisons, but on our ability to adapt old skills to new needs, on our desire for community and communication, and on our need to make a connection with the land by positive acts of the imagination.

## NOTES

1. I am indebted to the connections made between Jones' book and Frye's conclusion by Peter C. Noel-Bentley.
2. Ricou's "vertical" metaphor is taken from Wallace Stegner's *Wolf Willow* (271).
3. Nowhere in her study does McGregor acknowledge the similarity of her title to Robin D. Mathews' "The Wacousta Factor," which is the title of one of the sections of his book *Canadian Literature: Surrender or Revolution*, and to his article by that name. In the article, Mathews seeks to show how the Wacousta figure, "the betrayer or destroyer of community" (307), is rejected by the body of Canadian literature from the beginning as a version of the American heroic archetype. By McGregor's formulation, the "Wacousta Syndrome" in our literature is ever present, beginning with a garrison recoil and developing in several negative and positive directions.
4. This attitude towards earlier assessments of the tradition is expressed by Frank Davey in his *Surviving the Paraphrase*. The introduction to Davey's book of essays describes this "paraphrase." I agree with Davey's view of the restrictions of narrow "thematic criticism," but I cannot agree with his opinion that all the works he names as examples of this are as narrowly focused and reductive as he claims. At its best, "thematic criticism" is part of a broader structuralist approach to literature that can offer new ways to view a large body of literature and be most useful for establishing "difference."
5. My work on this subject actually began with Orest Rudzik's paper on Isabella Valancy Crawford, in which he uses Frye's garrison quotation to inform his essay, but posits a "radical sublimity" as being Valancy's typical reaction to the awesomeness of the wilderness.
6. In seeking this widening of our view of what is literature, I appeal to the same arguments expressed by Sandra Gilbert and Susan Gubar in *The Madwoman in the Attic*: that women have trouble fitting their stories into male-shaped genres, that much of a woman's "own story" can be hidden behind generic requirements (75–76).
7. When using the word "autobiographers" to describe women who wrote diaries, travel journals, memoirs, etc., I am reclaiming the word "autobiography"

to mean any significant life story written by the one who lived it. Thus, not only the forms typical of men (for example, spiritual and ego-development accounts), but also those typical of women may be included. My position springs from the work of such theorists as Mary G. Mason and Estelle Jelinek, and is outlined in my article "Canadian women's autobiography: some critical directions."

8.    Simcoe's account, written in the 1790s and in all strictness not a nineteenth-century document, is considered here with the justification that strict periodization, like strict generic requirements, is another way in which traditional criticism discriminates against women's literature. In the assumption of a more tolerant spirit, I also include Sarah Roberts' work which was written in 1906–1907 and 1915.

9.    Fowler theorizes a development of an "androgynous" personality resulting from women's encounter with the wilderness. I propose a more radically female experience of self in the spirit of Elaine Showalter's "wild zone" as described in "Feminist Criticism in the Wilderness."

10.    Mary Mason, in "The Other Voice: Autobiographies of Women Writers," posits the desire to be connected as one of the chief motivations of women's autobiographical writing.

11.    See Clara Thomas' "Journeys to Freedom" regarding Jameson's relationship with her husband.

12.    See Bina Freiwald's essay for insight into Jameson's friendship with von Goethe.

13.    The ability to "mythologize difficult reality" is identified by Patricia Meyer Spacks as a chief characteristic of women's autobiographical writing.

14.    See Lorraine McMullen's essay for an overview of Dougall's work.

15.    McClelland and Stewart's 1923 edition of *Roughing It in the Bush* contains this chapter and the new 1989 edition restores Moodie's full text.

## WORKS CITED

Allison, Susan. 1976. *A Pioneer Gentlewoman in British Columbia; The Recollections of Susan Allison*. Ed. Margaret A. Ormsby. Vancouver: Univ. of British Columbia Press.

Binnie-Clark, Georgina. 1914. *Wheat and Women*. Toronto: Bell and Cockburn.

Black, Martha. 1938. *My Seventy Years*. As told to Elizabeth Bailey Price. London: Thomas Nelson.

Buss, Helen. 1986. "Canadian women's autobiography: some critical directions." In *A Mazing Space: Writing Canadian Women Writing*. Ed. Shirley Neuman and Smaro Kamboureli. Edmonton: Longspoon-NeWest. 154–66.

Davey, Frank. 1983. *Surviving the Paraphrase, Eleven Essays on Canadian Literature*. Winnipeg: Turnstone Press. 1–12.

Fairbanks, Carol. 1986. *Prairie Women: Images in American and Canadian Fiction*. New Haven: Yale Univ. Press.

Fowler, Marian. 1982. *The Embroidered Tent: Five Gentlewomen in Early Canada*. Toronto: House of Anansi.

Freiwald, Bina. " 'Femininely speaking': Anna Jameson's *Winter Studies and Summer Rambles in Canada*." In *A Mazing Space*. 61–73.

Frye, Northrop. 1965. Conclusion. In *Literary History of Canada*. Ed. Carl F. Klinck. Toronto: Univ. of Toronto Press. 821–49.

Gilbert, Sandra M., and Susan Gubar. 1979. *The Madwoman in the Attic, The Woman Writer and the Nineteenth-Century Literary Imagination*. New Haven: Yale Univ. Press.

Godard, Barbara. "Voicing difference: the literary production of native women." In *A Mazing Space*. 87–107.

Hlus, Carolyn. "Writing womanly: theory and practice." In *A Mazing Space*. 287–97.

Jameson, Anna. *Winter Studies and Summer Rambles in Canada*. 1838, 3 vol. Cole Facsimile 1972. Toronto: Coles Publishing Company.

Jelinek, Estelle C. 1986. *The Tradition of Women's Autobiography: From Antiquity to the Present*. Boston: Twayne.

Jones, D. G. 1970. *Butterfly on Rock: A Study of the Themes and Images in Canadian Literature*. Toronto: Univ. of Toronto Press.

Langton, Anne. 1964. *A Gentlewoman in Upper Canada: The Journals of Anne Langton*. Toronto: Clarke, Irwin.

Mason, Mary G. 1980. "The Other Voice: Autobiographies of Women Writers." In *Autobiography: Essays Theoretical and Critical*. Ed. James Olney. Princeton: Princeton Univ. Press. 207–35.

Mathews, Robin. 1978. *Canadian Literature, Surrender or Revolution*. Ed. Gail Dexter. Toronto: Steel Rail.

———. 1978. "The Wacousta Factor." In *Figures in a Ground, Canadian Essays on Modern Literature Collected in Honour of Sheila Watson*. Ed. Diane Bessai and David Jackel. Saskatoon: Western Producer Prairie Books. 295–316.

Meese, Elizabeth. 1985. "The Languages of Oral Testimony and Women's Literature." *Women's Personal Narratives*. Ed. Lenore Hoffman and Margo Culley. New York: Modern Language Association of America. 18–28.

McGregor, Gaile. 1985. *The Wacousta Syndrome, Explorations in the Canadian Landscape*. Toronto: Univ. of Toronto Press.

McMullen, Lorraine. "Lily Dougall's Vision of Canada." In *A Mazing Space*. 137–47.

Moodie, Susanna. 1923. *Roughing It in the Bush, or Forest Life in Canada*. Toronto: McClelland and Stewart.

Moss, John. 1974. *Patterns of Isolation in English Canadian Fiction*. Toronto: McClelland and Stewart.

Neuman, Shirley. 1986. "Importing difference." In *A Mazing Space*. 392–406.

———, and Smaro Kamboureli, eds. 1986. *A Mazing Space: Writing Canadian Women Writing*. Edmonton: Longspoon-NeWest.

———, and Robert Wilson. 1982. *Labyrinths of Voice: Conversations with Robert Kroetsch*. Edmonton: NeWest.

Noel-Bentley, Peter C. 1970. "Our Garrison Mentality." *Mosaic: Literature and Ideas* 4, no. 1: 127–33.

Northey, Margot. 1976. *The Haunted Wilderness: The Gothic and Grotesque in Canadian Fiction*. Toronto: Univ. of Toronto Press.

O'Brien, Mary. 1968. *The Journals of Mary O'Brien, 1828–1838*. Ed. Audrey Saunders Miller. Toronto: Macmillan.

Ostenso, Martha. 1987. *Wild Geese*. 1961. Toronto: McClelland and Stewart.

Ricou, Laurence. 1973. *Vertical Man/Horizontal World: Man and Landscape in Canadian Prairie Fiction*. Vancouver: Univ. of British Columbia Press.

Roberts, Sarah Ellen. 1971. *Alberta Homestead: The Chronicle of a Pioneer Family.* Ed. Lathrop E. Roberts. 1968. Austin: Univ. of Texas Press.

Rudzik, Orest. 1979. "Myth in 'Malcolm's Katie.' " In *The Crawford Symposium.* Ed. Frank M. Tierney. Ottawa: Univ. of Ottawa Press. 49–60.

Showalter, Elaine. 1981. "Feminist Criticism in the Wilderness." *Critical Inquiry* 8, no. 2: 179–206.

Simcoe, Elizabeth. 1965. *Mrs. Simcoe's Diary.* Ed. Mary Quale Innis. Toronto: Macmillan.

Spacks, Patricia Meyer. 1973. "Reflecting Women." *Yale Review* 63.1: 26–42.

Stegner, Wallace. 1966. *Wolf Willow: A History, a Story, and a Memory of the Last Plains Frontier.* New York: Viking Press.

Tefs, Wayne. 1986. "Current Prairie Fiction: Openings/Beginnings." In *Trace: Prairie Writers on Writing.* Ed. Birk Sproxton. Winnipeg: Turnstone Press. 241–49.

Théoret, France. "Writings in the feminine: voicing consensus, practising difference." In *A Mazing Space.* 385–91.

Thomas, Clara. 1972. "Journeys to Freedom." *Canadian Literature* 51: 11–19.

# Susanna Moodie

## "The Embryo Blossom": Susanna Moodie's Letters to Her Husband in Relation to *Roughing It in the Bush*

### CARL BALLSTADT

The embryo blossom is an image from the poetic epigraph to "A Change in Our Prospects," a passage from *Roughing It in the Bush* which, in typical Susanna Moodie fashion, embraces notions of such opposites as growth and blight, hope and uncertainty:

> The future flower lies folded in the bud, —
> Its beauty, colour, fragrance, graceful form,
> Carefully shrouded in that tiny cell;
> Till time and circumstance, and sun and shower,
> Expand the embryo blossom—and it bursts
> Its narrow cerements, lifts its blushing head,
> Rejoicing in the light and dew of heaven.
> But if the canker-worm lies coil'd around
> The heart o' the bud, the summer sun and dew
> Visit in vain the sear'd and blighted flower.

This image is an appropriate title for this paper because a series of letters Moodie wrote to her husband between 1837 and 1840 are an embryonic version of some parts of *Roughing It in the Bush*. Like the poem, these letters give witness to health and sickness, anticipation and disappointment. The letters were written during the two years in which the Moodies' prospects changed, beginning with the Rebellion of 1837 and ending with their departure from the bush at the beginning of 1840. Susanna alludes to them several times in her book, most notably in "The Outbreak" when she observes that "the receipt of an occasional letter from him was my only solace during his long absence" and "a long-looked-for prize" and in the lengthy reflection on their correspondence and their spiritual communication in "A Change in Our Prospects."[1]

The letters were written during three periods of separation.[2] From January to August 1838, Dunbar Moodie served with the militia in Toronto and on the Niagara frontier; from this period, there are five letters from Dunbar to Susanna, none from her to him. From December 1838 to August 1839, Dunbar was paymaster to the militia companies in the Belleville area; there are five letters written by Dunbar to his wife in this period, nine from Susanna to him. From his period as Sheriff of the Victoria District, there is only one letter, Dunbar to Susanna, written in November 1839. The chapters of *Roughing It in the Bush* that relate to these letters, in large or small degree, are "The Outbreak," "The Whirlwind," "The Walk to Dummer," and "A Change in Our Prospects."

The relationship of letters and chapters offers several areas of investigation. First, the letters may serve as a gloss on *Roughing It in the Bush*, telling us more about persons who appear in the book, such as the dear and often-mentioned friend Emilia Shairp,[3] the Traills,[4] the Caddys,[5] who assist the women on their mercy mission to Dummer, and the Y——ys, or Jorys, to whom the Moodies owe money for farm labour. In the discussion of these and other people, the letters reveal more about the workings of backwoods society than does the book. They also reveal Dunbar's side of the story and convey his rather interesting perceptions of Canadian society and militia life during the period. In addition, they offer an account of Susanna's and Dunbar's first response to some of the motifs, persons, experiences, and events delineated in *Roughing It in the Bush* and, hence, an opportunity to see what Susanna selected from her material and how she adapted it for use in the book. Although some sources have permitted scrutiny of stages in the evolution of *Roughing It in the Bush*, most notably the serial publication of portions of it in *The Literary Garland* and *The Victoria Magazine*, these letters constitute the earliest version of Susanna's backwoods life in its darkest days.

I shall begin with some observations of the temporal rearrangement of events and then suggest some reasons for this rearrangement, reluctantly acknowledging, of course, that Susanna may not even have resorted to these letters and may simply have forgotten when things occurred. However, she was too much the creative writer to be unmindful of the effects her accounts would have, and one sees plenty of evidence of this in the letters themselves.

In "The Outbreak," the reader is presented with a Susanna coping quite determinedly and successfully with her husband's absence on the frontier during the winter and spring of 1838. In addition to managing the money sent by Dunbar and carrying on the operations of the bush farm during sugar-making and planting, she reports that she began to supplement their income by writing for John Lovell and by painting birds and butterflies on sugar-maple fungi for sale in Peterborough and in England. She writes of the pride she felt upon receiving the first twenty-dollar bill from Montreal and that she fancied it forming "the nucleus out of which a future independence for my family might arise'' (420) and of the painting enabling ''hope [to raise] at last her drooping head'' (423). The issue here is that neither of these activities took place until the spring of 1839, and I suggest that Susanna places them where she does because they fit with the essentially up-beat action of that chapter in which, although missing her husband exceedingly, she is managing effectively in his absence. So well, in fact, that in a letter to Dunbar dated May 24, 1838, Thomas Traill wrote:

> Your wife deserves all you say of her. She has commanded the esteem of every one. Your spring crops are nearly in. She was anxious to spare you every trouble when you came home. In fact she is farther advanced than her brother or me, or indeed any of the neighbours . . . . I am happy to say that all your children look fat fair and flourishing as do mine, and you will find on your return, which I hope will be soon, that every thing has been managed admirably in your absence and every difficulty met with energy constancy and courage. I am proud to do justice to the worth and value of your most excellent wife. She is indeed a treasure of which you may be proud (154).

If Susanna has indeed shuffled her report of the artistic endeavours so that they form part of the series of her accomplishments in the winter and spring of 1838,[6] the rearrangement takes on an even greater significance in light of the events that follow.

The next chapter is ''The Whirlwind,'' which deals with an adventure in August 1838 and briefly with the fall and winter of 1838–39. Immediately following is ''The Walk to Dummer,'' but the chronology of it is a bit ambiguous. Susanna indicates that the walk took place in the ''year of the Canadian rebellion,'' but she also places it in January 1839 during ''a short but severe spell of frost and snow'' following the ''unnaturally mild'' months of November and December 1838 (459). Furthermore, ''The Walk to Dummer'' is flanked by a paragraph at the end of ''The Whirlwind'' that succinctly outlines Susanna's physical and social deprivation and suffering, the illness of her children, and the visit of Dr. B—— in the winter of 1839 and by several paragraphs at the beginning of ''A Change in Our Prospects'' in which she again alludes to her own illness in that period. She also writes here of her loneliness when she suffers ''the three-fold chord of domestic love to be unravelled'' by the absence of her child and when her sister's removal renders her ''separation from [her] husband doubly lonely and irksome'' (484–85). It is at this point that she reflects most extensively upon the correspondence between herself and Dunbar.

That correspondence tells us that the walk to Dummer most certainly took place in January or February 1838, that Mrs. N—— was named Louisa Lloyd,[7] and that Susanna did indeed send a copy of her description of the situation to her husband. He in turn sent it to Dr. Strachan through a Mr. Maynard, having written ''a few lines of [his] own as an introduction or head-ing and quoted a considerable portion of [her] communication, which [he] was obliged to curtail a little'' (61). By placing the account where she does in *Roughing It in the Bush*, Susanna makes it a projection of her own experience and even of her own attitudes. The dreadful conditions of her life as depicted in the letters parallel those of Louisa Lloyd, with one exception: Dunbar, unlike Captain Frederick Lloyd, had not completely abandoned his family. In fact, when Emilia talks of "some plan of rescuing this unfortunate lady and her family from her present forlorn situation," Susanna observes: "tears sprang to my eyes, and I thought, in the bitterness of my heart, upon my own galling poverty, that my pockets did not contain even a single copper, and that I had scarcely garments enough to shield me from the inclemency of the weather'' (461). At least one other parallel between the Moodies and Lloyds is worth citing; like Dunbar, Captain Lloyd had taken that "rash and hazardous step for any officer to part with his half-pay,'' which is "generally followed by the same disastrous results'' (451–52). Susanna also reproves Captain Lloyd for having taken up wild land instead of settling on a good cleared farm.

The results of such folly in the Moodies' own case is most poignantly and pathetically revealed in her first letter to Dunbar, dated January 11, 1839. This letter, as well as many of the others, reveals just how remarkably restrained Susanna Moodie was in documenting her own condition in *Roughing It in the Bush*. Since Dunbar's departure just before Christmas, she had been confined to her bed suffering from mastitis.[8] Dr. Hutchison of Peterborough was sent for, and the account of his visit is worth quoting extensively both for its vividness and for Susanna's typical tinges of humour:

> During the Christmas week I was in great agony and did little else but cry and groan until the following Sunday night, when kind Traill went himself after dark and brought up the Dr at three o'clock in the bitter cold morning. He put the lancet immediately into my breast, and I was able to turn and move my left arm for the first time for ten days, for I lay like a crushed snake on my back unable to move or even to be raised forward without the most piteous cries. You may imagine what I suffered when I tell you that more than half a pint of matter must have followed the cut of the lancet and the wound has continued to discharge ever since. I was often quite out of my senses, and only recovered to weep over the probability that I might never see my beloved husband again. Poor Jenny nursed me somewhat like a she bear, her tenderest mercies were neglect. She is however behaving better now. Dr H. seemed greatly concerned for my situation. When he looked round the forlorn, cold, dirty room feebly lighted by the wretched lamp, he said with great emphasis, "In the name of God! Mrs Moodie get out of this—'' Well, I have got through it, and am once more able to crawl about the house, but I am very weak (80).

No sooner had she begun crawling about the house when Donald, her second boy, "got a dreadful fall on the stove and laid his skull bare above the right eye. Jenny called out that he was killed, and for a moment when I saw his ghastly face, the blood pouring in a torrent from the frightful wound I thought so too.''

Like Louisa Lloyd, Susanna is the recipient of kindnesses from her neighbours. Mrs. Caddy "came down through a heavy snow storm, and offered to stay and nurse me," and "Dear Mrs Hague and Mrs Crawford came to see me twice, and both wept much at my miserable state. Mrs H. sent me a gallon of old port wine, and so many nice things, I could not help shedding tears when I received them. She took away my poor little Aggy, and insists on keeping her through the winter." There are other kind offers, but again like Mrs. Lloyd, Susanna notes: "I seem no longer able to contend with my comfortless situation and the charity of my kind neighbours really distresses me" (80).

By February she is strong enough to undertake another mercy mission of her own, this time to Mrs. Caddy who "has been alarmingly ill, supposed dying . . . . I went to her and staid two days, during which period I thought she would die every moment . . . . I am sure I made a good doctor, and the poor dear thanked me when she recovered herself to know me with tears in her eyes" (81).

The challenges to her endurance, however, are almost unrelenting. On March 6, she describes the severe illness of several of her children (this is the illness she describes with such remarkable restraint at the end of "The Whirlwind"):

> I have been anxiously looking for a letter from you for some days past, and I can no longer repress the strong desire I feel to write to you. Since the date of my last, I have been occupied incessantly at the sick bed of two of our children, whom I expected every hour to breathe their last. You may imagine the anguish of your poor Susy, and you so far away. Poor little Donald, was first taken, with sudden inflamation on the lungs, attended with violent fever and every symptom of croup. I had to put him in a warm bath, force castor oil down his throat, and apply a large blister to his chest. Poor little fellow his cries were dreadful and his entreaties for me to take all the pins out of his belly which was the violent pains in his chest and at the pit of his stomach. Dear Mrs Traill came to me at the break of day, and Traill went down to get advice from the Doctor if he could not bring him up. That night my beloved baby was struck in the same manner, only he was to all appearance dead . . . all sense appeared to have fled. His jaws were relaxed the foam was running from his mouth and my lovely dear's beautiful limbs fell over my arms a dead weight. I burst into an agony of tears in which I was joined by poor Katey, and putting my insensible lamb into her arms, I ran and called Jenny . . . . We got him into the bath, but it was a long time before he gave any signs of returning life. In the meantime Cyprian Godard ran off for the Doctor, sending up in his way Mrs Strickland and dear Catharine . . . . Neither would give me any hopes of my darlings recov-

ery. But we did all we could for him, we put a blister on his white tender
chest and forced some tartar emetic down his throat and put hot flannels
to his cold feet, and sat down to watch through the dreary night the faint
heavings of his innocent breast. In the mean time my kind messenger sped
on to Peterboro' and met Mr Traill who was bringing up medicines for
Donald, and dear Mrs A Shairp who would come up when she heard my
dear child was so ill . . . . It was four o clock in the morning before Cyprian
returned faint and tired. Dr H. would not come, but said, that he would
send up Dr Dixon in the morning.
   The next was a dreadfully severe day of wind, frost, and drifting snow.
The dear babe was apparently worse and no Dr came when Cyprian, again
volunteered to go down for a Dr. but Dr H. would not be entreated. ''If
you do not come,'' Cyprian said, ''The sweet babe will die.'' ''I cant help
that,'' was the unfeeling reply. ''The roads are too bad, and I cant leave
Peterboro'.'' Cyprian then went to old Dr Bird, who came up in spite of
the bad roads and the dreadful night. Good old dear how kind he was—He
told me, that without medical aid the child must have died. That he was
still in great danger though the remidies we had applied had prolonged his
life—''I am an old man,'' he said to come thus far, through such weather,
but I did it to serve Mr Moodie, when I heard Hutchison would not come,
I was determined that the child should not be lost if I could save it.'' He
told me Donald was out of danger, but that I was very ill myself. I had not
even felt the effects of this horrible influenza—so great was my anxiety about
my children. Numbers of children have died with it (83).

Although the crisis has passed, Susanna must still sit up all night with the child,
suffering illness herself but following ''Dr Birds receipts'' and getting better.
How anticlimactic and ironic is her conclusion to this episode: ''In this time
of universal sickness, how anxiously my thoughts turn to you. I hope my dear
one is well. Do write me on the receipt of this, if only a few lines to dissipate
my fears—'' (83).
   Obviously, such vivid accounts of the children's suffering and her own
were not very soothing to Dunbar while he was fulfilling his responsibilities
as paymaster to the regiments in the Victoria District, and it is not surprising
to find Susanna beginning her next letter with ''Banish all your gloomy for-
bodings, our children are *quite* out of danger, though a cough hangs on both
of them . . .'' (84). While it is clear that Susanna does not mask her description
of ''Susie, the poor bush wacker'' (86) in the letters, neither does she mask
her love and admiration for Dunbar.
   The common impression of Dunbar as a bumbler and a rather shadowy
figure has been fostered by the editions that omit most of what he wrote for
the book, as well as by the fact that many of the key actions delineated in what
remains occur while he is away from home. And yet *Roughing It in the Bush*
makes it very apparent that he is of the utmost importance to Susanna, not
only economically. In ''A Change in Our Prospects,'' in the extended passage

about their correspondence, she writes of her sense that they are kindred spirits, communicating sympathetically even without the use of letters. She also uses some conventional but nevertheless interesting imagery to reflect their relationship. The day of his leaving at the time of the outbreak is "like our destiny, cold, dark, and lowering" (413) because "all joy had vanished with him who was my light of life" (414). Such contrasts of dark and light, depression and joy are remarkably sustained in *Roughing It in the Bush*. When Dunbar returns, she receives him "with delight" (417), but "his long-continued absence cast a gloom upon my spirit not easily to be shaken off" (417). As the winter of 1838 wears away, "the receipt of an occasional letter from him was [her] only solace" (423). Later on, when both she and the children are seriously ill and he writes in alarm, she asks: "Why did the dark cloud in his mind hang so heavily above his home? The burden of my weary and distressed spirit had reached him; and without knowing of our sufferings and danger, his own responded to the call" (486–87).

Such imagery is pertinent to some very complex issues in the relationship of husband and wife, such issues as dependency and choice, domestic obligation and literary aspiration, which frequently emerge in *Roughing It in the Bush*. But the imagery also expresses hope and longing and love, and we can look to the letters for a fuller expression of these feelings and for further revelations of the personalities of husband and wife.

The Moodie correspondence of the post-Rebellion period reveals that, to a very considerable extent, Dunbar was the restless one and Susanna much more stable and inclined to make the best of Canada. When he reports that he has sold Groote Valley, his farm in South Africa, she observes: "It will do more to reconcile you to Canada, than anything else, and I have no doubt that the hand of Providence guided us hither" (81). Dunbar, along with others in the neighbourhood, had been looking over the prospects of resettling in Texas, but Susanna's view is that they have "naught to do with brother Jonathan and his scampish progeny. But if our debts were all paid, we might live happily enough here and rear up our dear children in the fear and love of God—" (87). What she does hope for is that 1839 will be their last year in the bush, although she "should not wish to live in a town, but near one . . . a little Place with a few acres of ground within a ride of you, where we could keep a cow or two a few fowls and cultivate a nice garden" (84).

Interwoven with such reflections of domestic contentment are alternative aspirations to creative endeavour. Both the painting of the fungi for sale and the forwarding of items to Lovell will, she hopes, "open up a little fund for me which may enable me to pay Jenny's wages and get a few necessaries for the children" (87). There is even a proposal that she and Dunbar

> edit a Newspaper in some large town on conservative principles and endeavor
> to make it a valuable vehicle for conveying intelligence respecting the colony
> to the old country as well as this. I am sure we should get a multitude of

subscribers, and I should enjoy the thing amazingly. Mrs Shairp thinks, that such a paper would be taken by all the Peterboro' folks. Think over it a wee bit . . . . I could take all the light reading Tales, poetry etc. and you the political and statistical details. Without much effort I think our paper would soon be the first in the Provinces. Perhaps some wealthy bookseller might start such a thing paying us a salary for the first year, and giving us two thirds of the profits afterwards (83).

While this is one of Susanna's dreams, obviously she did not entirely forget it as the later appearance of *The Victoria Magazine* makes clear.

Nor was it her only dream. If there is one constant in these letters, it is her love for Dunbar and his for her. And sometimes as she longs for him, that love is expressed in a dream context. In March, after she and the children have recovered, she writes: "To know, that you love us, and think of us in all our sickness and privations atones for them all. How precious that love and sympathy is to your poor Susy no written language can tell . . . . There are times when I almost wish I could love you less. This weary longing after you makes my life pass away like a dream" (84). On April 4, their wedding anniversary, she tells of another dream: "I dreampt you returned last night, and I was so glad, but you pushed me away, and said you had taken a vow of celebacy and meant to live alone, and I burst into such fits of laughing that I awoke" (85).

While depression and privation is often the subject of these letters, the love seems to transcend them and the expressions of it to carry a deep conviction:

I am a very rich woman. *You love me*—my friends are kind to me—my dear children are well and happy, and we have united hearts and interests. Can poverty, ever outweigh these blessings? No dearest no?—we will defy temporary evils, and still enjoy the existence given us to improve for a better state of being, and be firm friends through a happy eternity, though the endearing tie which now unites us should be severed by death (87).

The aspects of the relationship between these Moodie letters and chapters in *Roughing It in the Bush* by no means exhaust the content and significance of the letters. I have focused largely on the "temporary evils" in order to show how restrained Susanna was in her account of her own condition in the book and yet how she was mirroring her own case in the story of Louisa Lloyd. In a variety of moods and tones, many other details of their days in the bush are fleshed out in the letters, including the continuing story of the steam boat stock, further adventures with the bear which "haunts the top of the clearing" (87), the management and disposal of the farm, and plans for the journey to Belleville, along with Dunbar's assessment of the politics of the "front" and his own plans for coping with them. Such a range of matters and the revelations of aspects of the personalities of Susanna and Dunbar Moodie make the letters a valuable resource for a better understanding of *Roughing It in the Bush* and their lives in general.

# NOTES

1.   References are to *Roughing It in the Bush or Life in Canada*. London: Virago Press, 1986. This edition, a reprint of parts of the Richard Bentley first edition, 1852, is used here because some of the quotations in the paper are not found in the Canadian editions thus far available. Susanna refers to the letters on three other occasions: in "The Outbreak" (429), in "The Walk to Dummer" (480), and in "A Change in Our Prospects" (497).

2.   The letters are part of the Patrick Hamilton Ewing Collection of Moodie-Strickland-Vickers-Ewing Family Papers in the National Library of Canada. A finding-aid numbers the letters by author and in chronological order and these numbers are used in this paper when letters are cited.

3.   Charlotte Emilia Shairp and her husband Major Alexander Mordaunt Shairp lived for a time near the Moodies, on the west half of Lot 21, Concession 5 in Douro Township. Shairp also had a dwelling in Peterborough. See OTAR, Peterborough County, Township of Douro, Abstract Index 1, GS 4959.

4.   Catharine Parr Traill, Susanna's sister, and her husband Thomas.

5.   Lieutenant Colonel John Thomas Caddy and his family lived on Lot 21, Concession 4 of Douro Township, two concessions east of the Moodies. His son George owned Lot 20 in the same concession. See OTAR, Municipal Records, RG 21, Newcastle District Census and Assessment, Douro, MS-16.

6.   Since Susanna altered the chronology of the Lovell connection and the fungi painting, perhaps she had also altered the time of the writing of the letter to Sir George Arthur that she tells of in the same chapter. The letter has not yet been located.

7.   Lieutenant Frederick Lloyd, his wife Louisa, and his family settled on land in Concession 1 Dummer in 1831. See OTAR, Locations in the Districts of Newcastle and Bathurst, Dummer, 1823–1842, RG 1, C-1-4, MS-693, Reel 159.

8.   Susanna gave birth to her third son, John Strickland, in October 1838, and when nursing him, one of her breasts became infected.

# WORKS CITED

Moodie, Susanna. 1986. *Roughing It in the Bush; or, Life in Canada*. 1852. London: Virago Press.

The Patrick Hamilton Ewing Collection of Moodie-Strickland-Vickers-Ewing Family Papers. National Library of Canada, Ottawa.

# Susanna Moodie

## The Function of the Sketches in Susanna Moodie's *Roughing It in the Bush*

ALEC LUCAS

$S$usanna Moodie's *Roughing It in the Bush* has seldom received the credit it merits as a work in which themes, characters, and narrative form a coherent whole. For many years the book seemed simply a lively, personal chronicle of life in early Canada written by one of the illustrious Strickland family. Some readers did note its humorous characters, "delightfully drawn," and the "charms and witcheries" of its narrative, but most praised its content rather than its style, admiring its "reflections on the picturesque" and its "wide variety of subjects." If British, readers lauded its "heroine" as a symbol of noble English womanhood; if Canadian, they sometimes damned Moodie for her condescending class-consciousness (Ballstadt et al., 108–109). Both views, however, are merely different sides of the same coin. As one of the upper middle-class, Mrs. Moodie tried, on the one hand, to demonstrate the strength that she shared with her class, and on the other, to affirm Britain's superiority to the crude overseas colony.

During recent years, the continuing popularity of the book has attracted the attention of many literary critics. To determine the basis of its success, some have continued to discuss it as personalized social history or as autobiography. Those focusing on the latter disregard everything but Mrs. Moodie's personality. She is a symbol of an alleged national paranoid schizophrenia, and the sketches (presented in chapters 1, 2, 4, 5, 7, 10, 17, 22, 23, and 25) are merely hit-and-miss affairs, warnings to settlers, tests of values, studies in failure, means of objectifying an inner world, almost anything but parts of an overall design. Such critics fail to recognize that these aspects of the book are part of the very essence of *Roughing It in the Bush* and that the autobiographical sketch was the only way, other than the essay, open to Moodie to write realistically and imaginatively of her experiences in the backwoods. Only through the autobiographical sketch could she describe and dramatize her setting and her characters. For Moodie writing in mid-nineteenth century, no other prose fictional mode lent itself so well to the depiction of such intractable New World material as confronted her. Since it would not fit the popular Old World romantic mould of the time, in *Roughing It in the Bush*, she had to forgo (fortunately for her reputation as a writer and for us as readers) the make-believe of her sentimental and gothic fiction. North America had to wait several years before mastering the art of realistic fiction, especially of the kind that concerns the rural world.

For other critics, the biographical approach has not seemed a satisfactory explanation of the success of *Roughing It in the Bush*, because that approach fails to provide a way of seeing the book as more than "roughly-hewn" social history filled with "rather pointless character sketches" (MacDonald, 21). Carl Ballstadt argues that it owes much to Mary Mitford's sketch book *Our Village*, published in 1832 (22–38). Mitford's book, however, is in the pastoral tradition, and *Roughing It in the Bush* is in the anti-pastoral, even the anti-rural, tradition (except for the half-hearted tribute to the rural in "Disappointed Hopes," when Moodie avows that manual toil is satisfying and that a "well-hoed ridge of potatoes" is a thing of delight [1913, 393]). Like Ballstadt, R. D. MacDonald recognizes the significance of the sketches, but unlike Ballstadt, he recognizes their relationship to the theme and narrative of the book as a whole. The sketches are, MacDonald affirms, not only "watersheds between the flows of action," but also prefigurations of the Moodies' failure, for him the controlling concept of the book (24). This generalization lacks support. Each sketch is not, as he holds, an "ominous picture of the British gentleman who fails in the bush" (28)—unless one elevates Uncle Joe, Old Satan, and John Monaghan to such a lofty rank. And each is not merely a transition in the study of social misfits, nor an "anecdotal" fragment in a movement "from romantic anticipation to disillusionment" (30). On the contrary, the sketches in *Roughing It in the Bush* comprise an integral part of a study, not merely of theme (whatever one believes it to be), but of the pioneer world, of Moodie's life, and of the design or structure of the book.

Some critics have suggested that *Roughing It in the Bush* should be read as fiction, and to give Moodie's contemporary readers their due, a review in *The Commercial Advertiser* of 1852 noted that *Roughing It in the Bush* reveals the "three great qualifications necessary to a novelist" (Ballstadt et al., 108). But it was not until years later, after Carl Klinck had commented on the book's fictional nature (xii), that critics paid heed to this insight. Generically the sketch is, of course, fictional. (Besides, Mrs. Moodie may stretch the truth a bit, as in her account of a hair-breadth escape when burning the fallow, or in other misadventures.) To read the whole book as a novel *manqué* is, however, still to misread it and to misconstrue the nature of the collections of sketches once popular in the seventeenth century. Moreover, the new interest in *Roughing*

*It in the Bush* as fiction has led to a concomitant neglect of the function of the set sketches (chapters 1, 2, 4, 5, 7, 10, 17, 22, 23, and 25).

Novelist and critic Carol Shields thinks them excellent but of little importance to the book. "Brian and Malcolm," she comments, "are not part of a story but are studies in themselves" (13). Less enthusiastic about the set sketches but more about the book as fiction, Marian Fowler complains that "Susanna interrupts the main narrative" with "unrelated stories . . . the whole helter-skelter collection [reproducing] the usual meanderings of the sentimental novel" (105). She tries to force the book deeper into the romantic cast by dividing Mrs. Moodie into a non-fiction "Dasher" narrator and a fictional "Hartshorn and Handkerchief" heroine. For Fowler, the sketches relate to the narrative, when they relate at all, only as reflections of Moodie's acidulous reaction to her environment. In keeping with the currently fashionable, urban thesis of a Canadian love-hate relationship with nature, Fowler considers the Yankee neighbours and Malcolm—a gothic villain in Fowler's romantic cast—to be mirrors of Moodie's antipathy towards a harsh and hostile land. Another interpretation, however, readily presents itself, one in which the Yankees may well symbolize an aversion to Americans (those "odious squatters" like Old Satan, that untutored natural man), with Malcolm representing a dislike of the sophisticated and arrogant Briton who would sneer at the efforts and achievements of people of the Moodies' class in Canada.

That Susanna Moodie thought of herself as a heroine of fiction is doubtful. Autobiography normally presents self in a good light, and although circumstances offered her many opportunities to display herself as a heroine, she does not portray herself in any way as the faultless heroine. If she thought herself a heroine at all, it was as a woman, a kind of proto-feminist, eager to demonstrate a woman's strength and right and ability to assume a responsible place in society. She is a romantic heroine only from a certain modern perspective, a twentieth-century standpoint that disregards her difference from the "weaker vessels" of Victorian fiction. Her behaviour derives essentially from the English gentry, not the English romance, from her desire to transplant the values of her upbringing, not of her reading.

Aside from studies of the book as local colour fiction or as women's travel writing, the search for design seems to have become a lost cause. David Jackel proclaims that the book has "no structure" (Peterman, 81). Michael Peterman regrets that there are always "loose ends no scheme can sufficiently account for" (80). More recently, John Thurston, writing from the linguistic angle that presumes all texts to be indeterminate, finds only loose ends. Lacking textual and generic stability, the book is for him a thing of "inadequacies of language . . . of contradictions, generic amorphousness, open-endedness, and disunity," but one that manages nonetheless "to articulate the contradictions at the root . . . of the Canadian consciousness" (195–203).

In general, *Roughing It in the Bush* is social history that centres on the tensions in pioneer Canadian society, which involved for the most part the cultured (European middle-class culture or Old World) and the uncultured (North American or New World), the civilized and the primitive (or nature and civilization). Since Susanna Moodie's intellect and emotions were always deeply involved in this struggle, the resulting tensions are a source of much of the power that lifts the book above the other similar descriptions of life in early Ontario—that, and Moodie's literary talent, of course. In more specific terms, *Roughing It in the Bush* is a personal narrative of the Moodies' experiences on the frontier from 1832 to 1840. The book falls into two parts. The first eleven chapters present Susanna Moodie as an emigrant, largely as observer and social historian, who through scenes involving visits to and from neighbours discloses innumerable facts about settlement life, from details about domestic matters to generalizations about religious and financial affairs, and manners and customs. The remainder of the book (chapters 12–26) focuses on Mrs. Moodie as wife and mother in a settler's home, a role that challenged her on every score and a role that, as family fortunes fell, helped her rise above the prideful woman who had come on stage at Grosse Isle.

Regarding the two-part division and the overall movement of the book, the sketches are neither "helter-skelter" fragments nor haphazardly-ordered fictional interludes. They follow a roughly chronological order in the book and involve its three major tensions sequentially: human beings in society, in nature, and as individuals. Many of the sketches, however, had been published previously in *The Literary Garland* and *The Victoria Magazine*, and in a different order from that of the book. Consequently, the rearrangement in the published book argues that the sketches constitute an integral part of the book's formal and thematic plan. (See Appendix.)

The first chapters introduce some of the major tensions—the past and English culture versus the future and North American pioneer culture—and lead directly to sketches involving Tom Wilson, which embody these conflicts. The opening chapters set the hopes of an elegant mansion on an estate against the actuality of a shanty amid stump-filled fields in a half-cleared countryside. They link the Moodies with a past, a time when they had lived graciously but when, like many of England's upper class, they had fallen on hard times. Wilson warns too of the threat of a bleak future in a land where gentlefolk of the Old World mean little, where they must be on guard against Old Satans (one of whom Wilson outwits) in the New World and where gentlemen unfitted for its rough life often fail. Finally, Wilson is one of a series of visitors (along with Monaghan, Malcolm, and John E——) who are touchstones for Moodie's behaviour and values, while serving to enrich and humanize the social history she relates. (Significantly, Wilson drops from the narrative when the Moodies leave for the wild lands of the north.) "Uncle Joe and His Family" focuses directly on a resident Canadian, as opposed to an emigrant, and so presents another, but different, aspect of backwoods society. Unfortunately, Uncle Joe substantiates none of Moodie's expectations, financial or cultural. She learns through him, though, that large land holdings in Canada are unrelated to the genteel life that they symbolized in England. Here, the land holder is a hard-pressed farmer; there, one of the leisure class.

The study of Canadian society continues with John Monaghan (one of the first in a long line of hired men, now an endangered species in our life and literature), but from a different point of view. A more intimate portrait than either Wilson's or Uncle Joe's, it would seem to come from a deeper level of Moodie's consciousness. Monaghan challenges her disposition towards the Irish. In the sketch "A Visit to Grosse Isle," written after "John Monaghan," she probably exaggerated her aversion to the Irish so that "John Monaghan" would demonstrate more forcibly the broadening of her humanitarianism under the influence of frontier life. Later she does introduce other Irishmen, one of whom, Mr. Y——, exemplifies for Moodie the kind of person who should come to Canada, whereas the other, Captain N——, indicates the gentleman immigrant completely out of place in the backwoods.

Having tested in the crucible of experience a preconceived notion of settlement society, Moodie then turns to her preconceived view of nature, a Wordsworthian view, as she reveals in her initiatory trip up the St. Lawrence River. She discovers that Wordsworth's concept of the natural world no more fits the reality of the Canadian wilderness than his solitaries, men supposedly living close to God in nature, resemble Uncle Joe and Old Satan. Poor Phoebe proves the point too that one finds God in nature only after finding him elsewhere. She lives in the rural world, but is godless. Accordingly, Moodie takes up the question of the relationship between revealed and natural religion, and in "Brian, the Still-Hunter," she examines it in some detail. Through Brian she learns indirectly that nature can be harsh and cruel, that wolves and lichens are as much parts of it as "noble" deer and beautiful flowers. Yet her central problem remains. Does an individual get close to nature by collecting scientific specimens (a fad of the period) or by living in it? Neither Brian nor the botanist demonstrates, however, that an individual *is* "alone with God in the great woods" (1913, 223). Fundamentally, Moodie is trying here to reach some kind of conclusion about the wilderness and society and about romantic nature, about God, human beings, and the great cyclical relationship of life to death, that other still-hunter who may feel "sorry for" the wild creatures even as he kills them.

The first half of *Roughing It in the Bush* closes with "The Charivari," using the indigenous folk custom to juxtapose the social world with the natural world of Brian the Still-Hunter; thus, Moodie brings the story full circle with reminiscences of emigration and a discussion of settlement mores and customs. It completes that aspect of the book that centres on general social history. In the first half of the book, at least seven of its eleven chapters are character sketches; of the last fourteen chapters, only two are, and of these, one is her husband's work, "The Ould Dhragoon," a half-humorous introduction to the Moodies' own rough times described next in "Disappointed Hopes."

Having already examined setting and society in broad personal terms, Moodie turns in the second half of the book to herself as individual and repeats the pattern of the first half. From chapter 13, "The Wilderness," to chapter 18, "Disappointed Hopes," she presents her daily life as she lived it in the clearing. The focus then narrows even further, with chapter 19, "The Little Stumpy Man," and chapter 20, "The Fire," both of which reflect her inner self. Finally, in "The Outbreak" (chapter 21) and "The Whirlwind" (chapter 22), she examines that same self, but now in isolation, using, in turn, the same frames of reference—society, nature, and the individual. "The Walk to Dummer" (chapter 23) broadens the focus to include all three parameters and sets the last two chapters in perspective, where she proves herself a woman of competence and human sympathy, and where, in closing, the narrative returns to pioneer society.

The second half of the book immediately reveals a new perspective. It opens with "A Journey to the Woods" (literally to and through the wilderness), which parallels the touristic "Our Journey up the Country," when the Moodies, full of fearful hope, made their way up the beautiful St. Lawrence River. As in the opening of the book, "Our Journey" immediately describes the Moodies' neighbours, but here as "our Indian friends," as if to expose by comparison Uncle Joe and his ilk as even greater reprobates. The second half of the book, however, centres on Mrs. Moodie's own reactions and activities rather than on those of neighbours.

"Our Logging Bee" dramatizes authentic social history but also discloses Moodie's failure to appreciate the levelling process that the bee symptomized, an incipient egalitarianism that was to have important political consequences. The following sketch, "A Trip to Stony Lake," is also important, although it is largely descriptive. Klinck unfortunately omitted it in his edition of the book, as if to stress the book's fictional mode and to play into the hands of those who consider Mrs. Moodie an incessant grouch. This omission is particularly regrettable for both the book itself and its usefulness in the classroom, since the deleted sketch again demonstrates her skillful use of contrast—a favourite device—for structuring narrative (in, for example, the opening sketches of the first and second halves of the book). This omitted sketch also reveals that for Moodie not all society was composed of ruffian squatters, such as gathered at the bee. She makes it plain here too that she recognizes the opportunities the New World does offer to the right kind of immigrant. Despite her life on the frontier, moreover, she finds her sensibilities neither dulled nor debased; the grandeur of nature moves her as deeply as ever. But she reveals as she returns home and greets her little boy that what is right is the experience of human community, rather than devotion to some romantic ideal of communion with nature.

The second half of the book reaches its centre with "The Little Stumpy Man" (the seventh chapter of the thirteen between "A Journey to the Woods" and "Adieu to the Woods"), which provides a centre in terms of both narrative and Moodie's study of self. The earlier sketches are generally societal and descriptive; "The Little Stumpy Man" is personal and experiential. It involves Moodie consciously and subconsciously, or intellectually and emotionally, as through Malcolm she figuratively confronts her inner and former self, thereby becoming aware of her own previously unacknowledged weaknesses and deficiencies. Others had criticized her, largely her social behaviour, criticism she readily attributed to her detractors' insensitivity and lack of breeding. Malcolm finds fault on different grounds. She is a prude. She is a farmer's wife who is afraid of cows (though significantly her response here differs from her response to the same criticism by Mrs. Joe). She suffers from mock-humility, a feeling of superiority, as she discovers later when she "astonished" poor "Dunbar" with her rudeness during tea with Malcolm and Mr. Crowe. Worst of all, she "needed to be a better cook" (1913, 432). Though an angry Mr. Moodie is on her side (he had helped with the meal), she finds Malcolm's disparagements, which are emphatically personal and from a man of her own class, hurtful. They mark a new phase in the growth of Mrs. Moodie's personality.

After Malcolm's visit, the narrative in "The Fire" immediately focuses on another "ordeal by fire." This time it is a real rather than an emotional fire, as Mrs. Moodie fights to save her children and home. As author, she wanted to point up the contrast between the terrified Mrs. Moodie of "Burning the Fallow" and the brave new self-reliant Moodie. Significantly, "The Fire" continues the process of self-recognition with the visit of John E——, a young gentleman who provides a perfect standard of reference for her personal and cultural values. In his presence, she can indulge her neglected femininity, disclose her softer side as woman of the house, and re-establish respect for her social status. "John," she notes, "always grieved . . . to see me iron a shirt, or wash the least article of clothing for him" (1913, 449).

In the sketches and episodes that follow "The Fire," the book maintains its subjective orientation as Moodie tests her new self in isolation, for with "The Outbreak," when Mr. Moodie goes soldiering, the book becomes a chronicle of roughing it in the bush alone. In the next chapter, "The Whirlwind," the storm (which actually occurred before, not after, the uprising of 1837 [1848, 192–93]) acts as a natural, symbolic parallel to the rebellion which, like the storm and Moodie's concurrent illness, represents a force beyond her control. Taken together, they emphasize the place of the social, natural, and personal in the pattern of the book and, in addition, accentuate her newly-discovered humility in her loneliness. "I felt," she laments as she concludes the chapter, "more solitary than ever" (1913, 495). And these were difficult years for her, as her recently discovered letters to her husband make clear.

"The Walk to Dummer" follows "The Whirlwind" logically, despite Klinck's implicit disavowal in his omission of it from his edition of the book. In "The Walk," Mrs. Moodie pays tribute to friendship, even to her Irish servant Jenny, just as she had in the first book to John Monaghan, and dramatizes a bleak winter-time event that brings home to her the meaning of charity and friendship in both personal and broad social terms. Here, then, Moodie synthesizes her chief preoccupations with society, nature, and self as never before. As setting, the winter scene is also significant for its social history; it presents the "pitiless wild," where the gentleman (as class or individual whose proper place is the old country) may live a desperate and poverty-stricken existence.

"Adieu to the Woods" brings the narrative to an end. Old Woodruff, the successful settler whose portrait closes the book, counterbalances the sketches of those failures, Tom Wilson and Uncle Joe, which opened it. Moodie has now examined pioneer society from numerous angles. Taken together, the sketches of *Roughing It in the Bush* form a mosaic, a designed pattern rather than a hodge-podge of reminiscences. Part of that pattern is the theme, a recurring motif that involves genteel emigrants who exemplify Moodie's belief that Canada was no fit place for them. Her final paragraph is apt, simply stating what the narrative has repeatedly illustrated from the beginning with Tom Wilson's misadventures: that no one should risk everything to emigrate hoping to recoup fortune and re-establish social prestige. Unlike in the first pages of the book, Moodie's Canada is, finally, the land of the "industrious working man" (1913, 562), now viewed not as someone who belongs to a lower order, but as someone who is part of a new society that is developing into a new class of educated and prosperous Canadians. She has learned a lesson she would have the English gentry learn as well: that one can no more successfully transport one's Old World society to the New World than one can transplant a Wordsworthian ideal of nature in the reality of the Canadian wilderness.

Susanna Moodie's story of "roughing it" is over, not simply because she has learned her lesson and leaves the woods, but also because she has completed the literary structure of *Roughing It in the Bush*: she has surveyed her life there as it relates to the community, the natural world, and her own development. In adversity, she has found the way to objectivity and maturity. More hard knocks would not further develop her personality or her "character." The reader may dislike the Susanna Moodie her story reveals, but such a judgement is beside the point. The merit of the book as art depends on art, not personality, on Moodie's ability to recreate character and to describe her experiences with imaginative sympathy. Even such apparent virtues as the narrative mode, unity of character, serious treatment of themes, and the skillfully wrought structure involving the depiction of settlement and clearing and the exploration of the inner self—even these are not the only bases for the long continuing interest in *Roughing It in the Bush*. Another strength derives from its setting, for the backwoods is no mere backdrop. It is a living frame of reference in the age-old struggle between human beings and nature. *Roughing It in the Bush* presents that conflict and society's response to it, not as a single response, but as many responses centring on the human situation when Canada was in the making.

## APPENDIX

The order of publication of Moodie's sketches as book chapters and in *The Victoria Magazine* (*VM*) and *The Literary Garland* (*LG*) is indicated below. The numbers in parentheses give the publication sequence for the periodicals.

| *Chapters* | | *Magazines* | | |
|---|---|---|---|---|
| 1 | A Visit to Grosse Isle | (6) | Sept. 1847 | *VM* |
| 2 | Quebec | (10) | Nov. 1847 | *VM* |
| 4 | Tom Wilson's Emigration | (4) | June 1847 | *LG* |
| 5 | Our First Settlement and the Borrowing System | (3) | May 1847 | *LG* |
| 7 | Uncle Joe and His Family | (5) | Aug. 1847 | *LG* |
| 10 | Brian, the Still-Hunter | (8) | Oct. 1847 | *LG* |
| 17 | Dandelion Coffee (pp. 394–96) | (7) | Sept. 1847 | *VM* |
| 22 | The Whirlwind | (9) | Jan. 1848 | *VM* |
| 23 | The Walk to Dummer | (2) | Mar. 1847 | *LG* |
| 25 | Adieu to the Woods (Old Woodruff and his Three Wives) | (1) | Jan. 1847 | *LG* |

## WORKS CITED

Ballstadt, Carl, et al., eds. 1985. *Susanna Moodie: Letters of a Lifetime.* Toronto: Univ. of Toronto Press.

Fowler, Marian. 1982. *The Embroidered Tent: Five Gentlewomen in Early Canada.* Toronto: House of Anansi.

Klinck, Carl. 1962. Introduction to *Roughing It in the Bush.* Toronto: McClelland and Stewart.

MacDonald, R. D. 1972. "Design and Purpose." *Canadian Literature* 51 (Winter).

Moodie, Susanna. 1848. "Description of a Whirlwind." *The Victoria Magazine* 1, no. 5 (January).

Moodie, Susanna. 1913. *Roughing It in the Bush.* Toronto: Bell & Cockburn. (This text is Susanna Moodie's final version [1871] and the first Canadian publication. See Alec Lucas, *The Otonabee School* [Montreal: Mansfield Book Mart, 1977].)

Peterman, Michael A. 1983. "Susanna Moodie." In *Canadian Writers and Their Works.* Ed. Robert Lecker et al. Downsview, Ont.: ECW Press.

Shields, Carol. 1977. *Susanna Moodie: Voice and Vision.* Ottawa: Borealis Press.

Thurston, John. 1987. "Rewriting *Roughing It.*" In *Future Indicative: Literary Theory and Canadian Literature.* Ed. John Moss. Ottawa: Univ. of Ottawa Press.

# Susanna Moodie

## "The tongue of woman": The Language of the Self in Moodie's *Roughing It in the Bush*

BINA FREIWALD

$\mathbf{T}$wo important moments are identified with the conception of this essay. The first is a personal one, best captured by my copy of the 1962 New Canadian Library edition of *Roughing It in the Bush*.[1] It is a slim volume, marked up savagely in fine-point red pen by a hand seeking out all references, literal or figurative, to mothers and children; and there is hardly a page that has escaped the red fury. The hand, I might add, belonged to a scholar hard at work on a manuscript dealing with artistic self-representation in nineteenth-century women's writing. While her infant daughter was being cared for in a nearby nursery, she read, marked, and eventually dismissed Moodie's narrative as only marginally relevant to the topic at hand. That scene of reading, however, was to be revisited. The second moment, a theoretical one, centres on a recent shift in feminist articulations of the gendered subject. An aspect of this shift that is particularly pertinent to the present discussion concerns the emergence of a new thematization of motherhood "that reflects the evaluation of motherhood as an essentially positive activity and insists on its disalienating recuperation by and, in the first instance, for women themselves" (Maroney, 41).

The shift in theorizations of the relationship between female experience and female expression, in relation to which my engagement with Moodie's narrative situates itself, might best be illustrated by juxtaposing two critical statements; interestingly, both are cast in the interrogatory mode. The first is from Nina Auerbach's unambiguously entitled essay "Artists and Mothers: A False Alliance," which opens with this rhetorical question:

> Did the Brontes, Jane Austen, and George Eliot write out of a thwarted need
> to give birth, sadly making substitute dream children out of their novels?
> Or did they produce art that allowed them a freer, finer, more expansive

world than the suppressions of nineteenth-century motherhood allowed?
(171).

Having formulated the predicament of the nineteenth-century woman writer
in terms of the antagonistic pull of the mutually exclusive cultural myths of
motherhood and artistic creativity—as prescribed by a climate of opinion which
dictated that "one can be a speaker or a mother but not both" (Homans, 1986,
38)—Auerbach celebrates the resolution of the double bind in the triumph of
creativity and the total rejection of motherhood: "In the lives of Jane Austen
and George Eliot, two woman artists made inescapably aware of the social
assumptions equating womanhood with motherhood, art is a liberation from
that demand, not a metaphoric submission to it . . . . Austen and Eliot both
turned away from motherhood and embraced a creativity they defined as more
spacious, more adult, more inclusive" (183). The second theoretical statement
introduces the parameters of a still novel and tentative investigation to which
the present essay seeks to contribute. Susan Rubin Suleiman reacts to
Auerbach's categorial dissociation of writing and motherhood by proposing
to interrogate the terms of this much maligned (mis)alliance, and at least provisionally introduce a different agenda: "Is there no alternative to the either/or?
Will we ever be forced to write the book and deny the child (not the child we
were but the child we have, or might have) or love the child and postpone/
renounce the book? . . . It is time to let mothers have their word" (360).
Suleiman calls upon another mother's inquiry—Kristeva's "que savons-nous
du discours que (se) fait une mère?"—to motivate and sustain a project which
she renders in her own mother tongue: " 'what do we know about the inner
discourse of a mother?' " (368).

From its whimsically humorous (and blatantly ethnocentric) opening
episode, in which Susanna Moodie describes the spectacle of a shrivelled-up
health inspector aboard the *Anne* screaming at the ship's captain—"'sacre, you
bete! you tink us dog, when you try to pass your puppies on us for babies?' "—to
its dramatic and sentimental conclusion, in which Moodie is reunited with her
daughter Addie and bids farewell to the backwoods, *Roughing It in the Bush*
unfolds as a narrative shaped by the complex vision and singular voice of its
first-person narrator. Already in its opening pages, where the pronominal "I"
first assumes the materiality of a character and the narrator begins to weave
her presence into the fabric of her tale, we witness a double figuration, a
doubling which is to mark the subject of this discourse, its speaking subject.
Standing amid "fat, chuckle-headed" bull-terrier puppies, surrounded by
"boats heavily laden with women and children," Moodie not only brings into
textual existence a universe populated by mothers and their offspring, but is
*always also* (in contradistinction to the deconstructive dictum of 'always already')
marked herself/marks herself as a figure of mothering. As she makes her first
appearance in the text, Moodie's entrance is not a solitary entrance, just as

it will not be her choice to stage a solitary exit. "I watched boat after boat depart for the island," Moodie observes as she insinuates herself into the narrated scene, stepping out of the shadowy "we" of the first paragraphs and into the mother-with-child figure that is to occupy centre stage: "I was left alone with my baby in the otherwise empty vessel" (21).

The originating moment of Moodie's story—the decision to emigrate—is presented as a specifically maternal moment: "I had bowed to a superior mandate, the command of duty; for my husband's sake, *for the sake of the infant, whose little bosom heaved against my swelling heart,* I had consented to bid adieu for ever to my native shores, and it seemed both useless and sinful to draw back" (137; emphasis added). From its moment of inception, Moodie's narrative is marked by a double logic signalled by the mother's separation from her own mother—the native "mother country" (xvi)—and her bonding with the child who is to sustain her gaze and reconcile her to the new "land of [her] adoption . . . [Canada] the great fostering mother of the orphans of civilization" (56). This maternal gaze will remain constitutive of the narrative perspective; within the framework of a feminist challenge to deconstructive valuations of language, it can be understood as more "speech" than "writing," more a manner of communicating than the substance of the tale. Questioning the deconstructive rejection of the possibility of a mode of communication that can create presence, Margaret Homans has sought to reclaim a form of "speech" less easily collapsed into identification with the Derridean understanding of "writing" as creating meaning in the *absence* of what it refers to. Homans argues that a presence, and more specifically a co-presence of the self and the other, is established (however provisionally) in "parents'—historically mothers'— talk with children who have not yet learned symbolic language, talk that has the aim not primarily of representation but rather of creating contact" (1987, 158–59). On one level of the narrative deployment of signs in *Roughing It in the Bush*, a maternal idiom is introduced that partakes of the character of this "speech" which exceeds and escapes the recognized economy of representation and self-representation. It is an idiom that embodies a "remembering of what androcentric culture represses," as it recreates the experience of listening to and producing speech that circumvents the symbolic order, the *logos*.

As we follow the narrator around, we are informed about conditions in this new and strange land. We are told of its cold winters and inhospitable inhabitants; we hear of the trials of a gentleman-turned-farmer and of the peculiarities of a large cast of characters. While busily painting these panoramic vistas for the reader, Moodie is always also doing something else, something that never fails to engage her, that never fails her: mothering. We can only sample here a few of these innumerable moments of homecoming, quick maternal glances seeking reassurance that the child is there, brief moments of discursive bonding, islands of relatedness in a stormy, unpredictable, often hostile sea. In "A Visit to Grosse Isle," Moodie writes: "My husband went off with the boats, to reconnoitre the island, and I was left alone with my baby in the otherwise empty vessel" (21). A few pages later: "The rough sailor-captain screwed his mouth on one side, and gave me one of his comical looks; but he said nothing until he assisted in placing me and the baby in the boat" (24). A little further: "the mosquitoes swarmed in myriads around us, tormenting the poor baby, who, not at all pleased with her visit to the new world, filled the air with cries" (27). In the second chapter entitled "Quebec," she writes: "I had just settled down my baby in her berth, when the vessel struck, with a sudden crash that sent a shiver through her whole frame" (33). There follows the episode of the near wreck where Moodie plays mother to another distraught girl whose own mother fails her. In the aftermath of the storm, Moodie enjoys the comforting intimacy of a cosy trio: mother, daughter, and the dog Oscar (himself a trusted mother-substitute): "When my arms were tired with nursing, I had only to lay my baby on my cloak on deck and tell Oscar to watch her, and the good dog would lie down by her, and suffer her to tangle his long curls in her little hands, and pull his tail and ears in the most approved baby fashion, without offering the least opposition; but if anyone dared to approach his charge, he was alive on the instant, placing his paws over the child and growling furiously" (35).

There is always a child at Susanna's side. In chapter three, "The Journey up the Country," she writes: "the fear and dread of [the cholera] on that first day caused me to throw many an anxious glance at my husband and my child" (38). Stopping for the night at a small inn, she approaches the innkeeper: "I asked him if he would allow me to take my infant into a room with a fire" (44). In chapter five, the Moodies are on their way to their first settlement, and as the spring morning turns chilly, Susanna observes: "the baby cried, and I drew my summer shawl as closely round as possible, to protect her from the sudden change in our hitherto delightful temperature" (68). On the occasion of the first visit of Old Satan's daughter, the first borrower, the scene opens with a crying child: the "poor baby . . . lying upon a pillow in the old cradle, trying the strength of her lungs, and not a little irritated that no one was at leisure to regard her laudable endeavors to make herself heard" (70). Moodie's exposition on the borrowing system is further accentuated by the very tangible presence of the "poor weanling child" who wants for milk, and the borrower's unfeeling mockery: "when I asked my liberal visitor if she kept cows, and would lend me a little milk for the baby, she burst out into high disdain" (73). The chapter closes with the episode of the borrowed candle, occurring years later, yet partaking of the same quality of maternal anxiety; the youngest boy is sick, and as Tom the cat has made away with the borrowed candle, the chapter ends on a sinister note only slightly alleviated by the temporal distance between the narrating and narrated instances: "My poor boy awoke ill and feverish, and I had no light to assist him, or even to look into his sweet face, to see how far I dared hope that the light of day would find him better'' (83).

It is a rare moment in *Roughing It in the Bush* when the narrator appears unaccompanied by one or more of her children. Discursively, the narrating 'I' is rarely a discrete, separate entity; her idiom, a maternal idiom, populates the discursive universe of *Roughing It in the Bush* with an endless procession of ''children'': her children and other people's, as well as figurative children—children of the Divine Mother Nature, of ''the Great Father of Mankind'' (220), the sons and daughters of England and Canada, the native children of the land. These children draw the self out of its convenient-conventional fictional mould; they blur the boundaries between 'I' and 'you' and obliterate the distinction between inner and outer. A recurrent stylistic pattern which is emblematic of this narrative positionality consists of a shift in focalization, within a single sentence, from mother to child: ''My teeth were chattering with the cold, and the children were crying over their aching fingers at the bottom of the sleigh'' (234).

Who, then, speaks in *Roughing It in the Bush*? The question is not meant to restore an originating subject, authorial or otherwise, an immutable essence which fixes meaning and circumscribes sense. Rather, the attempt to grasp the subject who speaks is an attempt to seize a subject in its ''functions, its interventions in discourse, and its system of dependencies'' (Foucault, 1977, 137). For the subject is inextricably implicated in the play of differences that constitutes discourse, inasmuch as the subject is a subject produced in language—''the basis of subjectivity is the exercise of language''[2]—and in the sense that ideology (as the work of discourse) can be seen to constitute individuals as subjects: ''ideology has the function (which defines it) of 'constituting' concrete individuals as subjects . . . all ideology hails or interpellates concrete individuals as concrete subjects, by the function of the category of the subject'' (Althusser, 160–62). The subjectivity I seek to identify, then, is a ''process, not a structure of the subject. If language is the site of the symbolic constitution of the subject in the movement of the signifier, then that constitution is always historical, multiple, heterogeneous, always specific and specifying subject effects'' (Heath, 1979, 40).

Who speaks in *Roughing It in the Bush*? It is a subject who is possessed of, to use Moodie's own words, ''the tongue of woman.'' The opening through which I enter her narrative is a brief digressive anecdote Moodie uses to illustrate her observation that ''strange names are to be found in this country.'' It is perhaps not accidental that it is a reflection on naming—on the subject-constituting gesture par excellence by which an individual is first and last interpellated—that allows us an insight into the narrator's own self-constructing idiom. Moodie writes:

> It was only yesterday that, in passing through one busy village, I stopped in astonishment before a tombstone headed thus: ''Sacred to the memory

of Silence Sharman, the beloved wife of Asa Sharman.'' Was the woman
deaf and dumb, or did her friends hope by bestowing upon her such an impossible name to still the voice of Nature, and check, by an admonitory appela-
tive, the active spirit that lives in the tongue of woman? Truly, Asa Sharman,
if thy wife was silent by name as well as by nature, thou wert a fortunate
man (94).

Digressions, according to that other fantastic narrator-autobiographer, Tristram
Shandy, ''are the life, the soul of reading;—take them out of this book for
instance,—you might as well take the book along with them'' (Sterne, 1980, 52).
It might well be that if we took out of Moodie's book that which her digression
ventures to identify, if we stilled or silenced the ''voice of nature'' which she
finds distilled in the ''active spirit that lives in the tongue of woman,'' little
would remain of the life of the story. A woman's tongue, nature's voice, native
idiom, mother tongue, the mother's tongue: these are the co-ordinates, the
discursive interventions and dependencies that constitute the language of the
self in *Roughing It in the Bush*. A subject interpellated and self-constituted as
speaking a female idiom, the mother's tongue, Moodie's is a complex and
multiple subjectivity doubly marked by the traces of women's historically paradoxical position in discourse and a defiant resistance of this anomalous
condition.

How does a maternal language of the self become constitutive of a speaking subject? The difficulties surrounding this question can be gleaned from
a brief survey of the critical literature on Moodie's generically hybrid text.
Although the narrator's professed intention in *Roughing It in the Bush* is to reveal
the ''secrets of the prison-house'' by giving a ''faithful picture of a life in the
backwoods of Canada'' (236–37), for her twentieth-century critics the prisoner,
not the prison-house, has held the greater attraction. Carl Klinck's introduction to the 1962 New Canadian Library edition of *Roughing It in the Bush* unequiv-
ocally asserts the work's autobiographical character and stresses the thematic
and structural significance of its narrator's personal voice:

> *Roughing It* was wholly autobiographical, her own book; she was the author-
> apprentice-heroine. Everything pointed to her trials and her [partial] salva-
> tion . . . . Sharing in all the actions, and progressively enlarging the image
> of herself, she gave a pattern of movement to the whole book (xiv).

Margaret Atwood's *The Journals of Susanna Moodie* (1970) has been
another particularly influential and exemplary reading of *Roughing It in the Bush*
as autobiographical writing, as a narrative primarily conceived to explore and
give voice to a tortured and agonistic subjectivity. Atwood inaugurates her
poetic cycle with a poem that announces the primacy of the perceiver over the
perceived, as the persona enacts a ritualistic gesture by which observation is
transformed into introspection:

I take this picture of myself
and with my sewing scissors
cut out the face.

Now it is more accurate:

where my eyes were,
every-
thing appears.

The last poem in the cycle reaffirms the power of the creator over the created, as a resurrected Susanna defiantly rearranges time and space to establish the co-ordinates of an all-devouring identity. She tells the person sitting across from her on the bus travelling along St. Clair:

Turn, look down:
there is no city;
this is the centre of a forest

your place is empty.

In her afterword to *The Journals of Susanna Moodie*, Atwood articulates a view that has become a critical commonplace: the prose of *Roughing It in the Bush* and *Life in the Clearings* is discursive and ornamental, and the books, which are collections of disconnected anecdotes, have little shape. The only thing that holds them together, Atwood contends, is the personality of Susanna Moodie. The emphasis on the narrator's writing of her self into a tale ostensibly concerned with an external reality—with other people and the harsh realities of a foreign land, etc.—has persisted.[3] Carl Ballstadt argues that Moodie seems unable to resist projecting herself into the scenes she describes, and Carol Shields contends that a unifying force of a greater validity than the "nature-God-spirit trinity" characteristic of much nineteenth-century writing might be found in Susanna's "overriding sense of her own personality . . . every scene is filtered through her sensibility; every character encountered is studied in context with herself" (6).

The self that has been observed to dominate the narrative of *Roughing It in the Bush* has most often been identified as a fragmented, vulnerable, and tormented self. Much has been made of Susanna's condition of alienation and estrangement, the cultural shock she suffers and the consequent fragmentation of identity. Carol Shields gleans, from beneath the persona's vigorous appearance, a self desperately seeking confirmation of its existence, without which it will dissolve, unwitnessed and unverified, in an alien environment. Marian Fowler describes Susanna as a "mass of contradictions and startling contrasts" and contrasts the "conventional, English Susanna," who "stubbornly clings to the English stereotype of the delicate female," with Susanna the pragmatist, the quick-acting Dasher and courageous frontierswoman (101). For critics like Atwood and Fowler, the mother's experience and a maternal idiom are associated with a constraining and disabling sphere of female existence, and thus fundamentally at odds with the artist's creative imperative. For Fowler, Susanna the mother is a predictable avatar of the all-too-familiar sentimental heroine: an anxious admirer of cherubic innocence, a passive, patient sufferer in the face of continual affliction. Since for Fowler the drama that makes *Roughing It in the Bush* a literary masterpiece consists of the challenge to female stereotypes by an androgynous self, which "wheels and soars in male preserves," she can only see in Susanna's mother tongue an artificial, hollow, borrowed idiom. The children are easily dismissed: "children in sentimental fiction are very [sic] touchstones of sensibility" (119, 108). For Atwood, Susanna's mother tongue speaks forcefully but in ominous tones of separation, loss, death. There is the poem "Death of a Young Child by Drowning," and in "The Deaths of the Other Children," Atwood writes:

> Did I spend all those years
> building up this edifice
> my composite
>           self, this crumbling hovel?
>
> My arms, my eyes, my grieving
> words, my disintegrated children
>
> Everywhere I walk, along
> the overgrowing paths, my skirt
> tugged at by the spreading briers
>
> they catch at my heels with their fingers

In Atwood's recent introduction to the Virago edition of *Roughing It in the Bush*, this linking of motherhood with the "crumbling hovel" of the flesh/self is again placed in the foreground, as Atwood reminds the contemporary reader:

> We should remember too that the years she spent in the bush were child-bearing ones for her; in those days before modern medicine, when a doctor, even if there had been one available, wouldn't have been much help, not all the children eventually survived. Mrs. Moodie is reticent on the subject, but she says at one point, rather chillingly, that she never felt really at home in Canada until she had buried some of her children in it (VP, xii).

Moodie's anxiety over the life-threatening crises suffered by the children, from food deprivation to a near-fatal typhus epidemic, are indeed movingly communicated in *Roughing It in the Bush*; her initial reluctance to let go of certain Victorian ideals of feminine conduct is indeed irritating. Yet a critical perspective that remains satisfied with such partial views of her character can hardly begin to account for the centrality and complexity of the mother's relation to language and to the discourses that define and are redefined by her. We might start to attend to these issues by reflecting on the vital links that connect the thematic focus of *Roughing It in the Bush*—a preoccupation with emigration as an experience of territorial, cultural, and psychic displacement—with its narrator's use of a maternal idiom. We would do well, however, to prepare for such a discussion by noting the conceptual and ideological hazards involved in such a task.

Drawing on the work of feminist theorists like Mary Jacobus and Nancy Chodorow, Margaret Homans has recently proposed a redefinition of the project of feminist criticism that underscores not only the challenges ahead but also the risks involved:

> feminist criticism aims to recover the women and the women's voices that have been lost or repressed, but only in such a way as to avoid replicating the structures that brought about that repression in the first place. The question is how to redefine our sense of what ''women's voices'' or ''women's experience'' might be—to change the conditions of representability . . . so as to recover those losses without losing them all over again (1987, 172–73).

How, then, to represent the mother tongue in *Roughing It in the Bush* in a way that will not result in losing Moodie to the idiom of the family romance, in which the mother's desire is absorbed into—subsumed under—the father's and the child's, without losing her to a script that places her sacrificial passivity in the foreground by hailing their expansive actions and unrelenting demands? A necessary precondition for a revisionary reading will thus involve a recognition of the historically specific moment into which Moodie's discourse inserts itself. Margaret Homans suggestively articulates a context within which a narrative like Moodie's can be better appreciated:

> In the nineteenth century, when women's lives were increasingly defined in relation to a standard of womanhood, regardless of whether or not they were of childbearing age, women who wrote did so within a framework of dominant cultural myths in which writing contradicts mothering. Paradoxically, the high value placed on mothering as a vocation for women is entirely consistent with the devaluation of everything women did relative to men's accomplishments (1986, 22).

Elaborating on this paradoxical subject-position which has marked women's fictions of self-representation, Sidonie Smith further observes:

> On one hand, she [the female autobiographer] engages the fictions of selfhood that constitute the discourse of man and that convey by the way a vision of the fabricating power of male subjectivity . . . . But the story of man is not exactly her story; and so her relationship to the empowering figure of male selfhood is inevitably problematic. To complicate matters further, she must also engage the fictions of selfhood that constitute the idea of woman

and that specify the parameters of female subjectivity, including women's problematic relationship to language, desire, power, and meaning. Since the ideology of gender makes of woman's life script a nonstory, a silent space, a gap in patriarchal culture, the ideal woman is self-effacing rather than self-promoting, and her 'natural' story shapes itself not around the public, heroic life but around the fluid, circumstantial, contingent responsiveness to others that, according to patriarchal ideology, characterizes the life of woman but not autobiography (1987, 50).

Viewed in the light of these observations, Moodie's predicament as a female narrator-autobiographer appears to parallel that of her feminist reader, for in both instances what is at stake is a reclamation of a range of historically specific female experiences and expressions which have been appropriated to serve the ends of an androcentric culture that denigrates them.

An uneasiness with this problematic discursive positionality of the female 'I' is, in turn, reflected in stories of reading which occlude or evade the terms of the dilemma. Atwood's reading, for example, ultimately elides the problematic ('personal') female subject by transforming her tale into the public story of a genderless Canadian psyche. One could easily substitute "he" for "she" in Atwood's paradigmatic description of Moodie in the afterword to *The Journals of Susanna Moodie* without disturbing the logic or the rhetoric of that description. Fowler seems to favour a similar position, for she valorizes a movement away from the feminine and towards the androgynous. In both cases, the interpretive matrix seems to involve a rejection of the mother—a gesture Sidonie Smith identifies as a further symptom of women's paradoxical condition within discourse:

> as she [the woman writing] appropriates the story and the speaking posture of the representative man, she silences that part of herself that identifies her as a daughter of her mother. Repressing the mother in her, she turns away from the locus of all that is domesticated and disempowered culturally and erases the trace of sexual difference and desire . . . . "[she] cannot assume this identification with the Father except by denying her difference as a woman, except by repressing the maternal within her" (1987, 53).

Has repression of the maternal been the only recourse for women writers? Susan Suleiman, who has undertaken an initial exploration of the mother's discourse, observes two major thematic clusters in women's writing: motherhood as obstacle or source of conflict and motherhood as link, as source of connection to work and world. *Roughing It in the Bush* exhibits the latter tendency. On the most basic level, the maternal idiom appears as perhaps the single constant in an otherwise fairly volatile and shifting self. Whatever her preoccupation at a given moment, whatever her inclination, mood, or circumstance, Moodie's narrating and narrated 'I' is always also a mother's 'I'. As we move from the category of character to the formal and rhetorical modalities that govern *Roughing It in the Bush*, we observe that the mother's tongue is articulated on three interrelated planes of the narrative complex. As a modality of being which marks the narrator's presence in her tale, it manifests itself through that co-presence of the self and other which brings together mother and child. This relational subject-position is thematized in the narrator's appeal to a maternal idiom for the purpose of self representation, as Moodie freely alternates between the poles of motherhood and childhood, between speaking as provider and source of power, and pleading as a needy child or a helpless supplicant. In a second instance, the mother's idiom is further thematized as an ethical principle, a principle by which Moodie—as the prime narrative mover—both constructs and judges her character creations. Finally, the mother's idiom manifests itself as a rhetorical operation of changing registers from figurative to literal and back to figurative, a rhetorical operation heavily charged with mythic and thematic significance as it suggests a negotiation between a paternal symbolic (figurative) writing—regarded as being outside the female sphere—and a 'properly' feminine (literal) mode of expression.

The last of the three practices of the mother tongue—the shifting of rhetorical registers from figurative to literal—is perhaps the least conspicuous yet most pervasive of the three, as it contains, frames, and supports the mother's discourse in *Roughing It in the Bush*. Indeed, the narrative's central thematic concern with the experiences of displacement, relocation, and eventual naturalization is most profoundly transformed by a practice which Margaret Homans has characterized as "bearing the word": "the literalization of a figure [which] occurs when some piece of overtly figurative language, a simile or an extended or conspicuous metaphor, is translated into an actual event or circumstance" (1986, 30). In Moodie's text, as in the works of the other nineteenth-century women writers studied by Homans, this literalization of figures, when more specifically connected to female themes, articulates the woman writer's "ambivalent turning toward female linguistic practices and yet at the same time associating such a choice with danger and death" (Homans, 1986, 30). On the microtextual level, such an instance of "bearing the word"—in which a figure is literalized to voice a peculiarly maternal anguish—is evident in a sentence like the following from "The Outbreak": "How often, during the winter season, have I wept over their little chapped feet, *literally* washing them with my tears" (215; emphasis added). On the macrotextual level, the originating matrix of *Roughing It in the Bush* constitutes an exemplary instance of 'bearing the word.' For the experience of emigration is articulated by Moodie through the extended figure—which is then literalized—of the loss of childhood and a separation from the mother. In relation to their native land, emigrants, for Moodie, forever remain children; they are the "high-souled children of a glorious land," and their memories are those of the "local attachments which stamp the scene amid which [their] childhood grew" (xv). Immigration and naturalization, in turn, are conceived in terms of adoption and the maternal embrace of a new parent. "British mothers of Canadian sons!" Moodie exhorts her female readers, "make your children proud of the land of their birth" (30).

When applied to Moodie herself, this extended maternal figure spells out the painful passage from childhood to motherhood. She bemoans the loss of the mother and the ending of childhood, mourning the severance of the strongest of bonds:

> Dear, dear England, why was I forced by a stern necessity to leave you? What heinous crime had I committed that I, who adored you, should be *torn from your sacred bosom*, to pine out my joyless existence in a foreign clime? (56; emphasis added).

In Canada, Moodie is no longer a child but a mother, and her experience of loss is no longer that of the orphan but of the bereaved mother. As she 'bears the word' here, the figure of the mother country is both sustained and literalized, and both the mother country and Moodie the mother become associated with those experiences most resistant to symbolic representation, life and death:

> Canada! thou art a noble, free, and rising country—the great fostering mother of the orphans of civilization. The offspring of Britain, thou must be great, and I will and do love thee, land of my adoption, and of my children's birth; and oh—dearer still to a mother's heart—land of their graves (56).

Finally, presiding over this human drama which shapes and determines the narrator's destiny is another maternal figure: "Nature, arrayed in her green loveliness, had ever smiled upon me like an indulgent mother, holding out her arms to enfold to her bosom her erring but devoted child" (56).

As the figure of the mother is literalized in *Roughing It in the Bush* through the innumerable instances of mothering which define and identify the narrator's position, a concomitant emphasis works to establish the mother's idiom as a general principle of character construction in the story. From Oscar the dog to Malcolm "the little stumpy man," through John Monaghan, Bell, Jenny, Wilson, Jacob, Brian the still-hunter and others, characters in *Roughing It in the Bush* are judged by their ability to interact with, care for, and communicate with children. These patterns of behaviour are grasped as fundamentally constitutive of both their pragmatic actions and moral conduct. The blessed in Moodie's ethical universe are characters like John Monaghan who, "standing alone in the wurld," is nonetheless capable of attaching himself "in an extraordinary manner." Moodie lovingly and gratefully recreates for us this exemplary maternal scene:

> All his spare time he spent in making little sleighs and toys for her [Katie, the baby], or in dragging her in the said sleighs up and down the steep hills in front of the house, wrapped up in a blanket. Of a night, he cooked her mess of bread and milk, as she sat by the fire, and his greatest delight was to feed her himself . . . . Katie always greeted his return from the woods

with a scream of joy, holding up her fair arms to clasp the neck of her dark favourite (109–10).

The most striking instance of a maternal idiom that literalizes the figurative, however, is found in the narrator's double vision of herself as both mother and child. Caught between her own mother country and her children's country of birth, between her own childhood (which the mother country will always represent) and her children's childhood (which turns her into a mother), Susanna learns a critical lesson: "you cannot exalt the one at the expense of the other without committing an act of treason against both" (30). Literally, the lesson learned is that of balancing and attending to the respective claims of mother and child. The most enabling function of Moodie's mother tongue is to allow her to be not only her child's mother but also her mother's child.

By coming to Canada, Moodie becomes a permanent exile, a "stranger in a strange land" (37) as she keeps reminding the reader and as other characters keep reminding her. "I am a stranger in the country," Moodie tells her first borrower, Old Satan's daughter; and in an aside to the reader: "In fact we were strangers, and the knowing ones took us in" (83). Brian the still-hunter greets them with "You are strangers; but I like you all" (125). In a recognizably Romantic moment of existential anguish Moodie reflects on her share in the human predicament of self-estrangement: "The holy and mysterious nature of man is yet hidden from himself; he is still a stranger to the movements of that inner life, and knows little of its capabilities and powers" (221).

A closer scrutiny of this critical moment, however, reveals a rhetorical strategy which is emblematic of the narrator's subject-position in *Roughing It in the Bush*. The passage cited in which Moodie's sense of alienation and displacement is projected onto the larger arena of the human psyche forms the middle part of a paradigmatic mini-narrative which opens the important penultimate chapter entitled "Of A Change in Our Prospects." The maternal idiom is already suggested in the poetic epigraph to the chapter, a poem which introduces at its very structural and thematic centre "the embryo blossom." The chapter opens with Moodie as a grieving mother and a forlorn child. An illness has forced a separation from her second daughter, who has been taken in by a kind, neighbouring family. Hardly ever excessive when speaking of the children, Moodie's tone is charged but restrained as she speaks of the separation and loss: "During that winter and through the ensuing summer, I only received occasional visits from my little girl, who, fairly established with her new friends, looked upon their house as her home" (220). In the next paragraph, it is Moodie who is the little girl, a motherless or fatherless child, longing to be reunited with the "Great Father of mankind" as she lays down her throbbing head on the pillow beside the other child, her firstborn son, and "sleep[s] tranquilly" (220). Moodie is delivered from misery as she becomes, as it were, her own mother, as she envisions "a purer religion," the Mother of Christianity giving birth to a "beauteous child of God"; deliverance lies in delivery as the mother's labour pains release her and the child-humankind into a brighter future. Moodie prophesies:

> Oh, for that glorious day! It is coming. The dark clouds of humanity are already tinged with the golden radiance of the dawn, but the sun of righteousness has not yet arisen upon the world with healing on his wings; the light of truth still struggles in the womb of darkness, and man stumbles on to the fulfilment of his sublime and mysterious destiny (221).

In Moodie's version of the family romance, Father and Mother merge in the all-encompassing, ever-expansive force of Nature. In her isolation and fear Moodie sees herself as one of Nature's children, a "little brook" with its "deep wailings and fretful sighs" which sobs and moans "like a fretful child" (100, 130). Threatened and besieged, Moodie is anxious as a fretful child but also fearful for the child she risks losing to sickness or to the darker force of nature, here epitomized by the wolves: "just as the day broke my friends the wolves set up a parting benediction, so loud and wild, and near to the house, that I was afraid lest they should break through the frail window, or come down the low, wide chimney, and *rob me of my child*" (130; emphasis added). Yet Mother Nature ultimately never fails Moodie: she is there at the break of dawn, solemn, majestic, and beautiful; she is there reassuring, unconditionally loving: "As long as we remain true to the Divine Mother, so long will she remain faithful to her suffering children" (100).

Nature is the mother Moodie can always return to as a child, but it is also the mother who takes her away from her child. On those occasions when Moodie is most self-conscious as a writer, we find her adopting a Romantic idiom which laments the inadequacy of words to capture the beauty of Nature and to express the "pure and unalloyed delight" that it offers the observer. In these moments, Moodie reclaims for herself the privilege of the child, gratefully acknowledging the indulgence of Mother Nature and the Great Father. This is the *writer's* primal scene as it materializes for Susanna aboard the *Anne* on her voyage from Grosse Isle to Quebec:

> Nature has lavished all her grandest elements to form this astonishing panorama. There frowns the cloud-capped mountain, and below, the cataract foams and thunders; . . . regardless of the eager crowds around me, I leant upon the side of the vessel and cried *like a child . . . my soul at that moment was alone with God* (29; emphasis added).

While being "alone with God" is the child's prerogative, it is also the mother's transgression. The concluding passage from "A Trip to Stony Lake" best dramatizes this tension between the mother's need to be mothered—to receive and indulge herself, to be sustained so she can grow and leave home, so she can write—and the mother's recognition of another's need. Susanna is returning from an exhilarating expedition with her husband on which she took the two older children, leaving the younger boy behind:

It was midnight when the children were placed on my cloak at the bottom of the canoe, and we bade adieu to this hospitable family . . . . The moonlight was as bright as day, the air warm and balmy; and the aromatic, resinous smell exuded by the heat from the balm-of-gilead and the pine-trees in the forest, added greatly to our sense of enjoyment as we floated past scenes so wild and lonely—isles that assumed a mysterious look and character in that witching hour. In moments like these, I ceased to regret my separation from my native land; and, *filled with the love of Nature, my heart forgot for the time the love of home* . . . . Amid these lonely wilds the soul draws nearer to God, and is filled to overflowing by the overwhelming sense of His presence.

It was two o'clock in the morning when we fastened the canoe to the landing, and Moodie carried up the children to the house. I found the girl still up with my boy, who had been very restless during our absence. *My heart reproached me, as I caught him to my breast, for leaving him so long*; in a few minutes he was consoled for past sorrows, and sleeping sweetly in my arms (VP, 338–39; emphasis added).

Framed and contained by the presence of the children—the children safely asleep at the bottom of the canoe, the infant son restlessly waiting at home—Moodie's moment of inspiration, of flight from the literal into the realm of the "mysterious," is significantly a 'forgetting' of "home." Transported by the experience of beauty and an aesthetic vision, the adult woman writer forgets not only the home of her childhood ("my native land") but also her children's home, that is, forgets herself as a mother. As a result, the moment becomes marked by those traces of maternal guilt that Susan Suleiman has found to be symptomatic of the discourse of "the mother-as-she writes":

I would suggest that in the case of the writing mother, the subtle undermining, the oppressive feeling of impotence and insignificance . . . are intimately linked to a sense of guilt about her child. Jean-Paul Sartre once said in an interview, when asked about the value of literature and of his own novels in particular: "En face d'un enfant qui meurt, *La Nausée* ne fait pas le poids" [freely translated: "When weighted against a dying child, *La Nausée* doesn't count"] . . . . What are we to say about the guilt of a mother who might weigh her books not against a stranger's dying child but merely against her own child who is crying? (364).

In the mother tongue, however, there is no outside-of-home (as we know there is no *hors texte* or outside-of-text), for the very assumptions upon which such a distinction would be based are apprehended as a false dichotomy. The heart that forgets is also the heart that remembers and reproaches.

As the mother writes, she engages with the cultural myths of her particular historical moment, myths that define her relation to nature, to language, and to the self. For Moodie, to create is to write within and against a literary tradition that reinforces her otherness through a conflation of woman and nature and through an exclusive identification of the speaking subject as male.[4]

Maternal guilt is the price she has to pay for entering the symbolic order, for breaking the daughter's silence and speaking the mother. Once this price has been paid, Moodie is freed and free to carry on the negotiation between mother and child, between the child in the mother and that mother's child. *Roughing It in the Bush*, then, is perhaps not only the expression of an ambivalent colonizing consciousness, nor merely the expression of a paranoid schizophrenic condition; it is more than a textual space inhabited by a personality "split by the institution and system of *la langue* as she [Moodie] carries it and *la parole* as she finds it actualized in Canada" (Thurston, 1987, 202). In one recent rewriting of *Roughing It in the Bush*, the critic tells of a divided house and a broken home, an invaded narrative and a frustrated, threatened narrator:

> Moodie is most at home in this text when she is writing in the lyrical, hortatory, or didactic modes. She is drawn to these monologic modes as potential systems of narrative but they continually let her down. The verbal home she [Moodie] attempts to build is invaded by the voices of others. The characters who enter speak in no generic mode known to her. She tries to reduce them to the low comic or diabolic. They reassert themselves as embodiments of the carnivalesque (Thurston, 1987, 201).

But isn't "home" also where the children are, and isn't Moodie indeed "at home" with them, in speaking of, to, and with them? And what of those peace gatherings, so unlike the scenes of (sexual?) violence suggested above, where Moodie speaks of, to, and with other characters (both male and female) similarly possessed of the mother tongue? *Roughing It in the Bush* may be about more than divided national loyalties, the pioneer experience and the challenge of the wilderness, man's existential anguish—all those worthy themes we have been taught to look for in the best works of art. It is perhaps also about something much closer to home, something that has been kept out of sight for too long, something Moodie calls "maternal feelings" (VP, 476). There is a story told in *Roughing It in the Bush* that we have not been reading. In one of its many beginnings, it goes like this: "old Jenny and I were left alone with the little children, in the depths of the dark forest, to help ourselves in the best way we could" (VP, 458). And very well they did, too!

## NOTES

I would like to acknowledge the assistance of the Social Sciences and Humanities Research Council of Canada in the preparation and writing of this paper.
1.   Since the New Canadian Library (NCL) edition of *Roughing It in the Bush* is still the most widely used one, I have used it as my text throughout. References to material left out of the NCL edition are to the 1986 Virago Press edition (identified as VP).
2.   Benveniste (226) cited in Silverman (44).

3. There have been, however, dissenting voices; see Groening.
4. On the predicament of the nineteenth-century woman writer, see Gilbert and Gubar, and Homans (1980).

# WORKS CITED

Althusser, Louis. 1971. "Ideology and Ideological State Apparatuses (Notes Towards an Investigation)." In his *Lenin and Philosophy*. New York: Monthly Review Press.
Atwood, Margaret. 1970. *The Journals of Susanna Moodie*. Toronto: Oxford Univ. Press.
Auerbach, Nina. 1986. *Romantic Imprisonment: Women and Other Glorified Outcasts*. New York: Columbia Univ. Press.
Ballstadt, Carl. 1972. "Susanna Moodie and the English Sketch." *Canadian Literature* 51: 32–37.
Benveniste, Emile. 1971. *Problems in General Linguistics*. Trans. Mary Elizabeth Meek. Coral Gables: Univ. of Miami Press.
Foucault, Michel. 1977. "What is an Author?" *Language, Counter-Memory, Practice*. Ed. Donald Bouchard. Trans. D. Bouchard and S. Simon. Ithaca: Cornell Univ. Press.
Fowler, Marian. 1982. *The Embroidered Tent: Five Gentlewomen in Early Canada*. Toronto: House of Anansi.
Gilbert, Sandra, and Susan Gubar. 1979. *The Madwoman in the Attic: The Woman Writer and the Nineteenth Century Literary Imagination*. New Haven: Yale Univ. Press.
Groening, Laura. 1982–83. "*The Journals of Susanna Moodie*: A Twentieth-Century Look at a Nineteenth-Century Life." *Studies in Canadian Literature* 7–8: 166–80.
Heath, Stephen. 1979. "The Turn of the Subject." *Cine-Tracts* 8: 32–48.
Homans, Margaret. 1987. "Feminist Criticism and Theory: The Ghost of Creusa." *The Yale Journal of Criticism* 1.1.
———. 1986. *Bearing the Word: Language and Female Experience in Nineteenth-Century Women's Writing*. Chicago: Univ. of Chicago Press.
———. 1980. *Women Writers and Poetic Identity*. Princeton: Princeton Univ. Press.
Kristeva, Julia. 1983. "Stabat Mater." In her *Histoires d'amour*. Paris: Denoel.
Maroney, Heather Jon. 1985. "Embracing Motherhood: New Feminist Theory." *Canadian Journal of Political and Social Theory* (special issue *Feminism Now*) IX, nos. 1, 2: 40–64.
Moodie, Susanna. 1962. *Roughing It in the Bush*. New Canadian Library. Toronto: McClelland and Stewart.
———. 1986. *Roughing It in the Bush*. Introduction. Margaret Atwood. London: Virago Press.
Shields, Carol. 1977. *Susanna Moodie: Voice and Vision*. Ottawa: Borealis Press.
Silverman, Kaja. 1983. *The Subject of Semiotics*. New York: Oxford Univ. Press.
Smith, Sidonie. 1987. *A Poetics of Women's Autobiography: Marginality and the Fictions of Self-Representation*. Indianapolis: Indiana Univ. Press.
Sterne, Laurence. 1980. *Tristram Shandy*. 1760–65. New York: W. W. Norton.
Suleiman, Susan Rubin. 1985. "Writing and Motherhood." In *The (M)other Tongue: Essays in Feminist Psychoanalytic Interpretation*. Ed. Shirley Nelson Garner, Claire

Kahane, Madelon Sprengnether. Ithaca: Cornell Univ. Press. 352–77.

Thurston, John. 1987. "Rewriting *Roughing It.*" *Future Indicative: Literary Theory and Canadian Literature*. Ed. John Moss. Ottawa: Univ. of Ottawa Press.

# "Splendid Anachronism": The Record of Catharine Parr Traill's Struggles as an Amateur Botanist in Nineteenth-Century Canada

## MICHAEL A. PETERMAN

**C**atharine Parr Traill's achievements as a "natural historian" have not gone entirely unnoticed in this century. In a number of brief descriptive articles published in the 1970s, she receives glowing praise for her two botanical studies, *Canadian Wild Flowers* (1868) and *Studies of Plant Life in Canada* (1885). Jean Cole argues that "so little work was done in the field in her day that her text [*Plant Life*] now stands as a unique record of Canada in its natural state, before the hand of man obliterated many of its tender and timid native plants" (79). For Elizabeth Collard, "Mrs. Traill not only achieved a place among recognized botanists, she made original contributions to that science" (32). Linking Traill's studies to her social role, Elizabeth MacCallum notes:

> The occupation of collecting flowers seems a more appropriate interest to a lady of Mrs. Traill's era than ecology, but the seriousness of her botanical pursuits went beyond a genteel taste for floral beauty. She was interested in every aspect of the plant: its appearance, its medicinal and nutritional value, its life cycle and its relation to other flora and fauna (45).

Tributes of this kind appear in a variety of contemporary books and magazines. They are characteristically descriptive and honorific, and they deserve praise as attempts to recognize an important and often overlooked aspect of Traill's work. At the same time, however, these commendations neglect the complexities and tensions of the world of nineteenth-century Canadian science in which Traill was a distant and small player.

Among more recent interpreters of nineteenth-century Canadian literature and culture, there has been a noticeable tendency to downplay or ignore the entire botanical aspect of Traill's work. At best, it is regarded as a matter of tangential concern. Traill is most likely to be studied as a counterpoint to her more dynamic and outspoken sister Susanna Moodie and as the author of pioneer memoir, settlers' guidebook, and instructive stories and sketches for children. Despite efforts of scholars like Clara Thomas, William Gairdner, David Jackel, and Carl Ballstadt, there is a tendency to be intellectually dismissive of Traill's work as a whole. This tone was set by Northrop Frye who in *The Literary History of Canada* criticizes Mrs. Traill for promoting in Canada a sentimental myth of nature derived from Wordsworth. Detecting an inclination to turn away from snakes and reptiles, Frye locates in her sensibility "a somewhat selective approach to the subject reminiscent of Miss Muffet" (845). In a later essay in *Divisions on a Ground*, he labels her more favourably as "a miniature Thoreau," a writer whose flower studies make her an "exceptional, if not unique" contributor of detailed "still life" in early Canadian writing (51). It has recently become increasingly fashionable to label her dismissively as a pioneer who used domesticity not only to evade the grim realities of life in the backwoods but also to disguise her own paranoia.[1]

This context draws attention, explicitly and implicitly, to a number of problems facing any attempt at serious inquiry into Catharine Parr Traill's achievements as botanist and natural historian. Among these are the literature student's lack of scientific expertise and resistance to science *per se*; the difficulty of getting beyond glowing generalizations in describing such scientific contributions; and the danger of seeing Traill too exclusively within the context of a contemporary thesis or from the point of view of contemporary psychological assumptions. Despite such pitfalls, it may still be possible, through a close look at Mrs. Traill's career and work as a natural historian, to foster inquiry that will deepen understanding not only of her personal struggles and achievements but also of the problems she faced as a woman and a scientific amateur in the developing, still fragile world of late nineteenth-century Canadian science.

With an eye particularly upon Traill's reputation as a student of botany in her own time, let me offer two indicative views. In the *Proceedings and Transactions of the Royal Society of Canada* for 1897, D. P. Penhallow, Professor of Botany at McGill University, contributed a well-received historiographic paper entitled "A Review of Canadian Botany from 1800 to 1895." An American with a degree in science from Boston University, Penhallow had become "an outstanding authority on the paleobotany of Canada" (Wallace, 657). His essay is a report to the élite and initiated, full of praise for important botanists like Frederick Pursh, a German who died in Montreal in 1820, George Lawson, John Macoun, the Abbé Léon Provancher, Sir William Hooker, and Canadian-born Sir William Dawson. In his bibliography, which lists over 100 names and nearly 500 pieces of writing, Professor Penhallow mentions no women. Catharine Parr Traill, then ninety-five years old and the subject of some government attention, is nowhere named, even as a gifted amateur. It is only in the context of Sir William Hooker's remark in his *Flora Boreali-Americana* (1840)—

"the more densely inhabited parts of Canada have produced many native botanists" (11)—that Penhallow names two women, Lady Dalhousie and Mrs.
(Anne Marie) Percival. He consigns them, however, to obscurity with these
words:

> It seems probable, therefore, that owing to their work being wholly confined
> to collecting, and in the absence of published writings, their names have
> gradually fallen into neglect, and the part they played in the advancement
> of Canadian botany—important if obscure—cannot now be ascertained, and
> it is more than probable that there were many others, of whom all trace has
> been completely lost (12).

His gracious bow to genteel amateurism suggests not only ignorance
of Lady Dalhousie and her work in the Literary and Historical Society of
Quebec but also an inadvertent smugness that follows from professional training, status, and advantages. When he later discusses the sorry state of the teaching of botany and botanical research in Canadian universities—"Our universities are yet doing in large measure what more properly belongs to the high
schools" (25)—and applauds the work of the newly formed Botanical Club of
Canada (c. 1892) in promoting "the study of botany among the various schools
throughout the country" (19), he might well have found a place to acknowledge Traill's efforts to promote and broaden the study of plants, ferns, and
trees among Canadians. That he does not may well betray a double professional
bias, against the amateur scientist on the one hand and against woman as
scientist on the other.

In his essay Penhallow does praise two self-educated Ottawa-based
scientists who were particularly friendly to Traill and sympathetic to her efforts.
Both John Macoun (1832–1920), author of many botanical treatises and
member of the Geological Survey of Canada, and James Fletcher (1852–1910),
who after serving as Librarian of Parliament became the Central Experimental
Farm's first entomologist and botanist, were instrumental in the process of
seeing *Studies of Plant Life in Canada* into print. In preparing the manuscript,
Traill closely studied Macoun's recent *Catalogue of Canadian Plants—Part I.
Polypetalae*, published by the Geological and Natural History Survey of Canada
in 1883. The copy he presented to her includes her pencilled annotations on
her own sightings of plants in Ontario and on special medicinal properties or
folkloric information pertaining to particular flowers.[2] Freeing time from his
busy schedule, Macoun was also helpful to Traill and her socially prominent
niece, Agnes Chamberlin (née Moodie, formerly Fitzgibbon), in locating both
a publisher and a number of prominent subscribers for *Plant Life*.

More important still was James Fletcher. Though overworked in his
capacity as parliamentary librarian, he found time to correct and edit Traill's
manuscripts and to see them through publication. A "valuable friend" to Traill,
he corresponded with her from January 1883, a year before they met, until

1898. His letters reveal his unwavering respect, courtesy, and admiration. In November 1883, he wrote:

> I am charmed with your style and find it so attractive after the irreverent materialistic philosophy, falsely so called, of too many of our modern naturalists. It is very charming to me to see such love for our beneficent creation, & reverence for his perfect works. In all my instructions in botany I have always endeavoured to draw attention to the marvelous & beautiful adaptations, of all objects presented to us in the study of nature, to their required ends and to show how much we have in this lovely world to make us happy.

A decade later, on July 26, 1894, Fletcher paid Traill a stirring tribute in response to her sending him yet another "collection of beautiful specimens":

> With regard to your disclaiming the title of botanist, all I can say is, that I wish a fraction of one percent of the students of plants who call themselves botanists, could use their eyes half as well as you have done. I think indeed your work of describing all the wild plants, in your book, so accurately that each one could have the name applied to it without doubt, is one of the greatest botanical triumphs which anyone could achieve, and one which I have frequently spoken of to illustrate how one can develope [sic] their powers of observation.

Juxtaposing the views of Penhallow and Fletcher, the one coolly professional, the other warmly personal, establishes a ground for considering Traill's work as a natural historian and botanist. She was not a trained scientist nor did she have the language training, books, equipment, or funds to carry on sophisticated study. She had very little knowledge of or exposure to what Penhallow calls the "higher" range of botanical interests that deeply engaged late nineteenth-century scientists. Financially strained and for the most part isolated in "the backwoods," either near Lakefield or Rice Lake, she was limited to the flora of the locales in which she lived, relying on her own observations, on letters, books, and magazines (when affordable), and on occasional visitors as the means to broaden the range of her inquiry.

Her "passion for flowers" (1836, 120), nurtured in Suffolk, England, and evident in her early English publications,[3] led to her initial gatherings ("my hortus siccus boasts of several elegant specimens of fern") soon after her arrival in Upper Canada. It also led to her desire to name, at first "according to inclination or fancy" (1836, 120), the unknown plants she was discovering in her Katchewanook rambles. She knew nothing of marine or Arctic vegetation, of the study and implications of fossils (paleobotany), of lichens and algae. She had little sense of ongoing botanical research. Nowhere in her writings, published or unpublished, is there mention of Charles Darwin, "the reluctant father of a revolution that," in Carl Berger's words, "ultimately destroyed traditional natural history and the amalgam of science and faith" (53). She had no desire to be more than descriptive, informative, evangelical, and useful in her cataloguing. As such, John Macoun, whom Traill regarded as "the Father of Canadian Botany" (1885, 209) and who zealously guarded his reputation as Canada's foremost professional botanist, could privately say of her, in the wake of *Plant Life*'s publication, that she "was not a critical botanist" (Berger, 83 n. 8). Ironically, Macoun later admitted in a letter: "I have no time for critical examination and must hand my material over to others" (Berger, 24). Berger, in fact, sees Macoun as representative of the state of organized botany in late nineteenth-century Canada; despite his reputation, he was a man who "cultivated, and became very dependent upon, expert correspondents" from elsewhere (25). By necessity so did Traill, but on a far more modest scale and from a sustainedly Paleyite perspective.

Macoun, Penhallow, and Traill herself seem implicitly to have accepted the Victorian assumption of separate spheres for men and women, especially for gentlemen and gentlewomen. It was for men to think—to be analytical, critical, and professional, to assume and perpetuate authority. It was for women to feel and nurture—to be decorous, familial, and retiring, to accept authority's wisdom and beneficence. Such assumptions were reinforced by the slow and belated process of professionalization of the sciences in colonial Canada. The Royal Society of Canada, founded in 1882 as a national medium for scientific activity, admitted, "by invitation, only men of recognized merit and achievement" (Berger, 19). Reading between the lines of Penhallow's academy study, one notes, not surprisingly, a zealous regard for separating the wheat from the chaff, the professional from the amateur, the methodologist from the observer, men of achievement from female collectors of flora. Thus, while Penhallow feels it worthwhile to devote several pages of his essay to the story of Frederick Pursh's gravesite, he completely ignores the work of such gifted amateurs as the then-forgotten Charles Fothergill and the more publicly prominent Catharine Parr Traill. Critical botany had become rigorously exclusive by the time Traill's *Studies of Plant Life in Canada* appeared.

In *Science, God, and Nature in Victorian Canada*, Carl Berger accurately describes Traill's *Studies of Plant Life in Canada* as "a splendid anachronism" (35). Her roots as a natural historian lay with Isaak Walton and Gilbert White, guides and mentors who were as vital to her in 1885 as they had been in her girlhood. She cherished the memory of reading *The Compleat Angler* with her father while fishing in the Waveney in rural Suffolk. In later years, she referred often to Walton and kept her father's copy of the book close by until her death. In a letter dated October 14, 1884, James Fletcher acknowledged Traill's gift of her "sketch of Walton": "it gives me much more of an interest in that grand old book than I ever had before" (Traill Family Papers, vol. I). In her preface to *Studies of Plant Life in Canada*, Traill is similarly nostalgic, hoping that her work might "become a household book, as Gilbert White's Natural History of Selborne is to this day among English readers" (xvii). She throws in her lot temperamentally with "the old florists and herbalists of former times [who] were more gallant than our modern botanists, for they gave many pretty names to the flowers instead of the harsh-sounding, unmeaning ones that we find in our scientific manuals of Botany" (1885, 85–86). At the same time, she clearly recognizes that "the student of botany [would] not be content merely with [her] superficial, desultory way for acquiring a more intimate acquaintance with the productions of the forest and the field" (1885, 209). Similarly, in the face of the increasing professionalization of medicine in her later years, she resisted the growing assumption that science and scientific method held the key to all. She came to see herself as a hold-out, "a regular old quack" who was often more comfortable with folk remedies than with the advice of modern doctors (1856).

American historian Henry Adams once ruefully defined himself as a nineteenth-century man given an eighteenth-century education to prepare him for the twentieth century. In this spirit, Catharine Parr Traill might be seen as a nineteenth-century woman given an eighteenth-century education to prepare her, not for the twentieth century, but for emigration and isolation in the backwoods of the New World. Once in rural Upper Canada and awakened to the botanical wonders around her, she sought to catch up as best she could, familiarizing herself with scientific method and classification in order to co-ordinate her study. Though she struggled over many decades to apply what she understood to be correct botanical categorization and nomenclature in her various inventories, her persistent desire was to create "short floral biographies" (1885, 150) or calendars in which the story—the name, season, appearance, lore, and useful properties—of the plant or flower were pleasingly presented.[4] The audience she imagined for herself was largely female, high-minded, and of British origin. "Mothers of Canada," she wrote in *Plant Life*,

> teach your children to know and love the wild flowers springing in their path, to love the soil in which God's hand has planted them, and in all their after wanderings through the world their hearts will turn back with loving reference to the land of their birth, to that dear country, endeared to them by the remembrance of the wild flowers which they plucked in the happy days of childhood (viii–ix).

For Traill, the study of flowers was a nurturing process, engendering not only peace of mind through all the stages of life but also a firm sense of identity and place, of rooted continuity. Flowers were "the first of nature's books," as accessible to children as to sensitive cultivated adults. They could awaken "that higher inward life that is the gift of God to man," and they could be "an enduring source of pleasure" (1863, 55). In personal terms, the study of nature and particularly of flora helped sustain Traill through the prolonged difficulties, deprivations, "home-longings," and deculturation of her backwoods experiences. One cannot gainsay the psychological worth of flowers to her. Her statement in *Plant Life*—"But for the Canadian forest flowers and trees and shrubs, and the lovely ferns and mosses, I think I should not have been as contented as I have been away from dear old England''—benignly masks much of her personal struggle simply to survive (xvi).

Flowers provided an invaluable emotional continuity for Traill, a continuity between past and present, childhood and maturity, Suffolk and Upper Canada, and cultivation (civilization) and wilderness (the state of wildness). They offered a distinctive measure by which she could personally apprehend and weigh matters of time, space, moral worth, and most importantly, the divine order affecting all life. In *Plant Life*, she praises the infinite wisdom and mercy of God's—''the Great Creator['s]''—''arrangements'' (25): ''There seems in the vegetable world, as well as in the moral, two opposite principles, the good and the evil. The gracious God has given to man the power, by the cultivation of his intellect, to elect the good and useful, separating it from the vile and injurious, thus turning that into a blessing which would otherwise be a curse'' (28). By inclination and choice, she refused to dwell upon the ''dark side of the picture'' (1836, 94). From her earliest to her final written work, she was remarkably consistent in her attitude towards, and uses of, natural history. Always without irony, she sustained her focus on nature's salutary qualities, and this is what distinguishes her writing from the works of her sisters and most of her contemporaries. The naturalist in her loomed very large; natural history was for her a kind of autobiography.

It is not my purpose here to make extravagant claims for Traill as an overlooked botanist. However important Traill's work is, it had little impact on the study of botany in Canada in the last half of the nineteenth century. Penhallow's historical observations are valid, though unnecessarily and insensitively restrictive. Suzanne Zeller confirms this in her placement of Traill in her recent and detailed study *Inventing Canada: Early Victorian Science and the Idea of a Transcontinental Nation.*

Traill was an outsider to the emerging, self-conscious, and self-promoting world of science in colonial Canada. Her interests and skills, rooted in her Suffolk upbringing, disposed her to follow a non-specialized and holistic direction in her studies of nature. Lack of access to scientific information and guidance frustrated her, as she noted in *Backwoods*, but it is unlikely that mere access to more information, even as early as the 1830s, would have significantly altered—which is to say professionalized—her approach. In fact, as an amateur with a passion for flowers, she already shared many of the philosophical and cultural imperatives underlying the work of most of the early eminent botanists of Canada. She had, however, no desire to be a methodological scientist.

For much of the nineteenth century, the natural historian and the practising scientist walked parallel paths in Canada in their response to ''nature's unpredictable and brutal force'' (Zeller, 3). The ''rational study of nature,'' according to Zeller, ''displac[ed] art as the 'dominant cultural mode' of Britain's new industrial civilization'' (3) and offered a hopeful ''counter-thrust'' to the problems of geography and a northern climate, a means of moving beyond ''mere survival'' to ''real prosperity'' (3). It was very much a part of the spirit of the era that ''Any individual could add piecemeal to the stock of knowledge,'' or more purposefully, to the ''common inventorial purpose'' (4) which characterized the emerging study of botany in colonial Canada. Indeed, it was not until the 1870s when the Geological Survey of Canada was expanded to include natural history that an ''obvious institutional focus for a [national] botanical inventory'' appeared (184). The emergence of university chairs in botany, of botanical and horticultural societies, and of scientific magazines like the *Canadian Naturalist* (1856–57) and the *Canadian Agriculturalist* (1849) also contributed significantly to that slow process of development.

At the same time, according to Carl Berger, the tradition of linking the study of nature with natural theology, a tradition rooted in seventeenth-century British thinking, ''went generally unchallenged until the later Victorian period'' (31). The inventorial thrust of nineteenth-century Canadian botany was supported by a deep-rooted conservatism. The assumption of and belief in ''the beneficence of the prevailing order'' (49), writes Berger, ''gave science a legitimacy in a profoundly religious culture'' such as Canada's (50). Darwin's ideas were critically attacked in Canadian scientific circles; indeed, a leading Canadian geologist, William Dawson, became perhaps Darwin's major antagonist in the 1870s (70, 60).

Traill shared with early Canadian scientists a commitment to natural history. It was a tradition particularly suited to literary ambitions. Carl Berger defines its salient features: ''It was an instrument for the appropriation and control of nature and a vehicle through which divine purpose stood revealed; it was at once an acceptable form of leisure and a path to recognition; it provided an outlet for intellectual activity in a colonial environment that seemed to have no past and no traditions to stimulate the literary imagination'' (77). The path Traill travelled, however, was marked by many frustrations and disappointments that were peculiar to her own situation. This goes some way towards explaining her anachronistic place even in the slow and conservative development of Canadian botanical study. Certain of her surviving letters provide glimpses of, if not explanations for, many of the problems she faced.

*The Backwoods of Canada* clearly establishes Traill's passionate interest in flowers and her struggles to overcome her ''scanty stock of [scientific] knowledge'' (233). But shortly after the book's publication in 1836, the fortunes of the Traill family took a turn for the worse. Thomas Traill's unfortunate investments and debts, his frequent depressions, and his sale of their Katchewanook farm in 1839 left them virtually impoverished in the mid-1840s. In at least one instance, their survival depended entirely on the charity of friends. Not surprisingly, her surviving letters during this decade tell little of botanical projects, except to show her sustained enthusiasm for the natural world, to ask friends for samples, or to comment on outings and discoveries of specimens.[5]

The letters of the 1850s reveal a somewhat more aggressive Catharine Parr Traill, almost desperately pursuing publishing opportunities in order to provide money for her impoverished family. Spurred by the publication of *Canadian Crusoes* in England in 1852 and by opportunities offered by various magazines, including the Rochester-based *Horticulturalist*, she was nevertheless frustrated in her attempt to find a publisher for her "Forest Gleanings" (which had appeared as sketches in *The Anglo-American Magazine*) and likely also for her plant and fern manuscripts. An invitation in 1855 to manage the women's department of a Hamilton magazine, "The Agriculturalist," fell through as well.[6] Meanwhile, still self-conscious about her expertise, she occasionally sent her "queries about plants" to leading scientists like Toronto-based William Hincks. She also entered her collections of dried flowers in various exhibitions in Toronto, Kingston, and Montreal.[7]

Traill was, as she admitted to her friend Frances Stewart, "the poor country mouse" when it came to exhibitions and publishing negotiations ([1862]). At the time, she was also extremely vulnerable, depending on friends and relatives in Belleville or Toronto for lodgings and keep while uncomfortably awaiting word from a publisher. After sending her plant manuscript to Mr. A. Brown of the Hamilton Horticultural Society, through late 1864 and early 1865 she desperately awaited a response, kept for months in "this suspense after all his fine words." Nearly a year later, she wrote to her eldest daughter Kate, "I begin to think there is some design in keeping the work back as there is another about to be brought out shortly. If it be so it is a mean trick but do not mention this idea as it may be unfounded and might injure me or the Hamilton Society" (1865a). As it turned out, no funds could be found for publication. A similar rebuff met Traill's submission of her fern manuscript to William Dawson of the *Canadian Naturalist*. Offering "no remark and no correction," Dawson kindly informed her that "they have all their matter for the *Naturalist* gratis." Puzzled by so unhelpful a rejection, Traill objected to Kate:

> Sir W. Hooker wrote word to Mr. Macoun that Canada was behind every one of the British Colonies and all civilized nations in Scientific literary effort especially in Botany, the only country that had not responded to his appeals. I think the Great man was right. There is certainly a great want of encouragement in this country for literary talent (1865b).

"Mary and I," she added, "are always concocting some notable scheme about *mss*, but the dear child has not succeeded and we are too poor to risk a great deal in postage for heavy paper and the chance of losing a copy" (1865c).[8]

The fact that *Plant Life* stands as "a splendid anachronism" in nineteenth-century "Scientific literary effort" owes much to Traill's vulnerability. Not only was she a shy woman living in rural Canada in impoverished circumstances. She was also often in ill health, and she lacked both business acumen and influential connections within the country. Moreover, publishing opportunities within the colony were few. By 1865, she was in her sixties, certainly less resilient and energetic than formerly, but still clinging to "a doubtful hope" that her serious botanical efforts might find publication (1865c).

The publication of *Canadian Wild Flowers* and *Studies of Plant Life in Canada* owes a great deal to her niece, Agnes Fitzgibbon. Charles Fitzgibbon, a Toronto lawyer, died in 1865, and despite six young children to raise, Traill's niece was eager to undertake a literary venture.

For *Canadian Wild Flowers*, Agnes Fitzgibbon not only taught herself lithography but found a publisher and co-ordinated a list of 500 subscribers for the first edition (1895). Then with some family help, she painstakingly coloured the ten plates for each of the books. Traill adapted some of her long-standing manuscript material to provide text for the plates and wrote a preface. For Traill, the business of selling subscriptions was as taxing as the preparation of the text. Writing to her daughter Annie Atwood, she described the comic adventures she and Kate shared as "agents" in Peterborough:

> A hard-fisted, hard-headed, hard-hearted hardware merchant . . . looked . . . as if he would have liked nothing better than throwing one of his hammers or hoes at [Kate's] head when he paid down hard cash for his book. One man kept us a long time in suspense, and at last declined on the plea that his children always tore all the books in his wife's drawing room to pieces, calling on a lean, ill-favoured vinegar bottle of a wife to endorse the fact which she did saying, "I guess they do." I merely hinted that it was rather a bad plan to let them destroy things. "Wal I guess it is but they will do it so it's no use buying things to be tore up," she said—so there was an end to the matter (1869).

There were great expectations following the success of *Canadian Wild Flowers*, but plans for a series of books and for English and American editions were thwarted in 1870 when Agnes Fitzgibbon married Brown Chamberlin and moved to Ottawa and "new duties." It was not until the early 1880s that Agnes once again encouraged Traill to publish her long-neglected plant and fern manuscripts. A wide range of connections in Ottawa society and the newly formed Ottawa Field Naturalists' Club (c. 1879) helped reawaken Agnes's ambitions. Visiting Ottawa in January 1884, two years after her niece's initial overture, Traill found herself the toast of the town. Meeting John A. Macdonald, entertained by the Governor General (the Marquis of Lorne) and his wife, and visited by some of the leading scientists and social figures of the day, she took pleasure in unusual attention and adulation. To Kate, she wrote:

> I am paid more attention to here in Ottawa than I have ever been, by the heads of society of the place, being made much of for my literary talents which of course few care for at Lakefield and which I never bring forward

myself keeping quietly the even tenor of my way—without obtruding myself, or introducing topics of this kind among my friends in our little world— there are always little matters to talk about besides books. Those that interest me most on Botany and flowers and natural history have not much charm for any out of our own, but here I find many friends among the Professors and we get on charmingly (1884).

The result of this visit—and of her niece's initiatives and enterprise, as well as John Macoun's help and James Fletcher's sustained advice and editing —was *Studies of Plant Life in Canada*, which under more congenial circumstances might have been published twenty, perhaps thirty, years earlier. Ever sensitive to her errors, ever doubtful of her scientific reference, Traill in subsequent letters expressed dissatisfaction with her contributions in the book. But at age eighty-four, when *Plant Life* at last appeared, she was doubtless grateful simply to see it in book form. While editing the manuscripts, James Fletcher had written to her: "Allow me to say I have seldom enjoyed any 'communing with nature' more than I have the perusal of your thoroughly and patently original notes on . . . 'The flowers of the field' " (1883a).

Traill's originality belongs to the gentle way in which she blended her scientific and literary interests. At a time when, in George Lawson's words, botany in Canada was "at a lower ebb than in most civilized or half-civilized countries on the face of the earth" (Zeller, 232), she was well advanced in her *Plant Life* manuscript to which she had devoted so much attention and which, in 1857, she had narrowly managed to save from the fire that destroyed Oaklands and almost all the Traill family possessions. In that text, while carefully observing botanical classification and nomenclature, and while showing deference to scientific authority, she insists upon her literary role. Thus, not only is she the beneficent creator, the namer, playing "floral godmother" by giving new-found plants identities "of [her] own choosing" (1836, 144); she is also the integrator of those literary and oral traditions (both rural and native) that reflect and celebrate a holistic sense of nature's divine and conservative order. The result is that, except among observers of similar inclinations, her work as natural historian has fallen between the disciplinary stools of botany and literature both in her own century and in our own. Recognition and under-standing of her commitment and achievement still await Catharine Parr Traill.

## NOTES

1.  See Marian Fowler's *The Embroidered Tent* and Gaile McGregor's *The Wacousta Syndrome*.
2.  The annotated text is part of the Traill Family Papers.
3.  Consider, for instance, *Sketches from Nature; or, Hints to Juvenile Naturalists*.
4.  *Wild Flowers of Canada* and *Studies of Plant Life in Canada* show numerous signs

of her scientific inquiry and correspondence. The books include references to Pursh, Dr. Charles Lee, Sir James Smith, Asa Gray, John Lindley, George Lawson, and William Hincks. In a letter to the author (June 14, 1989), Suzanne Zeller speculates that, at some point in *Wild Flowers of Canada*, Traill may have switched her system of classification from Linnean to De Candollean, a sign perhaps of her struggle to cope with the scientific resources available to her. But Traill is equally attentive to the poets of nature and to various sources of "oral tradition" (1885, 122). Several traditions converge to inform her vision.

5.    Relatively few letters survive from the 1840s.

6.    The provision of "useful articles for the colonists" was Traill's expressed aim. She was more inclined to read agricultural and farming magazines than scientific matter and to focus on what was practical and applicable. Such was the place and career she saw for herself in "the literary history of this new country," as she wrote to Ellen Dunlop on June 22, 1856 (Metropolitan Toronto Library).

7.    In the fall issue of 1856, the *Canadian Agriculturalist* (vol. 8, no. 11) records Traill's prize at the Kingston Provincial Fair for best collection of native plants, dried and named. The winter issue of 1862 (vol. 14, no. 24) reports that her collection of dried plants won second prize in the Provincial Exhibition in Toronto.

8.    Traill was conducting her negotiations from Belleville where her third daughter, Mary Muchall, was then living, as was her sister, Susanna Moodie.

## WORKS CITED

Berger, Carl. 1983. *Science, God, and Nature in Victorian Canada*. Toronto: Univ. of Toronto Press.

Ballstadt, Carl. 1983. "Catharine Parr Traill." In *Canadian Writers and Their Works*. Fiction Series, vol. I. Ed. Robert Lecker, Jack David, Ellen Quigley. Toronto: ECW Press. 149–93.

Chamberlin, Agnes Fitzgibbon. 1895. "Introductory Notes" to *Canadian Wild Flowers*, by Catharine Parr Traill. 4th ed. Toronto: Briggs.

Cole, Jean. 1975. "Catharine Parr Traill—Botanist." In *Portraits: Peterborough Area Women Past and Present*. Ed. Gail Corbett. Woodview, Ont.: Portraits' Group. 73–79.

Collard, Elizabeth. 1978. "Flowers to heal and comfort: Mrs. Traill's Books for Collectors." *Canadian Collector* 13 (May/June): 32–36.

Fletcher, James. 1883a. Letter to Catharine Parr Traill. June 25. Traill Family Papers. Public Archives of Canada, Ottawa.

————. 1883b. Letter to Catharine Parr Traill. Nov. Traill Family Papers. Public Archives of Canada, Ottawa.

————. 1894. Letter to Catharine Parr Traill. July 26. Traill Family Papers. Public Archives of Canada, Ottawa.

Fowler, Marian. 1982. *The Embroidered Tent. Five Gentlewomen in Early Canada*. Toronto: House of Anansi.

Frye, Northrop. 1965. Conclusion. *The Literary History of Canada*. Ed. Carl F. Klinck. Toronto: Univ. of Toronto Press.

———. 1971. *The Bush Garden: Essays on the Canadian Imagination*. Toronto: House of Anansi.

———. 1982. *Divisions on a Ground: Essays on Canadian Culture*. Toronto: House of Anansi.

Gairdner, William. 1973. "Traill and Moodie: the Two Realities." *Journal of Canadian Fiction* 2, no. 3: 75–81.

Jackel, David. 1979. "Mrs. Moodie and Mrs. Traill, and the Fabrication of a Canadian Tradition." *The Compass* 6: 1–22.

MacCallum, Elizabeth. 1975. "Catharine Parr Traill: A Nineteenth-Century Ontario Naturalist." *The Beaver* 306 (Autumn): 39–45.

MacGregor, Gaile. 1985. *The Wacousta Syndrome*. Toronto: Univ. of Toronto Press.

Penhallow, D. P. 1897. "A Review of Canadian Botany from 1800 to 1895." *Proceedings and Transactions of the Royal Society*, 2nd series. Vol. 3, sec. 4. 3–56.

Traill, Catharine Parr. 1830. *Sketches from Nature; or, Hints to Juvenile Naturalists*. London: Harvey and Darton.

———. 1836. *The Backwoods of Canada*. London: Charles Knight.

———. 1854. *The Female Emigrant's Guide, and Hints on Canadian Housekeeping*. Toronto: Maclear.

———. 1856. Letter to Ellen Dunlop. May 26. Metropolitan Toronto Library.

———. [1862]. Letter to Frances Stewart. May 5. Metropolitan Toronto Library.

———. 1863. "Flowers and their Moral Teaching." *British American Magazine* 1 (May): 55–59.

———. 1865a. Letter to Kate Traill. Feb. 2. Traill Family Papers. Public Archives of Canada, Ottawa.

———. 1865b. Letter to Kate Traill. Mar. 2. Traill Family Papers. Public Archives of Canada, Ottawa.

———. 1865c. Letter to Kate Traill. Mar. 17. Traill Family Papers. Public Archives of Canada, Ottawa.

———. 1868. *Canadian Wild Flowers*. Montreal: Lovell.

———. 1869. Letter to Annie Atwood. Jan. 31. Traill Family Papers. Public Archives of Canada, Ottawa.

———. 1884. Letter to Kate Traill. Traill Family Papers. Public Archives of Canada, Ottawa.

———. 1885. *Studies of Plant Life in Canada; or Gleanings from Forest, Lake and Plain*. Ottawa: A. S. Woodburn.

———. 1895. *Canadian Wild Flowers*. 4th ed. Toronto: Briggs.

———. 1906. *Studies of Plant Life in Canada; Wild Flowers, Flowering Shrubs, and Grasses*. Toronto: Briggs.

Thomas, Clara. 1972. "Journeys to Freedom." *Canadian Literature* 51 (Winter): 11–19.

Wallace, W. Stewart, ed. 1978. *Dictionary of Canadian Biography*. Toronto: Macmillan.

Zeller, Suzanne. 1987. *Inventing Canada: Early Victorian Science and the Idea of a Transcontinental Nation*. Toronto: Univ. of Toronto Press.

# "You may imagine my feelings": Reading Sara Jeannette Duncan's Challenge to Narrative

MISAO DEAN

When Mamie Wick is seated beside a formidable-looking Englishwoman at dinner in the first few pages of *An American Girl in London*, she exclaims to the reader: "you may imagine my feelings . . . or as you are probably English you can't" (11). Mamie's remark displays Sara Jeannette Duncan's characteristic interest in word play that exploits the differences between North American and British English—the U.S. "you may imagine my feelings" versus the British "you can't imagine my feelings." But there is a private meaning as well, shared by only some of her readers; for a colonial, who brings to the statement a knowledge of the self-centred Briton who patronizes mere colonials, Mamie's words are more than a linguistic joke. The insular Briton she addresses is unlikely to understand colonial experience; to the extent that her readers are British, they simply can't imagine her feelings. Mamie is self-consciously aware that the clash of cultures which is the subject of her story is repeated in the form of her narrative.

Like Mamie Wick, Canadian Sara Jeannette Duncan addresses an audience that could rarely be expected to share her "point of view."[1] Duncan published her books in England and the United States and often self-consciously addressed her readers as British or American; such readers would bring to her text expectations about political and literary issues that would be foreign to her. As a Canadian and a woman, Duncan was doubly removed from the ideological centre of the societies she addressed; as part of the Anglo-Indian community of Calcutta and Simla, fearful of the "subject races" and accused of luxury, feudalism, and racism by the opposition benches in Parliament, she possessed another point of view on imperial politics and colonial society which would not be shared by most of her readers.[2] Like her narrators, Duncan is also self-consciously aware that the clash of cultures she depicts in her "international'' novels is repeated in her narrative; the novels challenge the political, social, and literary assumptions of a British reader from the point of view of a colonial.

Although she was an outsider because of her nationality and her sex, Duncan was also joined to the imperial ideological centre by her race, her class, her sense of participation in the English literary tradition, and her idealist support for the British Empire. Virginia Woolf describes the ''double consciousness'' of living both inside and outside British culture as typical of women: ''one is often surprised by a sudden splitting off of consciousness, say in walking down Whitehall, when from being the natural inheritor of that civilization, she becomes, on the contrary, outside of it, alien and critical'' (91).

Woolf's words apply to Duncan as a woman, but they also describe the relationship of the Canadian imperialist to England, both inside and outside the tradition of British culture. The double consciousness of being female and Canadian yet middle-class and British, an inheritor of British civilization yet alien from it, makes Duncan the kind of writer that Rachel Blau DuPlessis calls ''(ambiguously) non-hegemonic,'' one who is ''in marginalised dialogue with the orders she may also affirm'' (33). In order to express her colonial experience, Duncan could not fundamentally challenge the structure of the popular novel in the way of modern feminists like Woolf; Duncan's commitment to the popular reader and her qualified affirmation of the political centre did not allow such radical experiments in form. But true to her definition of a Canadian personality as the middle ground between conventionality and freedom, she subverts the conventions of the popular novel to express her marginalization, while clinging to the framework they offer.

Duncan expresses her ''(ambiguous)'' commitment to the colonial point of view in the literary form of her novels, adopting strategies that allow her to covertly criticize the assumptions of the ideological centre without betraying her own or her reader's allegiance to them. Chief among these strategies is the ironic narrator, who explains and qualifies the colonial ''point of view'' by directly addressing the way that it differs from that of the centre. The narrator of the ''international novel'' compares and contrasts the British reader's assumptions about social and political conventions with those standards prevailing in the colonies,[3] concluding that in the material realm at least such truths are relative to a person's point of view.

But the narrator of Duncan's books is self-consciously the writer of them as well; the narrator represents in the novel the process of shaping the story for the reader. Just as her favourite eighteenth- and nineteenth-century novelists directly address the reader in their narratives, Duncan's narrator also writes ''metafiction'' that represents not only real life but the situation and the process of composing fiction. As she challenges social and political conventions, she also challenges the literary conventions that represent them. The narrator understands that general ideas of the ''correct'' way to portray material reality depend upon a shared conception of what that reality is, and when that conception is broken by the perspective of an outsider, the way is open for a challenge to literary conventions as well. In other words, literary form follows social form (DuPlessis, 2). The narrator invokes the reader's expectations about literary form in order to show the artificiality of the conventional popular novel which claims to represent reality and to assert a different literary reality which includes colonial and female experience.

That Duncan was able to see such conventions as the happy ending, the passive heroine, the stereotyped memsahib, and the intense literary romance as artificial and unrealistic means that to some extent such conventions had already been outgrown. In an attempt to reform romantic fiction, American realists had commented on literary convention: W. D. Howells had reversed the usual order of the romantic novel by beginning with a marriage in *A Modern Instance*, and Henry James had deplored the "happy ending" of the nineteenth-century novel which required tying up all the loose ends in an implausible final paragraph. In her essay in *The Week*, "Outworn Literary Methods," Duncan uses Thomas Carlyle's clothes metaphor to portray such clichés of fiction as "cast off garments" which still live in "the attic of every writer's brain." She writes: "Very well he knows they are there, but he is much too tender a parent to send his offspring forth into a gibing world tricked out in them" (June 9, 1887, 450). In an attempt to express the "practical spirit of the age" and to make method conform to matter, the modern novelist must discard "the old rules by which any habitual reader of fiction would prophesy truly at the end of the third chapter how the story would 'come out' . . ." (451). But Duncan writes that "the themes of civilization are as old as civilization": change comes only within limits. While the outward manifestations of truth in literature must change to conform to the new perspective of modern life, that change must be reconciled to the persistence of the old truths. So Duncan preserves the framework of the old stereotypes even as she challenges them, seeing in the reconciliation of the two a way to reconcile the chaotic difference of perspective of the colonies and the Empire with the old ideals.

Mamie Wick quite consciously addresses the expectations of a British reader when she introduces herself in the first chapter of *An American Girl*. She makes her first statement, "I am an American girl" (1), in order to explain any deviation she represents from the British norm: "I have observed, since I came to England, that this statement made by a third person in connection with any question of my own conduct is always broadly explanatory" (1). She introduces herself by way of her family history because she knows the British reader expects it. As she describes her impressions of England, she carefully qualifies her judgements by reminding the reader that she means no offence.

The narrative voice of *An American Girl* manipulates not only the reader's social expectations, but her literary ones as well. The novel sets up the expectation of a "happy ending" to the romance between Mamie and Charlie

Mafferton, an English gentleman who is looking for an American heiress to marry. Mamie finds him merely innocuous and pleasant, but his constant attendance as well as hints from other characters indicate to the reader that he intends marriage. The reader has every right to expect that when he reveals his feelings, she will accede and the story will end with a wedding. But the different customs of courtship in England and in the United States mean that, until the last chapter, Mamie remains unaware that Charlie Mafferton looks upon her as a future bride. When she finally realizes what his intentions are, she hurriedly boards the first ship home, explaining that she is already engaged. After spending 300 pages establishing the expectation of a "happy ending," the novel deflates that expectation in one short chapter. The new social customs inaugurated by the colonial United States require a new approach to the conventional ending.

Contemporary reviews confirm that readers found the novel's ending surprising, and intriguing. The reviewer in *The Week* points out the initial similarity between *An American Girl* and the then ubiquitous American-girl-marries-a-Lord-and-becomes-a-Lady plot: "we feel we shall not be surprised if the usual fate which pursues pretty American girls overtakes our heroine," the usual fate being, of course, marriage. The reviewer remarks that the lack of the expected marriage "is perhaps the cleverest thing in the book" (Apr. 3, 1891, 288).

In *The Imperialist*, the narrator's "(ambiguously) non-hegemonic" attitude towards her British readers allows her to assume the point of view of Elgin, Ontario, in order to challenge preconceptions about stories and about Canada. The novel opens with a description of Mother Beggarlegs, the ancient woman who sells gingerbread in the Elgin Market Square. British social convention demands a formal introduction to the lady; literary conventions derived from the eighteenth-century novel also prescribe a formal introduction by way of a genealogy. As Mamie Wick discovers in Britain, the English reader expects an account of a character's past and present history: "I have learned that in England you like to know a great deal about people who are introduced to you—who their fathers and mothers are, their grandfathers and grandmothers, and even further back than that" (*American Girl*, 3). But the narrator protests, "it would have been idle to inquire in to the antecedents" of Mother Beggarlegs; she belongs to a society so new that such information is often unobtainable, and irrelevant. The "antecedents or even the circumstances, of old Mother Beggarlegs" are lost in history; but what places her distinctly for the residents of Elgin is the Canadian indicator of social class, her occupation, which "was clear" (11).[4] In her description of Mother Beggarlegs, the narrator ironically links the conventions of the literary biography and of British society and then dismisses them as irrelevant, calling upon the British readers to imagine the effect of transporting their own prejudices to the new world.

The narrator "(ambiguously)" recognizes the views of both the British reader and the colonial when she describes the attitudes of recent immigrants to Elgin, John Murchison and Dr. Drummond. She tells in some detail how the two came to Canada and explains their attitude towards Britain with the exactness of one aware that she is talking to an audience with its own ideas of Canadian loyalty. "A sentiment of affection for the reigning house" is all that Elgin feels, "an anachronism of the heart" (58) which has no connection to actual Royals who spend money. Elgin is much less concerned with England than England would like to think:

> But the Government might become the sole employer of labour in those islands, Church and school might part company forever, landlords might be deprived of all but compassionate allowances and, except for the degree of extravagance involved in these propositions, they would hardly be current in Elgin (59).

Elgin is not particularly interested even in the affairs of the Empire: "It was recognized dimly that England had a foreign policy, more or less had to have it, as they would have said in Elgin . . ." (59). While certainly these passages point out the narrow Elgin concentration on "the immediate, the vital, the municipal" (60), they also ironically denigrate the ethnocentric British view that the citizens of the colonies must be interested in everything that happens "at home." In the novel, the British focus just as vitally on "parish affairs" (125) as do the citizens of Elgin and are, in their way, more provincial than the Canadians, as Lorne Murchison finds out: "more interested in a back garden fence than anything else" (132). The British make the mistake of assuming that their interests and views are universal at least throughout the Empire; Duncan points out that in Elgin, the immediate issues of "the town, the Province, the Dominion" (59) are quite justifiably more important.

Duncan intimately links her deviation from the reader's political and social expectations to her breaking of literary conventions to express colonial reality. When Hugh and Advena are in the library alone one evening, the narrator metaphorically waits in the hall, trying to decide whether to break in on them or not. The social convention of chaperonage (which Duncan takes as a serious English custom in *Those Delightful Americans*) and the literary convention of the romantic tête-à-tête seem to demand that the narrator enter the library and witness the scene between Hugh and Advena. But she takes the Elgin point of view on both conventions: "It would simply have been considered, in Elgin, stupid to go into the library" (88). The narrator concurs with Canadian social practice and takes the reader into the dining room, where Lorne and his parents are meeting with Lawyer Cruikshank. The clash of cultures which results in Duncan's taking the part of Elgin is repeated as she represents the Elgin form of fictional narrative.

The Imperialist also illustrates the link between the social conventions which restrict women's actions and the literary conventions which prescribe the proper deportment of a romantic heroine. The heroines of *The Imperialist* reflect Duncan's belief that fiction should reflect the changing situation of women in real life.

> The woman of today is no longer an exceptional being surrounded by exceptional circumstances. She bears a translatable relation to the world; and the novelists who translate it correctly have ceased to mark it by unduly exalting one woman by virtue of her sex to a position of interest in their books which dwarfs all the other characters . . . . The novel of today is a reflection of our present social state. The women who enter into its composition are but intelligent agents in this reflection, and show themselves as they are, not as a false ideal would have them (*The Week*, October 28, 1886, 772).

Catherine Sheldrick Ross points out in her article, "Calling Back the Ghost of the Old-Time Heroine," that Duncan evokes the stereotype of the passive, decorative heroine in Dora Milburn, who jilts Lorne Murchison in favour of his superficial British friend, Alfred Hesketh, and creates a new heroine in Lorne's sister Advena. Ross sees Advena's later lapse into self-sacrifice as a flaw in Duncan's execution (45). But Advena's attempt to become a romance stereotype by sacrificing her love for Hugh illustrates her allegiance to the old ideals and her inability to see how to embody them in the new world. Advena, in writing her own life script, has cast herself in the stereotyped role of sacrificial heroine, seeing herself a martyr to Hugh's honour and declaring that by becoming a "friendship of spirit" their love will be purified of the body. But Advena does not finally submit to the stereotype, realizing that the pose of the self-sacrificing heroine is only satisfying in novels; she eventually goes to Finlay with her discovery of "what is possible and what is not" (250). Brought literally back to her senses after a meeting with Christie Cameron, she expresses "the desire of her heart" in no uncertain terms: "Send her away!" (250), she says. The "ideal" of self-sacrifice is one that human frailty can only aspire to; like Lorne's imperialist vision, Advena's self-sacrificing role founders on the new reality of the new world. Advena becomes a new kind of heroine, who recognizes her own desire and her human need in rejecting the passivity of the heroine and actively pursuing the "desire of her heart."

The new reality of women's lives also clashes with the stereotype of the passive heroine in *The Path of a Star*. Like *The Imperialist*, *The Path of a Star* has two heroines, Alicia Livingstone and Hilda Howe, the former a member of conventional Calcutta society and the latter a talented actress. Both women consciously choose the men they plan to marry but adopt very different strategies to win them. Hilda openly expresses her desire for the celibate clergyman, Stephen Arnold, while Alicia, who falls in love with the socialite Duff Lindsay, takes the more traditional course of self-sacrifice by refusing to declare her feelings and actually helping Lindsay marry someone else. Hilda scolds her: " 'We are an intolerably self-sacrificing sex' . . . . 'They've taught us well, the men; it's a blood disease now, running everywhere in the female line . . . It's a deformity, like the dachshund's legs' " (99).

Alicia proposes to sacrifice her love for the happiness of Duff Lindsay's life, and Hilda will have none of it. "And what about the happiness of yours? Do you imagine it's laudable, admirable, this attitude? Do you see yourself in it with pleasure?" (99). Hilda insists that Alicia use her own powers of judgement to condemn Lindsay's proposed marriage, and to thwart it.

Both women win the love of their chosen men. Although Stephen Arnold dies before his love for Hilda is consummated, his final words as she attends his death bed several months later indicate that she wins her point: "I would have married you" (308), he says. When he dies, he repudiates his celibacy: "he trusted to the new wings of his mortal love to bear his soul to its immortality" (309). But Alicia also wins her lover, Duff Lindsay, who finally recognizes her loyal support as repressed love. Hilda is the focus of the novel, which seems to imply a value judgement in favour of her forthright behaviour and her choice to pursue her vocation, yet that judgement is undercut by Alicia's success. The story embodies the contradictions of Duncan's feminism by creating a new, independent heroine but tacitly approving the traditional, self-sacrificing role as well.

The stereotype of the conventional heroine as young, beautiful, and competent forms the background for reading Miss Lavinia Moffat of *Vernon's Aunt*. Miss Moffat is an unmarried woman who undertakes an unaccompanied trip to India with expectations of exotic adventures. From this description, she might be one of the heroines of Duncan's earlier bestseller, *A Social Departure*. However, Miss Lavinia Moffat expresses the reality that not all women are twenty and beautiful: she is forty-two, a spinster, and rather sure of her ability to guide the rest of the world on questions of courtesy to middle-aged ladies. Just as Miss Moffat is not the sort of heroine the reader expects, India is not quite what Miss Moffat expects; her civil servant nephew seems in no physical danger and her ride on an elephant is uneventful. The romance that is required by the conventions of the popular novel does materialize in a roundabout way, in the person of Mr. Ali Karam Bux, whose attempts to gain Miss Moffat's assistance in a legal matter are misinterpreted as a proposal of marriage. Even the animal that Miss Moffat hears chewing in the dark of her tent in Nudiwallah turns out to be no more exotic than a stray cat with a mutton bone from the kitchen tent.

The conventional literary traveller to India offers commentary on the major issues of Indian government. Miss Moffat tries to do the same. Her genuine puzzlement over the Indian reluctance to discuss suttee and purdah on a train with a strange Englishwoman resonates with all the Anglo-Indian resentments against know-nothing British interference and the "public opinion" fostered by fiction and the press. She enters a society that was unfamiliar to the British reader of Kipling, but that "insiders" could know through the works of contemporary Anglo-Indian novelists or through personal experience: a community haunted by memories of the Mutiny of 1857, plagued by serious illness, and engaged in daily cultural clashes with the Indian majority. Although Anglo-India was the representative of the imperial power, Anglo-Indians felt as though they themselves were part of an overlooked, misunderstood colony. The reader familiar with and sympathetic to this Anglo-Indian self-portrait would have a focus of knowledge to apply to the portrait of Miss Lavinia Moffat. The ignorant globe-trotters who appear in Duncan's fiction become less figures of fun and more objects of serious alarm when one realizes, with the Anglo-Indian, that they have the power to materially affect the government of the country—more power, in fact, than the "old India hands" with whom they are contrasted.

As in the other novels, readers are made aware of the challenge to their social and literary expectations by the self-consciousness of the narrative voice. Miss Moffat is writing her adventures for the readers' benefit, and she often comments on literary conventions in order to caution readers against them. Travelling across Europe by train, she describes her experience of officers at the Italian stations:

> There were officers, too, at the various stations, just such Italian officers in cocked hats, and swords, and long cloaks, as one reads of in novels, but also, judging from the novels, I expected more from them in the way of impertinent advances than I saw. In works of fiction lady-travellers through Italy are always subjected to stares and smiles . . . but that I now believe to be a literary artifice (11).

Miss Moffat's suspicion of literary conventions that claim to represent reality is transferred to the readers, who begin to suspect that literary depictions of India leave something to be desired.

The clash between the Anglo-Indian point of view and the "know-nothing British" is repeated in *The Simple Adventures of a Memsahib*. The plot involves the initiation of Helen Peachey into Anglo-Indian society as the wife of "young Browne," a member of an import-export firm in Calcutta. The story is told by Mrs. Perth-MacIntyre, wife of a senior partner in Browne's firm, whose self-conscious narrative includes references to the literary expectations of British readers well versed in Kipling and the social expectations of a British visitor to Calcutta; but the narrator is committed to the Anglo-Indian point of view and looks forward to her own retirement to England with regret.

Mrs. Perth-MacIntyre self-consciously contrasts the literary conventions of "modern fiction" with the story of Helen Browne in order to ridicule readers' expectations and create a contrasting reality. The narrator knows that readers expect a story "of a young man and woman who fell in love according to approved analytical methods, with subtle silent scruples and mysterious mis-understandings, in the modern way'' (4–5). Mrs. Perth-MacIntyre knows the "modern way" demands extraordinary and original main characters, but Helen Browne is emphatically not original (26) and George Browne is equally lacking "the equipment proper for a young man of whom anything is expected in the nature of modern fiction" (50). "Modern fiction" as the narrator understands it begins with a courtship and ends with a wedding. Helen Browne's courtship takes up only one chapter of the novel and so the novel begins with a wedding. Having placed her "happy ending" at the beginning, Mrs. Perth-MacIntyre ends with two beginnings: the beginning of Helen Browne's family and the beginning of her own retirement to England.

Contemporary reviewers found Mrs. Perth-MacIntyre's innovations in the line of narrative disconcerting. The anonymous reviewer of *The Simple Adventures* in *The Athenaeum* declared that the novel had "no plot whatsoever" and "practically no love interest." The review pronounces the book to be "of real value to young ladies contemplating matrimony under similar circumstances" (August 5, 1893, 191) as a kind of conduct book or manual but implies that, because the book lacks a developing romance and a marriage ending, it is emphatically not a novel.

The preconceptions of British readers who have formed their ideas of Anglo-Indian women on the stories of Rudyard Kipling are ridiculed in the narrator's attack on Mr. Jonas Batcham, a British M.P. who visits the Brownes in Calcutta. Expecting the "possible Mrs. Hawksbees and Mrs. Mallowes" (194) of Kipling's stories to be incarnate in the wives of Government House officials, Batcham accuses any woman who is polite to him of having deeper designs upon his corpulent person. The fact that no one he meets lives up to his expectations has little effect upon his judgement. When his hopes of finding immorality in the Browne household are dashed, he privately concludes that the Brownes must be exceptions to the rule.

The stereotype of the memsahib as a woman constantly on the verge of adultery is also challenged in *Set in Authority*, where the recently arrived Mrs. Biscuit is quite disappointed by the respectability of society:

> She had even looked forward, I think, to the many interesting situations from which she should extricate herself within a hair's breadth of compromise; but always with the hair quite visible. Her sense that such things were inevitable suggested to her that she might as well make the most of them. But by this time Mrs. Biscuit had reached the private conclusion that either Pilaghur was far from being a "typical" Indian station, or the novelists were simply not to be trusted (36).

In fact, all the memsahibs of Duncan's books have "no notion of [their] responsibilities to fiction" (36) and simply refuse to be the stereotypes that British readers expect. Even Mrs. Jack Lovitt of *Simple Adventures*, who has a very close relationship with a single man, never contemplates anything that is not strictly respectable according to the lights of Calcutta society.

Like the writers she discusses in "Outworn Literary Methods," Duncan is much too tender a parent to send her novels into the world tricked out in old stereotypes. Yet she knows that the political, social, and literary expectations of every "habitual novel reader" are part of the process of creating meaning through reading. Duncan creates a narrator who challenges the expectations of the reader by sympathetically depicting the colonial "point of view" of social and political affairs; her self-conscious introduction of the colonial "point of view" on reality challenges the hegemonic values of the reader who is part of the imperial centre. But the narrator is also self-consciously the writer of the story; she repeats in her narrative the clash of cultures which is the thematic content of the novels. Duncan subverts the literary conventions that portray reality in the popular novel in order to assert the colonial perspective on reality.

## NOTES

1.   Duncan often uses the phrase "point of view" to indicate the outlook of a Canadian. The Cruikshank delegation in *The Imperialist*, for example, "kept their point of view" in England, and Graham Trent in *Cousin Cinderella* remarks that Canadians have a "point of view" on England.
2.   See Nagarajan (1975) and Howe (1949, 74–84).
3.   For critical discussion of Duncan's "international" narrator, see Allen (1984) and Thomas (1976).
4.   Compare with the discussion of occupation as a social indicator on p. 47.

## WORKS CITED

Allen, Peter. 1984. "Narrative Uncertainties in Duncan's *The Imperialist.*" *Studies in Canadian Literature* 9, no. 1: 41–60.
Duncan, Sara Jeannette. 1887. "Outworn Literary Methods." *The Week* IV, no. 28 (9 June): 450–51.
———. 1891. *An American Girl in London*. New York: D. Appleton.
———. 1971. *The Imperialist*. 1904. Toronto: McClelland and Stewart.
———. 1899. *The Path of a Star*. Toronto: W. J. Gage.
———. 1906. *Set In Authority*. New York: Doubleday and Page.
———. 1893. *The Simple Adventures of a Memsahib*. New York: D. Appleton.
———. 1894. *Vernon's Aunt*. London: Chatto and Windus.
DuPlessis, Rachel Blau. 1985. *Writing Beyond the Ending*. Bloomington, Ill.: Indiana Univ. Press.

Howe, Susanna. 1949. *Novels of Empire*. New York: Columbia Univ. Press.

Nagarajan, S. 1975. "The Anglo-Indian Novels of Sara Jeannette Duncan." *Journal of Canadian Fiction* 3, no. 4: 74–84.

Ross, Catherine Sheldrick. 1979. "Calling Back the Ghost of the Old-Time Heroine: Duncan, Montgomery, Atwood, Laurence, Munro." *Studies in Canadian Literature* 4, no. 1: 43–58.

Thomas, Clara. 1976. "*Cousin Cinderella* and the Empire Game." *Studies in Canadian Literature* 1, no. 2: 183–93.

Woolf, Virginia. 1984. *A Room of One's Own and Three Guineas*. 1929, 1938. London: Hogarth Press.

# Afterword

## ELIZABETH WATERSTON

**E**ach of the previous volumes in this series has nourished the development of criticism and literary history in this country by reappraising important or familiar Canadian writers or groups of writers. This 1989 collection continues that tradition, but there is something new here as well. A significant number of contributors have taken a first look at a world of writers previously unexplored.

This year, as in the past, some critics shed new light on writers who have already attracted critical attention. Thus we get, from Alec Lucas, Michael Peterman, David Bentley, Carl Ballstadt, and Bina Freiwald, a fresh perspective on Susanna Moodie and Catharine Parr Traill, and from Misao Dean, a new view of Sara Jeannette Duncan. And we learn from Carole Gerson how the works of many nineteenth-century Canadian women writers have been ignored by our own anthologists.

What has emerged in the essays by other contributors are many new names that are worthy of a first critical look—Fleming, Laut, Machar, Beckwith Hart, the Herbert sisters, Dougall, Armour, and Wetherald. Francess Halpenny presents a long catalogue of nineteenth-century women writers whose first work has yet to be published, and she adds a second list of writers—Margaret Murray Robertson, Harriett Wilkins Cameron, Mrs. Cushing, Roselda Thoms, Emily Shaw Beaven, Ann Cuthbert Rae—whose lives have been researched for the *Dictionary of Canadian Biography* but whose works still await our critical analysis. Marion Beyea gives us a key for beginning research: befriend an archivist and don't sneer at genealogists. James Doyle proposes another research key: follow the path of the periodicals, taking along Bliss Carman as a guide. From Helen Buss, Marjory Lang, and Donna Smyth, we hear of underprivileged genres— journalism, diaries, autobiographies—where we can look for new material.

These are the ingredients of this volume. What should Canadian literary scholars turn to next? Having broken "the cake of custom," we need to consider the soup. The *soupe du jour* has been excellent. Using this as a base, we need only to continue chopping and mincing and cubing and crushing to produce a good *soupe de demain*.

As Carol Shields reminds us, the things we add in later stages must be carefully prepared. What will we choose to put into this polysystemic soup next? We live now, not in a wilderness, not even in a "bush garden," but in a tough inner city. But if we walk carefully, who knows what herb of grace we may find growing through the cracks in the concrete?

## CONTRIBUTORS

| | |
|---|---|
| CARL BALLSTADT | McMaster University |
| D.M.R. BENTLEY | University of Western Ontario |
| MARION BEYEA | Provincial Archives of New Brunswick |
| HELEN M. BUSS | University of Manitoba |
| MISAO DEAN | University of Victoria |
| JAMES DOYLE | Wilfrid Laurier University |
| BINA FREIWALD | Concordia University |
| CAROLE GERSON | Vancouver, British Columbia |
| FRANCESS G. HALPENNY | Dictionary of Canadian Biography, Toronto, Ontario |
| MARJORY LANG | Vancouver, British Columbia |
| ALEC LUCAS | McGill University |
| CARRIE MACMILLAN | Mount Allison University |
| MICHAEL A. PETERMAN | Trent University |
| CAROL SHIELDS | University of Manitoba |
| DONNA E. SMYTH | Acadia University |
| CLARA THOMAS | York University |
| ELIZABETH WATERSTON | University of Guelph |

REAPPRAISALS: Canadian Writers

This series is the outcome of symposia on Canadian writers presented by the Department of English, University of Ottawa. The object is to make permanently available the criticism and evaluation of writers as presented by scholars and literary figures at the symposia. Where considered significant by the editor, additional critical articles and bibliographical material are included.

Lorraine McMullen
General Editor

Other titles in the series:

THE GROVE SYMPOSIUM, edited and with an introduction by John Nause

The A. M. KLEIN SYMPOSIUM, edited and with an introduction by Seymour Mayne

THE LAMPMAN SYMPOSIUM, edited and with an introduction by Lorraine McMullen

THE E. J. PRATT SYMPOSIUM, edited and with an introduction by Glenn Clever

THE ISABELLA VALANCY CRAWFORD SYMPOSIUM, edited and with an introduction by Frank M. Tierney

THE DUNCAN CAMPBELL SCOTT SYMPOSIUM, edited and with an introduction by K. P. Stich

THE ETHEL WILSON SYMPOSIUM, edited and with an introduction by Lorraine McMullen

THE CALLAGHAN SYMPOSIUM, edited and with an introduction by David Staines

TRANSLATION IN CANADIAN LITERATURE, edited and with an introduction by Camille La Bossière

THE CHARLES G. D. ROBERTS SYMPOSIUM, edited and with an introduction by Glenn Clever

THE THOMAS CHANDLER HALIBURTON SYMPOSIUM, edited and with an introduction by Frank M. Tierney

STEPHEN LEACOCK: A REAPPRAISAL, edited and with an introduction by David Staines

FUTURE INDICATIVE: LITERARY THEORY AND CANADIAN LITERATURE, edited and with an introduction by John Moss

REFLECTIONS: AUTOBIOGRAPHY AND CANADIAN LITERATURE, edited and with an introduction by K. P. Stich

Achevé d'imprimer
sur les presses de

Goulet. Létourneau Imprimeurs inc.
à Sherbrooke (Québec)

1379